Dying, Death, and Bereavement
in Social Work Practice

END-OF-LIFE CARE: A SERIES

END-OF-LIFE CARE: A SERIES

Series editor: Virginia E. Richardson

We all confront end-of-life issues. As people live longer and suffer from more chronic illnesses, all of us face difficult decisions about death, dying, and terminal care. This series aspires to articulate the issues surrounding end-of-life care in the twenty-first century. It will be a resource for practitioners and scholars who seek information about advance directives, hospice, palliative care, bereavement, and other death-related topics. The interdisciplinary approach makes the series invaluable for social workers, physicians, nurses, attorneys, and pastoral counselors.

The press seeks manuscripts that reflect the interdisiciplinary, biopsychosocial essence of end-of-life care. We welcome manuscripts that address specific topics on ethical dilemmas in end-of-life care, death, and dying among marginalized groups, palliative care, spirituality, and end-of-life care in special medical areas, such as oncology, AIDS, diabetes, and transplantation. While writers should integrate theory and practice, the series is open to diverse methodologies and perspectives.

Joan Berzoff and Phyllis R. Silverman, *Living with Dying: A Handbook for End-of-Life Healthcare Practitioners*

Virginia E. Richardson and Amanda S. Barusch, *Gerontological Practice for the Twenty-first Century: A Social Work Perspective*

Ruth Ray, *Endnotes: An Intimate Look at the End of Life*

Dying, Death, & Bereavement in Social Work Practice

DECISION CASES FOR ADVANCED PRACTICE

Terry A. Wolfer
and Vicki M. Runnion

COLUMBIA UNIVERSITY PRESS ⚜ NEW YORK

Columbia University Press
Publishers Since 1893
New York   Chichester, West Sussex
Copyright © 2008 Columbia University Press
All rights reserved

Library of Congress Cataloging-in-Publication Data
Wolfer, Terry A.
   Dying, death, and bereavement in social work practice : decision cases for
advanced practice / Terry A. Wolfer and Vicki M. Runnion.
      p.   cm. — (End-of-life care)
   Includes bibliographical references.
   ISBN 978-0-231-14174-1 (cloth : alk. paper) — ISBN 978-0-231-14175-8 (pbk.) —
   ISBN 978-0-231-51262-6 (electronic)
   1. Social work with the terminally ill.   2. Social work—Moral and ethical aspects.
3. Death—Social aspects.   4. Bereavement.   I. Runnion, Vicki M.   II. Title.
HV3000.W65   2008
362.1'0425—dc22   2007043083

Columbia University Press books are printed on
permanent and durable acid-free paper.

This book was printed on paper with recycled content.

Printed in the United States of America

c 10 9 8 7 6 5 4 3 2 1
p 10 9 8 7 6 5 4 3 2 1

References to Internet Web sites (URLs) were accurate at the time of writing. Neither the author nor Columbia University Press is responsible for URLs that may
have expired or changed since the manuscript was prepared.

Contents

To Instructors

AS EXPLAINED IN THE INTRODUCTION, the decision cases in this collection differ from the cases commonly used in social work education. Whatever their experience with the case method of teaching or with end-of-life care, most instructors will benefit from the extensive teaching notes written for each of the cases. These notes are available at the Columbia University Press Web site but accessible to instructors only.

The teaching notes have two basic purposes: to help instructors select particular cases and to help instructors prepare to lead case discussions. To help in case selection, each note begins with a case synopsis, intended case use, and possible learning outcomes. To help in preparation for class discussion, each note provides possible discussion questions organized into four sequential categories: facts, analysis, action, and personal reflection. Next, the note includes suggestions for possible activities to supplement the case discussion. A final section identifies recommended print, electronic, and media resources.

To Readers

AS EXPLAINED FURTHER in the introduction, the cases in this collection came from social workers telling about their experiences. They depict, in considerable detail, difficult and challenging situations these social workers actually encountered in professional practice. This is not always true of cases published in social work textbooks, and makes these cases more like the sort of cases you will encounter in your field placement or employment or that you might hear about in case conferences or peer supervision.

But these cases are like the ones you may encounter professionally in another very important way. They end at a point where the social worker protagonist must make a decision about how to respond. While social work cases traditionally illustrate practice theories or interventions, demonstrating how something should work, these cases depict unresolved situations and thus allow you to analyze the information presented and decide what to do. Indeed, if you must discuss these cases or write a case analysis in a social work course, you will have to carefully analyze the situation and draw your own conclusion about what needs to be done. That may be quite different from what you're accustomed to doing in the classroom. Some students find this learning process challenging, uncomfortable, and even distressing. But it closely approximates the kind of thinking and deciding that will be required of you in professional practice, and for which you no doubt wish to be prepared. These cases will provide opportunities for you to practice and refine those skills.

In addition, these particular cases raise issues related to dying, death, and bereavement in social work practice. In certain practice situations these issues may be expected; in others, unexpected. They are often perplexing and disturbing, especially for novice social workers. Reflecting upon and discussing these cases can help you to develop some professional skill and judgment in the safety of the classroom before you inevitably happen upon similar situations in the field. In short, studying these cases will introduce you to the messy world of professional practice in ways that textbooks and lectures alone cannot.

Beyond graduate education, these cases may also be used for continuing education or for discussion in supervisory sessions. Professional social workers have reported that they provide an appropriate level of challenge and vividly portray real-life struggles similar to those encountered in practice. Experienced social workers may disagree about how to respond in some instances, as happens frequently in social work practice, but still benefit from discussing these situations.

Preface and Acknowledgments

THE SEED FOR THIS PROJECT was planted in January 2001. From a chance encounter at the Society for Social Work and Research, Terry learned of funding for educational projects related to death and dying in social work practice. Terry had extensive experience writing, editing, and teaching M.S.W. students using decision cases, and he enlisted Vicki to help create a proposal for this collection. Vicki had written and taught using decision cases and, more significantly for this project, had nearly twenty years of experience in end-of-life social work practice. Work formally began in 2002, with grant funding from the Soros Foundation's Project on Death in America. We are very grateful to the foundation for funding this project and to Project Director Grace Christ for direction and encouragement. In addition, we benefited from annual retreats with the other grant recipients, where we became acquainted with and learned from many of the social work leaders in the area of death and dying. Their contributions have greatly enriched this collection.

The cases in this book are based on field research with professional social workers. Although they must remain anonymous, we are deeply grateful for their time and effort in giving interviews and reviewing case drafts, and for their openness with us throughout the writing process. The interviews required that they recall and reflect upon situations they often found personally challenging, even disturbing. They were not always proud of or pleased with their responses, but nevertheless perservered in sharing their experiences for the benefit of students. Without endorsing all their perceptions or reactions, we consistently found these social workers to be caring, competent, and ethical practitioners. If they were otherwise, their cases would be less compelling. Obviously, the case collection would not be possible without these professionals and their deeply personal contributions.

We found most of the cases by asking experienced social workers about memorable dilemmas they had experienced in professional practice. In a few instances, professionals familiar with decision cases volunteered to report cases when they learned about the project. We sought cases from a variety of professional settings, both those obviously associated with death and dying and those where the association is unexpected, because we wished to provide a curriculum resource broadly applicable to social work education. For the same reason, we sought cases portraying a variety of intervention levels, from direct practice to supervisory and administrative practice. As a result, particular cases can be used across the social work practice curriculum or in courses focused on death and dying.

We researched and wrote the cases using a highly collaborative process developed by a friend and colleague, Mike Welsh (1999). It involved repeatedly assembling small groups of social workers as case-writing teams led by the authors. Teams typically met for initial reporting sessions lasting 90 to 120 minutes. The case-writing process consisted of 5 steps. First, the case reporter prepared a brief written account of a problem or dilemma he or she actually faced in social work practice. Second, during the initial team meeting, the case reporter told the story in detail. Other team members asked questions to elicit information about the situation on multiple levels (e.g., intrapersonal dynamics, interpersonal and social relations, organizational factors, policy issues). These reporting sessions were tape recorded to collect detailed descriptions and quotations of dialogue. Third, immediately after the initial team meeting, a case writer prepared a working draft of the case that included a title, an introductory "hook," a basic narrative, and a dilemma-posing ending. Fourth, at a subsequent meeting or via e-mail, the case writer distributed the working draft to other members of the team, who asked further questions of the case reporter to correct, clarify, or amplify the case. Fifth, the case writer used the additional information that emerged from this discussion to revise the case. In addition, analysis from the follow-up discussion was used to prepare teaching notes for the completed case. This writing process promoted in-depth collaboration with experienced practitioners from a variety of social service settings.

The cases are carefully disguised to protect the confidentiality of the case reporters, clients, co-workers of the case reporters, and organizations. For example, cases may be placed in other states, in organizations with fictitious names, and of course all names of individuals have been changed. However, in order to maintain the integrity of each case and portray the issues and dynamics as accurately as possible, we have tried to retain details such as ethnicity, gender, socioeconomic status of individuals, characteristics of the community, personal history and characteristics of the individuals as it affected their interactions, and so on, either very close to or unchanged from the actual situation.

Many of the case coauthors were students or former students, and several were faculty colleagues. For everyone, Terry provided formal instruction or at least written guidelines and informal guidance for writing decision cases and teaching notes. More than other forms of academic writing, decision cases require an unusual combination of technical expertise and familiarity with practice settings. Details matter. Sometimes, for example, a decision turns on a seemingly minor fact, a matter of timing, or an overlooked policy. For that reason, it was important to collaborate with practitioners in this project.

We enjoyed collaborating on this project with several social work students, graduates, and faculty colleagues. As M.S.W. graduate assistants, Carmella Barton, Heather Bennett, Gecole Harley, Llora Negro, Rachel Parker, Laura Poindexter, and Jeannette Ucci worked on the project in various capacities, including case coauthorship. Laura Cox, Rich Schlauch, and Georgianne Thornburgh were M.S.W. graduates who also coauthored cases. Now social work instructors themselves, Sarah Cearley, Barbara Head, and Mary Hylton coauthored cases as doctoral students. Miriam Johnson and Karen Gray are faculty colleagues who also teach the case-based M.S.W. capstone course at the University of South Carolina College of Social Work

After completing a draft of each case and the accompanying teaching note, we solicited a review by an expert consultant familiar with death and dying and sometimes also by a second expert consultant familiar with the particular field of practice in which it took place. For serving as reviewers, we wish to thank Elizabeth Mayfield Arnold (Wake Forest University Baptist Medical Center), Mercedes Bern-Klug (University of Iowa), Susan Blacker (St. Michael's Hospital, Toronto), Cheryl Brandsen (Calvin College), Elizabeth K. Chaitin (University of Pittsburgh Medical Center), Darienne DeSalvo (Family and Children's Service of the Capital Region, Albany, NY), Sheila R. Enders (University of California Davis Cancer Center), Cynthia Forrest (Winthrop University), Barbara Head (University of Louisville), Barbara Jones (University of Texas at Austin), Johnny Jones (University of South Carolina), Betty J. Kramer (University of Wisconsin-Madison), Shanti Kulkarni (University of Texas at Austin), John F. Linder (University of California Davis Cancer Center), Julie Miller-Cribbs (University of Oklahoma), Joan Pendergast (University of South Carolina), Pat W. Priest (Lutheran Family Services, Greensboro, NC), Mary Raymer (Raymer Psychotherapy and Consultation Services, Acme, MI), Steve Walker (Richland County [SC] School District One), and Sherri Weisenfluh (Hospice of the Bluegrass, Lexington, KY).

Collaboration with case reporters, coauthors, graduate assistants, expert consultants, and external reviewers helped to ensure the veracity and readability of the cases and the thoroughness of the teaching notes. We and others have already piloted many of these cases—in an M.S.W. capstone course, an M.S.W. elective on death and dying, and continuing education workshops for social work practitioners or instructors—and we used those experiences to refine the cases and notes. We cannot guarantee the absence of substantive errors but trust they will be minor as a result of these multiple forms of collaboration and review.

Finally, we wish to thank several people connected with Columbia University Press. Series editor Virginia Richardson (Ohio State University) welcomed our book prospectus and put it forward as part of the Press's series on end-of-life care. Executive editor Lauren Dockett guided the prospectus through multiple levels of internal review, two anonymous external reviewers helped us clarify and elaborate the project, and copyeditor Leslie Kriesel corrected and clarified our writing at many points.

We hope these accounts will stimulate and intrigue you. More importantly, we hope they will provoke significant learning and growth, better preparing you for professional practice with people who, like you, will face dying, death, and bereavement.

Introduction to the Cases

FOR MORE THAN 100 YEARS, social work instructors have used cases in the classroom to educate students (Fisher 1978; Reitmeier 2002; e.g., Reynolds 1942; Towle 1954). Over time, these cases have taken many forms, ranging from brief vignettes only a few sentences or paragraphs long to complex, book-length accounts.

Merseth (1996) identifies three basic educational purposes of using cases: as examples or exemplars to illustrate practice, as foci for reflecting on practice, or as opportunities to practice decision making. For the first purpose, cases provide concrete and specific examples of how professional theories or interventions apply in practice situations and can help students understand theoretical content and practice skills. During the past few decades, most of the available social work casebooks have included cases for this purpose (e.g., Amodeo et al. 1997; Haulotte and Kretzschmar 2001; LeCroy 1999; McClelland, Austin, and Este 1998; Rivas and Hull 2003). Less frequently, cases have also been used as stimuli for student reflection.

In contrast, the case method of teaching uses cases as a site to practice collaborative decision making. This requires open-ended "decision" cases, a particular type specifically developed for this teaching approach. Such cases present students with unresolved situations that incorporate the ambiguities and dilemmas of social work practice and require active decision making (e.g., Cossom 1991; Golembiewski and Stevenson 1998; Lynn 1999; Rothman 2004; Wolfer and Scales 2006). They describe actual situations practitioners have encountered in great detail, reflecting the messiness and ambiguity of professional practice. Typically based on one practitioner's account, they sometimes include conflicting statements by the various participants involved, time constraints, competing ethical values, extraneous details, and incomplete information (only what was available to the practitioner at the time). Because the cases are open-ended, they do not tell what the practitioner ultimately did or how the case turned out. For that reason, they compel

1

students to use their analytic and critical thinking skills, their knowledge of social work theory and research, and their common sense and collective wisdom to identify and analyze problems, evaluate possible solutions, and formulate a preferred intervention.

What Decision Cases Are Not

Just to be clear, it may be helpful to point out what decision cases are not.

First, despite the fact that decision cases explicitly invite problem solving—in the sense of solving a puzzle or responding to a challenge—they do not require or imply a problem-focused approach, in the sense of having a primary focus on pathology or requiring use of a medical model. (For that matter, decision cases also do not require or imply a solution-focused approach—if that refers to a currently popular brief treatment approach.) Readers may actually assume a strengths perspective when discussing decision cases. However, either a problem-focused or a strengths perspective can be too dichotomous (McMillen, Morris, and Sherraden 2004), distorting the reality of a situation and potentially causing readers to overlook important aspects of the case.

Second, decision cases do not purposefully illustrate particular theories or intervention approaches. Decision cases seldom include much explicit theory unless the protagonist mentions it; rather, they are designed to provide detailed descriptive data about actual situations for use in case method teaching. Students and instructors are free to apply whatever theories they find useful. In fact, they will usually find it necessary to use some theory to make sense of a situation and decide how to respond. Students and instructors can draw potential theories from several sources. To prepare for particular case discussions, instructors may refer students to previous course materials or past experience; assign new readings on theory or intervention approaches; or require students to research appropriate resources on their own (much as they must do in the field following graduation). Although case discussions seldom include theory directly, they often clarify the fundamental importance of applying theory to practice—as students recognize the power of theory to provide a "handle" on complex situations—and also supply a means for understanding and assessing the relative value of alternative theories and intervention approaches—as students propose and consider various alternatives.

Third, decision cases do not imply that social workers can or should solve a problem without remainder (i.e., unambiguously, completely, permanently, for all parties). On the contrary, the best decision cases are ones about which competent practitioners will disagree. Obviously, the cases stimulate efforts to resolve problems. When we refer to resolving a problem, however, it is not to imply that all problems can be solved, but simply to acknowledge that the social worker must decide how to proceed from the point where the decision case ends. Such decision making will tend to be more effective if the social worker takes account of the underlying and interlocking reasons that have created or exacerbated the problem and addresses these in his or her decision. Increased decision-making skill is a major outcome of learning with decision cases.

Fourth, decision cases generally do not report how the case turned out. Pedagogically, the open-ended nature of the cases provides powerful incentive for problem solving. It also better replicates what students will experience in practice: they will need to make difficult decisions with limited and ill-structured information, under time constraints, and with uncertain consequences. Usually, they must make decisions going forward rather than with the luxury of hindsight to critique decisions by other professionals. In that way, discussing decision cases emulates practice and helps prepare students for it.

General Case Method Learning Outcomes

The cases in this collection are all decision cases. Properly used, they provide opportunities for the general types of learning associated with case method discussions. As suggested by Barnes, Christensen, and Hansen (1994), decision cases help students to adopt at least six aspects of a professional practitioner's point of view: 1) a focus on understanding the specific context; 2) a sense of appropriate boundaries; 3) sensitivity to interrelationships; 4) examining and understanding any situation from a multidimensional point of view; 5) accepting personal responsibility for the solution of organizational problems; and 6) an action orientation (50–51). Writing as business educators, they argue that case method instruction helps to develop in students an applied, "administrative point of view" (50). The concept of an administrative or practitioner point of view shifts students' attention from what they know to how they can use their knowledge. We refer to this as "thinking like a social worker" and will elaborate on it here.

First, the cases give ample detail about the background and context of the situations they depict. As students wrestle with the practice dilemmas, they come to understand the critical significance of context for problem framing and intervention. The relevant context varies across cases. For some it will include a combination of culture, law, policy, society, community, or organization. Many of the cases also include specific dates because timing—whether internally (relative to events within the case) or externally (relative to events in the broader environment)—is another important aspect of context. But not all the details turn out to be significant. Just as they must do in actual practice situations, students (social workers in training) must sort through the contextual information, selecting what is relevant and significant and disregarding what is not. Occasionally, addressing the dilemma will require gathering information not provided in the case because overlooking some aspect of context may have contributed to the practitioner's dilemma. Discussing these cases provides opportunities to practice deciding what is relevant and incorporating selected information into problem formulations and subsequent interventions.

Second, appropriate handling of the contextual information requires clear delineation of boundaries, sorting out what is separate and what is related. As students wrestle with the practice dilemmas in these cases, they come to appreciate the need to distinguish aspects of situations. For example, many of the cases turn on proper distinctions between social workers and clients, between individual clients and their families, between children and parents (or other adults), between professions, or between organizations. Sometimes these boundaries do not seem apparent to the protagonist. In fact, lack of clarity regarding boundaries often contributes to the reported dilemmas. Of special importance, some cases cannot be resolved without specifying the client system. In hospice practice, for example, the commitment to seeing the families of dying patients as clients sometimes obscures the boundaries between patients and their families, creating dilemmas for social workers. Likewise, social workers must consider whether addressing a particular client need falls within the scope of their employing organization's mission, license, expertise, or priorities. As suggested above, discussion offers opportunities for students to practice identifying and taking account of such boundaries in concrete situations.

Third, students must consider the webs of relationships present in these cases on multiple levels. Quite concretely, the cases depict relationships within families, professional work teams, or organizations that reflect the subtleties of behavior, cognition, emotion, and motivation. Many of the cases include both spoken and internal dialogue to more fully portray how the social workers who reported them experienced these situations and relationships. More abstractly, the cases also depict relationships between programs and policies, between professionals and host organizations, between events and their temporal context, and between theory and practice. In general, they require that students interpret the "raw" data to draw their own conclusions. Where the cases include assumptions held or conclusions drawn by the protagonist or others involved, students must decide what to accept. Assumptions and conclusions always shape how people understand situations, and sometimes contribute to the problem.

Relationships serve not only as background for the cases. Several cases also reflect the evolution over time of helping relationships (with individuals, families, or groups) or professional relationships (in supervision, interdisciplinary conferences, or work teams). Whatever has contributed to the current dilemma, the social worker must decide what to do next. There is no opportunity to go back in time to revise these relationships; change is only possible from the current point forward.

Fourth, although the cases were all based on interviews with individual social workers, they do not provide information from the protagonist's perspective alone. As much as possible, the interviews explored perspectives held by other participants, as reported by the social worker. For that reason, the cases include other perspectives as filtered through the eyes and ears of the social worker protagonist. While most involve relatively new practitioners, a few depict the experiences of longtime clinicians, supervisors, and administrators. As a result, they may be useful for experienced practitioners as well as social work students. The cases often include detailed dialogue that reflects differences in perspective and invites interpretation.

Fifth, the cases demonstrate the essential role of the social workers. Each case poses one or more dilemmas experienced by the social workers who reported it, highlighting their critical role as decision maker and actor. Often the reporting social worker was the only person who could intervene in the particular situation. Choosing not to intervene was seldom a real option and would carry its own consequences. Furthermore, the social workers often labored under time pressure because some imminent event required their decision and intervention. Because the cases are drawn from actual practice, the social workers must not only decide under time pressure but also often do so with incomplete information. As much as possible, the cases attempt to provide the full context for decision making (i.e., personal, professional, organizational, policy factors) of which the social worker was aware at the time.

In addition, many of the cases implicate the social workers themselves in the decision-making context. In other words, these detailed cases often reflect how the social workers' personal background, professional training, previous work experience, and time on the current job may contribute to their preparation and ability to respond. More specifically, the cases reflect how the social workers' personalities, values, ethics, knowledge, and skills influence their decision making. Discussing these cases will help students to understand how their own characteristics limit, focus, or enhance what they can understand and decide—in short, how the self of the social worker affects professional practice.

Sixth, the cases also clarify the necessity of moving from analysis to action. Whether the information appeared complete and clear or not, the social workers had to make decisions and act. Often, the situation could not wait: for example, a person was dying or another deadline looming, leaving limited time for deciding and intervening. As suggested above, not deciding or intervening would also be a kind of intervention, with its own set of consequences, and should be chosen just as carefully as any more active intervention rather than by default. The case discussions often explore the potentially harmful consequences of ill-considered or precipitous action. Discussion can help students to understand the fundamental necessity of intervening, and the importance of doing so based on thorough analysis of available data.

Specific End-of-Life Care Learning Outcomes

In addition to learning to "think like a social worker"—a skill vital in any area of social work practice—these cases provide a vehicle for students to develop their understanding of a somewhat specialized field of practice: end of life. Although case method teaching in general is intended to help students integrate and apply knowledge they already have, it also, like actual practice, requires them to identify gaps in their knowledge and take steps to fill them, under similar time pressures.

The collection of cases as a whole portrays the reality that sometimes serious illness precedes death, allowing time for reflection and opportunity for making choices about the end of one's life, and sometimes death occurs suddenly, unexpectedly. Half of the cases were in hospice settings, where end of life is clearly expected and social workers are prepared (to various degrees) to assist clients with concerns that are relatively predictable. The other half occurred in a range of social work practice settings. In some, death is expected for some clients but is not the major focus for social workers (e.g., hospital, dialysis center, AIDS clinic, support group for family members of individuals with AIDS, death row within a prison). In others, death impinges infrequently enough to be surprising (e.g., schools, residential treatment for children, group home for adults with profound disabilities). Some of the cases reflect various aspects of illness and the process of dying for a client, while others begin with the death of a person and focus more on the aftermath for the survivors.

In cases where death is expected and there is opportunity for choices related to the quality of living and dying for a client, predictable issues are presented: advance directives and the extent to which they are honored in various settings; the capacity of various clients to give informed consent; the tensions inherent in decisions to withhold or withdraw life-prolonging treatment; conflicts among health professionals, between people who are dying and their family members, and between health professionals and clients regarding client autonomy; and clients' right to define quality of life for themselves.

Social workers whose focus is on end-of-life care need a working knowledge of the biological and medical processes their clients are likely to experience throughout the dying process, and clear recognition of the limitations of their own knowledge and scope of practice. They must be familiar with the legal protections for clients' choices and self-determination regarding the care they do or do not wish to receive, and the issues involved in terminating some treatments when the burden begins to outweigh the benefit. They must be able to participate in resolving a wide range of dilemmas in light of ethical principles. They must have the knowledge and the clinical skills to be able to help both those who are dying and those who will survive them with their grieving, and be able to distinguish uncomplicated from complicated bereavement in survivors. They must understand the functioning of groups, organizations, institutions, and society, and be prepared to help clients deal with the pressures they may feel from health care systems, employers, and governmental and other organizational bureaucracies. Working their way through these cases provides social workers and students an opportunity to acquire factual information, integrate it with their prior knowledge and experience, apply it to a specific actual situation regarding which their knowledge is still likely to be incomplete, and reflect on their own values, beliefs, feelings, and life experiences as they affect and are affected by the situations portrayed.

Although end-of-life care constitutes a specialized field of practice, dying is a universal experience. It brings social workers into contact with clients who are usually considered the focus of an entirely different field of practice. Social workers in hospice and other end-of-life care settings—the social workers in many of these cases—have clients who have multiple and profound disabilities, or who abuse a variety of substances, or who do not speak English, or who have been physically or sexually abused. Conversely, social workers in residential treatment for adolescents and in elementary schools are called upon to respond to unexpected loss and grief.

In cases based in settings where death occurs less often and is not usually the focus of social work practice, different issues arise. Several cases present the possibility of a client's suicide—a university student who has experienced sexual trauma, a bereaved widower who is alcoholic, a young mother with a history of suicide gestures and a baby with stage 4 cancer, a Vietnamese refugee for whom suicide may be a way of saving face. The social workers in the cases—and the students who read and respond to them—must assess the level of imminent risk, make choices about their interventions, and sort out the degree of responsibility they bear for preventing suicide. Other cases present social workers' efforts to understand grief and be supportive of bereaved clients or co-workers while still being accountable for the goals of their work settings—for example, learning in elementary schools or maintaining a therapeutic milieu in a residential treatment center for adolescents.

A number of the cases reflect the need for social workers to take into account various legal and regulatory requirements. Although they are neither bankers nor lawyers, social workers in these cases (and thus the students who temporarily "step into their shoes") must help clients navigate financial trusts, state institutions for people with profound disability, statutory provisions for advanced care planning, and parental planning for the future care of dependent minors. They must assess and decide how to proceed in light of clients' questionable capacity to make decisions about their own care and clients' shifting expectations of health care providers as diseases, treatments, and funding sources change. They must take into account setting-specific definitions of privacy and confidentiality, personal and organizational liability and risk management, organizational budgeting priorities and constraints, evolving criteria for program eligibility, and possible malpractice by professionals of other disciplines in settings where they have higher status than social workers.

Social work as a profession is concerned with systems and boundaries, and especially with conflicts between and among them. Practitioners in these cases interact with professionals from other disciplines—including nurses, doctors, law enforcement officials, ethics committees, educators, and administrators for whom the financial bottom line is the final determinant of a decision—and organizational cultures, such as hospitals, nursing homes, schools, residential treatment centers, specialty health clinics, universities, prisons, social service agencies, and courts. The social workers must decide how to handle a range of conflicts among and with clients, co-workers, supervisors/supervisees, and administrators. In one instance, a social worker has to acknowledge her dislike and distrust of a dying woman's daughter and decide how, and how hard, to advocate for the patient's wishes, at the risk of further alienating the daughter. In another instance, nursing home staff members initiate artificial nutrition for a patient who is no longer eating, disregarding the patient's clear advance directive to the contrary. The hospice social worker must decide how firmly to press for the patient's wishes to be honored, realizing that if she antagonizes the facility staff it may adversely affect both the quality of care given to this patient and the likelihood of future referrals.

Although the cases do not always identify specific ethical principles, concepts such as autonomy, beneficence, nonmaleficence, informed consent, quality of life, and justice serve to inform or heighten the dilemmas presented. The social workers are faced with questions, for example, about whether or not a client has the capacity to make important decisions about his or her care at multiple points through the course of illness, about who should determine what is best for a client, and about the meaning of quality of life or suffering when the client cannot clearly communicate his or her own perspective.

As is true in all practice settings, social workers in these cases have to grapple with the integration of, and conflicts between, their personal and professional lives. One must balance her own worsening chronic health problems with the needs of her clients, and another must decide whether her own safety is threatened to the extent that she could justify denying or delaying services to a client. Several must decide how to handle their discomfort with or dislike of a client or co-worker or, conversely, their identification with, admiration for, and possibly even friendship with a client or co-worker. Others must deal with their own past trauma in order to know how to help their clients deal with trauma, and with their own grief in order to know how to help their clients grieve.

Finally, social workers must deal with their own beliefs about and responses to pain, suffering, illness, disability, disfigurement, grief, and the dying process in all its variations. They need to be keenly aware of the ways their own personal histories may hinder their work with or serve as a resource for clients in similar circumstances. And they need to be aware of the ways their exposure to dying and grieving affects them, both professionally and as human beings who will personally experience death and grief.

Diversity Within the Collection

This casebook is based on research funded by the Project on Death in America (PDIA). For budgetary reasons, as recommended by the PDIA selection committee, most of the cases come from the southeastern United States and reflect regional demographics. Nevertheless, we sought diversity on a variety of demographic dimensions (e.g., gender, age, race/ethnicity, socioeconomic status, sexual orientation, religion, immigrant status). The cases involve varying client system levels and ecological contexts. In addition, we included many fields of practice (not just those where people traditionally die), causes of death, and dying trajectories. The cases incorporate a variety of ethical, technical, and medical issues related to death and dying. The case matrix identifies selected dimensions of the decision cases and reflects their diversity and complexity.

Although these decision cases include people from a relatively limited range of demographic and cultural groups, what students learn about particular diversities may be secondary to what they learn about how to take account of diversities in professional practice. In other words, though content knowledge is necessary, it is not sufficient for decision making in these cases or in professional practice. Students can learn by dealing with familiar as well as unfamiliar types of diversity. For example, thought experiments that consider how a case might differ if some demographic element were substituted can be enlightening.

We trust that this collection of decision cases will provide stimulating and challenging opportunities for you to practice professional social work decision making, especially as it relates to end-of-life care. The cases may give new information about this and other aspects of professional social work practice. In addition, they will help you appreciate how end-of-life issues may crop up in many forms across diverse fields of practice, intricately interact with other aspects of the situations, and often have profound implications for everyone involved. At times, the learning that results from discussing these cases may be somewhat uncomfortable and difficult, even distressing. However, it will better prepare you for professional social work practice, and especially increase your sensitivity to and understanding of dying, death, and bereavement.

References

Amodeo, M., R. Schofield, T. Duffy, K. Jones, T. Zimmerman, and M. Delgado, eds. 1997. *Social Work Approaches to Alcohol and Other Drug Problems: Case Studies and Teaching Tools.* Alexandria, VA: Council on Social Work Education.

Barnes, L. B., C. R. Christensen, and A. J. Hansen. 1994. *Teaching and the Case Method.* 3rd ed. Boston: Harvard Business School Press.

Cossom, J. 1991. "Teaching from Cases: Education for Critical Thinking." *Journal of Teaching in Social Work* 5, no. 1: 139–155.

Fisher, C. F. 1978. "Being There Vicariously by Case Studies." In M. Ohmer and Associates, ed., *On College Teaching: A Guide to Contemporary Practices,* 258–285. San Francisco: Jossey-Bass.

Golembiewski, R. T. and J. G. Stevenson, eds. 1998. *Cases and Applications in Nonprofit Management.* Itasca, IL: F. E. Peacock.

Haulotte, S.M. and J. A. Kretzschmar, eds. 2001. *Case Scenarios for Teaching and Learning Social Work Practice.* Alexandria, VA: Council on Social Work Education.

LeCroy, C.W. 1999 *Case Studies in Social Work Practice,* 2nd ed. Pacific Grove, CA: Brooks/Cole.

Lynn, L.E., Jr. 1999. *Teaching and Learning with Cases: A Guidebook.* New York: Chatham House.

McClelland, R.W., C. D. Austin, and D. Este. 1998. *Macro Case Studies in Social Work.* Milwaukee: Families International.

McMillen, J.C., L. Morris, and M. Sherraden. 2004. "Ending Social Work's Grudge Match: Problems Versus Strengths." *Families in Society: The Journal of Contemporary Social Services* 85, no. 3: 317–325.

Merseth, K.K. 1996. "Cases and Case Methods in Teacher Education." In J. Sikula, T.J. Buttery, and E. Guyton, eds., *Handbook of Research on Teacher Education,* 2nd ed., 722–744. New York: Simon and Schuster Macmillan.

Reitmeier, M. 2002. *Use of Cases in Social Work Education.* Unpublished manuscript, University of South Carolina, Columbia.

Reynolds, B. C. 1942. *Learning and Teaching in the Practice of Social Work.* New York: Farrar and Rinehart.

Rivas, R.F. and G. H. Hull. 2003. *Case Studies in Generalist Practice.* 3rd ed. Belmont, CA: Wadsworth.

Rothman, J.C. 2004. *From the Front Lines: Student Cases in Social Work Ethics.* Boston: Allyn and Bacon.

Towle, C. 1954. *The Learner in Education for the Professions: As Seen in Education for Social Work.* Chicago: University of Chicago Press.

Wolfer, T. A. and T. L. Scales, eds. 2006. *Decision Cases for Advanced Social Work Practice: Thinking Like a Social Worker.* Belmont, CA: Thomson Brooks/Cole.

Case Summaries

1. The Request

Born with severe hydrocephalus, Timmy Jenkins was expected to die soon but survived to age fourteen, though he was unresponsive to stimuli. Timmy's mother, facing multiple life stressors, sought the help of hospice staff to obtain a Do Not Resuscitate (DNR) order to stop nursing home staff from treating Timmy's chronic infections. Kathy Scott, the hospice social worker, was not sure how to assist her.

2. ResponsAbilities

Hospice of Bayview developed a new program, Living Alone, to extend its usual hospice services to patients without primary caregivers. However, team members experienced increasing anxiety while serving Ms. Altman, their first Living Alone patient. Sharon Taylor, the director of social services, faced conflict about whether to replace a novice social worker with someone more experienced and confident—thus increasing the likelihood of the team's work with Ms. Altman going well—or leaving her on the case, so as to build her skills and not to undermine her confidence.

3. Family Matters

Lou Montgomery, a relatively new hospice social worker, began work with Leonard Morrison, a sixty-eight-year-old man dying of lung cancer. She was puzzled by his family's divergent reactions—Mrs. Morrison remained distant, allowing daughter Barbara to handle the details of Leonard's care—and surprised by a family secret.

4. Drug Interactions

Frank Barr, a middle-aged man who was HIV positive and dying of AIDS, sought hospice services after he had decided to stop antiviral medication and his physician confirmed that he had a prognosis of six months or less. From the outset, hospice social worker Cheryl Peak (and her colleagues) had questions about the appropriateness of hospice care in his case, first because he did not appear imminently terminal and then because he was suspected of misusing prescribed medications and using illegal street drugs.

5. Whose Will When?

Allen Robinson had experienced significantly diminishing health over the last six months. His daughter, to whom he had given power of attorney, and his wife decided to implement his living will and have tube feedings and liquids discontinued. However, the nursing home's assistant director of nursing decided to restart these treatments, stating that the nursing home had a policy that patients could not go without nutrition and hydration for more than seven days. Social worker Marianne Thornwell felt torn between the family's need for prompt resolution and her own need to stay in the good graces of the nursing home staff.

6. Unusual Appeal

Cynthia Sanders worked as a mitigation investigator at Florida Project for Human Justice, a nonprofit law firm that represented inmates on death row. Because of Cynthia's experience with clients who have schizophrenia, her boss, Diane Epps, asked her to work on José Aranda's case. José had schizophrenia and did not want to appeal his death sentence. Cynthia was not sure what her own responsibility as a social worker was to José.

7. The Last Dose

Lisa Parker, a pediatric hospice social worker, participated along with other team members in the death vigil for twelve-year-old Jason at Children's Hospital. She witnessed two interventions by the hospital nurse that seemed unusual to her, and began to question whether Jason's death might have been hastened by the nurse's actions. Her teammates apparently did not notice them or did not find them unusual, and were focused on supporting Jason's mother. Lisa had to decide whether to report what she saw.

8. No Place for Grief

Deb Weston's nephew, Shane McKinsey, had just been killed in a four-wheeler accident. As the social worker for the school district where he was a student, Deb had to provide grief counseling to his classmates, and she was surprised by her own reactions.

9. Right Before Their Eyes

In front of students on a morning school bus route, the former boyfriend of a student committed suicide with a fatal gunshot. School social worker Caroline Eastman only learned of the situation after the bus driver had already delivered the children to school. To intervene in this crisis, Caroline had to immediately identify and prioritize the competing needs of everyone involved.

10. Private Charity

Social worker Melissa Sinclair was the first manager of a new refugee resettlement program. She hired some very talented staff, including a Vietnamese refugee, Hao Tran, as a translator. Hao began borrowing money from various people and sources, getting himself ever deeper into debt, and when confronted he considered suicide as a way to save face.

11. Suicidal Co-ed

Lisa Conway, a social worker at a university sexual trauma center, initially responded to a sexual assault at a local hospital emergency room, where she met the survivor, Mary Williams, a first-year undergraduate student. Over time, Lisa faced several challenging situations with Mary, including her alleged history of sexual abuse by her father, her repeated calls to the twenty-four-hour crisis line, and finally, a suicide threat.

12. What Can I Tell?

In 1993, social worker Carolyn Johnson worked as a case manager for a medical clinic serving a homeless population. There she encountered Mark and Karen White, a common-law couple who sought medical care. When Mark was diagnosed as HIV positive, he refused to give Karen this information or to permit the clinic staff to do so. Unable to persuade Mark to inform Karen, Carolyn felt torn by her obligation to respect Mark's privacy and her desire to protect Karen's health and life.

13. Grief at Work

Mike Owens was a novice supervisor of the weekend shift at a residential treatment facility for children. Brian Stanfield was one of the staff members Mike recruited as a residential counselor. He and Mike had been acquaintances in school and became fast friends after they began to work together. Brian's work performance and accountability drastically diminished after the death of his father, leaving Mike to determine his responsibilities to Brian both as his supervisor and as his friend.

14. Dying on Time

As Director of Social Services, Bonnie Delaney supervised Miriam Goldstein, a hospice social worker who had a reputation as idealistic and demanding. Miriam was assigned to Jean, a hospice patient who had been diagnosed with ALS (Lou Gehrig's disease) and was about to enter her final hospice benefit period with Medicare, but had not been exhibiting symptoms that her illness had clearly reached the terminal phase. In 1995, because of increased government scrutiny regarding reimbursements, hospice administration decided to review whether Jean and other patients met Medicare criteria for the final benefit period.

15. Just Thinking About It

Eugenia Rollins, grandmother of a pediatric hospice patient, asked hospice social worker Cindy Burnett to assess the suicide risk of her daughter, Tiffany, the baby's mother, while Eugenia took the baby, who had a high fever, to the doctor's office. Tiffany had a history of suicide attempts, the most recent of which had occurred at the time of the baby's diagnosis, and Eugenia had just found an ambiguous note.

16. A Painful Predicament

Mindy Callahan, an experienced social worker providing services to dialysis patients, was confronted with a case in which the end-of-life wishes of her client, Elliott Marshall, were not honored. With Mindy's support and educational efforts, Elliott had decided to end the treatments that were only prolonging his suffering and no longer contributed to his quality of life. Mindy did her best to document, communicate, and advocate for his wishes, but another member of the health care team overrode Elliot's advance directive.

17. Til Death Do Us Part?

Linda Nickels, a geriatric social worker at Fredonia Hospital, was covering the discharge of an elderly woman for her colleague, Michelle Humphrey. As the patient, Mrs. Anderson, left the hospital, her husband of more than sixty years broke down in tears. His wife had had radical abdominal surgery that required complex dressing changes. She could not return to their home because he had a visual impairment and the conditions in their farmhouse were not sufficiently sanitary. Mr. Anderson insisted he would not have agreed to the surgery if he had known the consequences. Linda became quite concerned about the informed consent procedure at the hospital.

18. I Want to Talk to Your Supervisor!

Hospice social worker Marie Vincent found it difficult to connect and communicate with Suzanne Winters, the daughter of hospice patient Doris Blackwell. In particular, Marie found Suzanne superficial, unwilling to be inconvenienced for her mother's sake, and even deceitful. Marie faced an apparent choice between advocating for Doris's wishes to go home at the risk of alienating her daughter and helping Doris to grieve and hopefully adjust to life in an extended care facility in accordance with her daughter's wishes.

19. Drowning Sorrows

Hospice social worker Karla Thomas had a recently bereaved client, Howard Harriman, whom she assessed to be at high risk for suicide. Howard had a long history of alcohol use and had recently resumed drinking to ease the pain of his loss. He lived in a very rural, isolated setting. During her first visit, he touched Karla in an inappropriate way, and she feared being alone with him again, especially when he had been drinking. She asked him to refrain from drinking prior to her visits and he agreed, but then drank anyway.

20. Seizing Hope

Case manager Tim Reilly, M.S.W., coordinated services for individuals with developmental disabilities and their families. One of his clients, Gilbert, age thirty-five, had moderate mental retardation and a severe seizure disorder that threatened his life. He and a colleague felt compelled to advocate for Gilbert when they learned that medication for the seizure disorder would cause him to die within the next eighteen months unless he had a radical and risky surgery. Together, they decided to talk to Gilbert in a developmentally appropriate way about his prognosis and medical options.

21. Gifts

Phyllis Watts, an experienced hospice social worker, agreed to assume responsibility for leading Mothers and Others, a support group composed largely of white, middle-class and upper middle-class parents and grandparents of gay men who contracted HIV when the disease first appeared in the United States. Phyllis found herself struggling to define her role within the group. She worried that she was not effectively mediating between the needs of the founding members and those of the new members, and that the group was not responding adequately to the changing nature and demographics of the epidemic.

CASE SUMMARIES | 19

22. Patty's Girls

As a social work student intern, Patty Morris worked with two young girls whose mother was killed in a car accident. They went to live with their grandmother in a different part of town, which involved a change of schools. Patty felt torn between following the instructions of the children's grandmother, to wait before having any further contact with the girls, and the instructions of her field instructor, to immediately contact them at their new school to offer support and guidance. Making the situation more difficult, Patty herself had an extensive history of losses.

23. I Don't Want Them Mad at Me

Emily Prentice, hospice social worker, had to prioritize her work on multiple issues and needs presented by the Jones family. Donald Jones was dying of leukemia at age forty-two; his wife had died of complications of diabetes five years before. Donald had made no arrangements for the custody or guardianship of his two daughters, ages sixteen and twelve. Emily's efforts to facilitate this were complicated by Donald's changing desires, avoidance of conflict with his daughters, and deteriorating condition. When the hospice team first met him, his speech was already slurred and difficult to understand, and it became more so as he quickly grew weaker, to the point that it was difficult to converse at all.

	1. The Request	2. ResponsAbilities	3. Family Matters	4. Drug Interactions	5. Whose Will When?	6. Unusual Appeal	7. The Last Dose	8. No Place for Grief	9. Right Before Their Eyes	10. Private Charity	11. Suicidal Co-ed	12. What Can I Tell?
Case Settings												
Hospice	X	X	X	X	X		X					
Hospital							X					
Nursing home					X							
Residential care	X											
Outpatient medical clinic											X	X
Criminal justice						X						
School								X	X		X	
Other agency / community									X	X		
Client System / Target of Change												
Individual	X	X		X		X	X		X		X	X
Family			X		X			X				
Group		X						X	X			
Supervisee		X								X		
Organization	X	X			X	X	X		X			X
Ecological Context												
Client / patient		X		X	X	X	X				X	X
Family	X		X					X				X
Task or treatment group		X						X		X		
Organization	X	X		X	X	X	X		X	X	X	X
Community								X	X	X	X	
Populations at Risk												
Elderly		X	X		X							
Children	X						X	X	X	X		
Women	X	X	X		X			X			X	X
Racial / ethnic minorities						X				X		X
Sexual minorities												
Developmental disabilities	X											
Poverty							X					X
Immigrants / refugees							X			X		
Other Critical Factors												
Mental illness							X				X	
Substance abuse				X							X	X
Violence							X		X	X	X	
Religion / spirituality									X			

	13. Grief at Work	14. Dying on Time	15. Just Thinking About It	16. Painful Predicament	17. 'Til Death Do Us Part...	18. I Want to Talk...	19. Drowning Sorrows	20. Seizing Hope	21. Gifts	22. Patty's Girls	23. I Don't Want Them...
Case Settings											
Hospice		X	X			X	X				X
Hospital				X	X						
Nursing home											
Residential care	X							X			
Outpatient medical clinic				X							
Criminal justice											
School										X	
Other agency / community								X	X		
Client System/Target of Change											
Individual			X	X	X	X	X	X		X	X
Family			X		X	X			X	X	X
Group									X		
Supervisee	X	X									
Organization	X	X		X	X			X			
Ecological Context											
Client / patient				X	X	X	X	X			X
Family			X			X					X
Task or treatment group		X							X		
Organization	X	X		X			X	X		X	
Community									X		
Populations at Risk											
Elderly					X	X	X			X	
Children	X		X							X	X
Women		X	X			X			X	X	
Racial / ethnic minorities		X							X	X	
Sexual minorities		X							X		
Developmental disabilities								X			
Poverty				X					X	X	X
Immigrants / refugees											
Other Critical Factors											
Mental illness											
Substance abuse								X			
Violence			X	X							
Religion / spirituality				X					X		

	1. The Request	2. ResponsAbilities	3. Family Matters	4. Drug Interactions	5. Whose Will When?	6. Unusual Appeal	7. The Last Dose	8. No Place for Grief	9. Right Before Their Eyes	10. Private Charity	11. Suicidal Co-ed	12. What Can I Tell?
Chronology												
Suicide risk							X			X	X	
Dying	X	X	X	X	X	X	X					X
Death			X				X	X	X			
Bereavement			X						X	X		X
Ethical Issues												
Client competence and decision-making capacity	X	X		X	X	X				X	X	
Autonomy and self-determination	X	X	X	X	X	X		X		X	X	X
Informed consent		X										
Quality of life	X	X			X	X	X					
Withholding / withdrawing life-prolonging care	X			X	X		X					
Hastening death	X			X	X	X	X					
Suicide										X	X	
Confidentiality			X	X						X	X	X
Professional collegiality								X		X	X	
Professional competence		X										
Social Work Role in End-of-Life Care												
Host settings	X			X	X	X	X	X	X	X	X	X
Interdisciplinary settings	X	X		X	X	X	X	X	X		X	X
Interdisciplinary relationships			X		X	X	X				X	X
Biological and Medical Aspects												
Social worker use of / need for medical knowledge	X	X	X	X	X	X	X			X	X	X
Pain / symptom management	X			X	X	X	X					
Withholding / withdrawing life-prolonging care	X			X	X		X					
Dying process	X	X	X				X					
Hastening death	X						X					

	13. Grief at Work	14. Dying on Time	15. Just Thinking About It	16. Painful Predicament	17. 'Til Death Do Us Part…	18. I Want to Talk…	19. Drowning Sorrows	20. Seizing Hope	21. Gifts	22. Patty's Girls	23. I Don't Want Them…
Chronology											
Suicide risk	X		X				X				
Dying		X	X	X	X	X		X	X		X
Death				X						X	
Bereavement	X						X		X	X	
Ethical Issues											
Client competence and decision-making capacity		X		X	X	X		X			X
Autonomy and self-determination					X	X	X	X		X	
Informed consent				X	X			X		X	
Quality of life		X		X	X		X	X			
Withholding / withdrawing life-prolonging care				X				X			
Hastening death								X			
Suicide			X				X				
Confidentiality			X							X	X
Professional collegiality	X	X		X	X					X	
Professional competence								X	X		
Social Work Role in End-of-Life Care											
Host settings	X			X	X					X	
Interdisciplinary settings		X		X	X			X		X	
Interdisciplinary relationships		X		X	X	X		X			
Biological and Medical Aspects											
Social worker use of / need for medical knowledge		X		X	X	X		X	X		X
Pain / symptom management			X					X			
Withholding / withdrawing life-prolonging care				X				X			
Dying process		X		X		X		X			X
Hastening death							X				

	1. The Request	2. ResponsAbilities	3. Family Matters	4. Drug Interactions	5. Whose Will When?	6. Unusual Appeal	7. The Last Dose	8. No Place for Grief	9. Right Before Their Eyes	10. Private Charity	11. Suicidal Co-ed	12. What Can I Tell?
Technical Knowledge												
Advance directives		X			X							
Informed consent		X			X						X	
Withholding / withdrawing life-prolonging care	X				X		X					
Governmental / organizational policies related to EOL care	X			X					X			X
Dying process	X	X	X	X	X		X					
Grief		X						X	X	X		X
Developmental issues related to illness, death, grief	X						X	X	X			
Family relationships and dying / grief	X		X		X			X		X		X
Social worker use of / need for medical knowledge	X			X		X	X					X
Trauma / crisis situations								X	X	X	X	
Client competence / capacity	X	X		X		X						
Suicide									X	X	X	
Major Social Trends												
Quality of life	X	X		X	X	X						
Good death		X			X							
Cost containment												
Medical advances					X							

	13. Grief at Work	14. Dying on Time	15. Just Thinking About It	16. Painful Predicament	17. 'Til Death Do Us Part?	18. I Want to Talk...	19. Drowning Sorrows	20. Seizing Hope	21. Gifts	22. Patty's Girls	23. I Don't Want Them...
Technical Knowledge											
Advance directives				X							
Informed consent				X	X			X			
Withholding / withdrawing life-prolonging care				X				X			
Governmental / organizational policies related to EOL care		X		X				X			X
Dying process		X		X		X		X			X
Grief	X			X		X	X		X	X	
Developmental issues related to illness, death, grief			X		X			X		X	X
Family relationships and dying / grief	X		X		X	X			X	X	X
Social worker use of / need for medical knowledge		X		X	X			X			X
Trauma / crisis situations			X							X	
Client competence / capacity						X		X			X
Suicide			X				X				
Major Social Trends											
Quality of life				X				X			
Good death		X		X							
Cost containment		X						X			
Medical advances		X			X			X	X		

1 | The Request

Mary Hylton and Terry A. Wolfer

AS THE MEETING AT PINECREST Intermediate Care Facility for the Mentally Retarded ended, hospice social worker Kathy Scott had more questions than before the meeting began. To judge by the expressions on their faces, her hospice colleagues were equally perplexed.

As she wedged her notebook into her briefcase, Kathy thought about Evelyn's request. She was torn about whether or not the hospice should support Evelyn's demand for termination of all life-prolonging treatments for her fourteen-year-old son, Timmy Jenkins. It had seemed to Kathy since her first meeting with Evelyn that Evelyn wanted Timmy to die. More than one family had expressed to her a readiness for a child to die in order to end his suffering, but this felt different. As Evelyn saw it, obtaining a Do Not Resuscitate (DNR) order and termination of antibiotics were steps toward facilitating his death. It was also obvious to Kathy that the Pinecrest staff did not share Evelyn's wishes for her son.

Although hospice staff members often supported requests for the termination of life-prolonging treatments, Timmy's situation was unusual. Although

Development of this decision case was supported in part by funding from the Project on Death in America and the University of South Carolina College of Social Work. It was prepared solely to provide material for class discussion and not to suggest either effective or ineffective handling of the situation depicted. Although the case is based on field research regarding an actual situation, names and certain facts may have been disguised to protect confidentiality. The authors wish to thank the anonymous case reporter for cooperation in making this account available for the benefit of social work students and instructors.

Kathy and her team members had agreed to assess his case, they had not yet determined whether to admit him to the pediatric program. After today's meeting, Kathy wondered if Evelyn would still want to have hospice involved if they did not support her request. She also understood that if they did admit Timmy, they would have to decide to what extent they were willing to advocate on Evelyn's behalf, given that Timmy was completely unable to participate in the decision.

Kathy looked at her hospice colleagues as they headed toward the door and thought, *We have some difficult decisions to make.*

Pinecrest Intermediate Care Facility for the Mentally Retarded

Pinecrest was one of four intermediate care facilities for the mentally retarded operated and regulated by the state since the 1920s. The imposing old four-story Gothic-style building, clearly separated from the neighborhood by its location high up on a hill, was surrounded by pine trees and a six-foot stone wall and accessible only by a narrow, winding, recently blacktopped road. The 120 residents were, almost without exception, profoundly disabled (although not in need of skilled nursing care on a regular basis), and most lived virtually their entire lives there. In contrast with common staff retention problems experienced in other nursing facilities, a majority of the staff at Pinecrest had worked there for more than 10 years and took pride in their longevity in a job that others rejected as too depressing or difficult.

Hospice of Springville

Hospice of Springville was the only hospice in the city of Springville, and was well regarded and well supported by the community. Local corporations and foundations had established a sort of rotating responsibility for funding the pediatric program, since in the early 1990s insurance companies were just beginning to recognize the need for hospice care for children.

The pediatric program at Hospice of Springville had expanded its admission criteria for children to include "life-threatening" conditions in addition to those more clearly recognized as "terminal." The forceful personality and strong convictions of one early board member, who also happened to be a pediatrician, persuaded the hospice board to adopt these unusually broad criteria, and community support made it possible. Although one local home health agency also provided home care for pediatric clients, Hospice of Springville's pediatric team had established a reputation for being able to bring some stability and calm into even the most chaotic situations, resulting in improved care for children by their families and far less stress for busy physicians. The "peds team" members often laughed about how they seemed to get "only the really messy cases," but generally they enjoyed the challenges and the opportunity to make a significant difference for families and children as they dealt with difficult life circumstances.

The Referral

That's odd, Kathy thought as she hung up the phone.

Contrary to the agency's regular intake procedure, Dana Bruer, one of the pediatric team nurses, had called to request that the team meet to discuss the referral of Timmy Jenkins, an adolescent boy with severe hydrocephalus. Dana had stated that she felt it was important that the team talk before seeing Timmy or his mother, Evelyn, who was requesting hospice's assistance in obtaining a DNR order. Although they were common among hospice clients, something in Dana's voice indicated to Kathy that this situation was unusual.

At Evelyn's request, Timmy had been referred to Hospice of Springville by the staff of Children's Hospital following a single brief admission due to a seizure. Timmy had been born with severe hydrocephalus. Due to an accumulation of excess fluid in his skull, his head was approximately twenty-nine inches in diameter from ear to ear, and almost that large from front to back. His facial features appeared just slightly stretched. Although his eyes remained open, Timmy did not interact with others nor respond to visual or auditory stimuli. He had limited movement and had to be repositioned every two or three hours to prevent pressure sores. Due to the size of his head, it took three people to turn Timmy: two to turn his head while a third simultaneously turned his body. It was unknown whether he could see or hear.

Dana reported that she had gone with Timmy's mother to visit him at Pinecrest Intermediate Care Facility, and that Evelyn was "watching me like a hawk" to ascertain her reactions to Timmy. Although Dana had worked as a pediatric nurse for many years and then in hospice for several years, she admitted that she was shocked by Timmy's appearance and had to consciously suppress her reactions. She didn't want others on the team to have the same experience. Dana suggested that team members might need time to deal with their own responses before talking with Evelyn.

Meeting Timmy

The next day, after receiving the referral, Kathy stood next to Hope Kirkland, the hospice chaplain, and stared at the young man in the bed. Although she had seen a great deal of variety in the human condition during her ten years working in the hospice field, she was decidedly unsettled by what she saw. Clad in a blue T-shirt and diaper, Timmy lay on his side with his eyes open. His sparse, soft brown hair had been cut close to his enormous head. Because he had lived the entirety of his fourteen years inside institutions, Timmy's skin appeared nearly translucent. His thin, underdeveloped body resembled that of a ten-year-old rather than an adolescent. With his abnormally large head and small body, Kathy thought Timmy looked like a large embryo attached to a slightly flattened beach ball.

How can this be? she pondered. *How can someone in this condition survive?*

Kathy struggled to make meaning of Timmy's situation. Although she had worked with people with severe mental retardation and with people who were comatose, nothing in her prior experience directly matched this. Timmy's condition and life history raised questions for her regarding the meaning of being human. She felt unsure about how to relate to Timmy and unsure whether he could relate to others.

Kathy pulled a chair close to Timmy's bed and sat down. For the first time since she had arrived, she began to look around. The small private room Timmy occupied at Pinecrest was decorated with stuffed animals and cards. She observed the room and its contents to be clean and noted that Timmy did not show any of the signs indicative of neglectful care. Although the Pinecrest nurses and aides seemed guarded with her and Hope, they appeared genuinely affectionate toward Timmy. On several occasions she heard them refer to Timmy as "my Timmy" or "our Timmy." It seemed clear that he was well cared for.

Kathy Scott

At age thirty-three, Kathy Scott, a Caucasian woman from a middle-class background, had completed master's degrees in both theology and social work. She was a thoughtful and reflective person who had earned the respect of her co-workers. Having worked for eight years at another hospice prior to Hospice of Springville, she was also an experienced social worker. Kathy had worked with the pediatric team at Hospice of Springville for almost two years.

Encountering Evelyn Brampton

The day after meeting Timmy, Kathy and Hope returned to Pinecrest, this time, to meet his mother, Evelyn Brampton. At Evelyn's request, Dana had arranged for a meeting with all the hospice pediatric team members. Dana reported that Evelyn did not want to have to tell Timmy's story repeatedly and requested the meeting so that she would only have to go through it once. Although the meeting was being held at Pinecrest, the purpose was to provide the hospice team members with essential background information, much of which was already known to Pinecrest staff. Evelyn had requested to meet with just the hospice team this first time, so none of the Pinecrest staff had been invited.

Kathy looked around the small room and smiled at her co-workers. Dana and Chris Tinsley, the expressive therapist who would be working with Timmy's adolescent brother, were already seated in two of the five metal chairs surrounding the small conference table. A Caucasian woman with short dark hair, whom Kathy assumed to be Evelyn, sat stiffly across the table from them. Dana introduced Evelyn to the team and asked her to provide the group with some background information, including the details of Timmy's birth and the incidents that had led up to the referral to hospice.

"Timmy's birth was traumatic, and nearly cost me my life," Evelyn began. "Due to the size of his head, the doctors had to perform a c-section. I nearly died in the process."

Evelyn spoke matter-of-factly, but with an intensity that betrayed her surface calm. Kathy noted immediately that she was articulate and bright. However, something in her manner made Kathy feel uncomfortable.

"His doctors told us that he would not survive long," Evelyn continued. "Because they believed he would die quickly, they decided against placing a shunt to drain the fluid accumulating on his brain. He was placed in a pediatric skilled nursing facility. I didn't see him for weeks. I was still recovering physically from the birth, and I was maybe suffering from some depression.

"After several months it became apparent that Timmy was not going to die immediately, that he was living longer than was expected. His doctors decided that he would need to be moved to a less intensive and less costly facility. It was at this point that he was moved to Pinecrest."

Dana interrupted Evelyn. "How old was Timmy when he was moved to Pinecrest?"

"About six months," Evelyn responded.

"Has he remained here since that point?" Kathy inquired.

"Yes, excluding the hospitalizations," Evelyn replied curtly. Kathy quickly calculated in her head that Timmy had resided at Pinecrest for thirteen years.

"Recently, Timmy's condition has been deteriorating. In addition to the seizure that landed him in the hospital, he has been having increasingly frequent infections—urinary tract and pneumonia. I have repeatedly requested that a DNR be written, but the staff and doctors at Pinecrest refuse to listen to my request. That's why I asked the nurse at Children's Hospital to contact hospice." Evelyn leaned across the table and spoke forcefully. "They continue to disregard my request for the DNR despite the fact that Timmy continues to get worse physically. As Timmy's parent, don't I have the right to decide what's going to happen to him now?"

Evelyn's voice sounded angry. "I have visited Timmy several times every week for the last fourteen years. I am tired, and I am ready for this to be over. I am ready for Timmy to die. I want hospice to help with my request."

During her tenure in the hospice field Kathy had heard numerous family members say that they were ready for a loved one to die, but something about how Evelyn had said it made her uneasy. In Kathy's experience, family members tended to be tired, sad, or even resolute. Evelyn was angry. There was a coldness, a hardness, about her that Kathy had never encountered before. She sensed that Evelyn was not merely ready for Timmy to die but actually wanted him to die. *It almost feels like she would want us to help euthanize him if she thought we would do that,* Kathy thought.

"You said you believe Timmy is getting worse. Can you tell us a little bit more about the infections and anything else that leads you to believe that his condition is deteriorating?" Dana asked.

"He has had several seizures recently and has had to be hospitalized. He has also had numerous urinary tract infections, and he had pneumonia a couple of months ago. Timmy is getting worse. The doctors and Pinecrest staff just can't seem to see that. They persist in believing that he is responsive to their interventions. I think they refuse to see Timmy's limitations because they don't want to accept the futility of their work." Evelyn paused to look around the room and then continued tersely, "There is a quarterly care-planning meeting in a couple of weeks and I would like for you to be there. The Pinecrest staff will not listen to me. Timmy is getting worse. I want that DNR and I need your help to get it. I am ready for him to die."

The team was momentarily silent. Kathy noticed that Evelyn had never fully articulated what it was about Timmy's current condition that indicated extensive deterioration. According to information Dana had provided, Timmy's infections had been relatively minor and easily treated with antibiotics. She wondered whether Evelyn might be exaggerating. Kathy also thought she remembered that, as a state facility, Pinecrest could not honor a DNR order, but wondered why that information had not been shared with Evelyn. *I'll have to check that out,* she thought.

"Perhaps we can visit Timmy during the week, if that would help you— maybe you could take a day off from visiting, knowing that one of us would be here. The visits would also give us an opportunity to assess Timmy," Dana offered.

Evelyn straightened her back and nodded agreement. After a hurried thank you, she abruptly exited the room, leaving the team members alone. Hope let out a sigh and looked toward Kathy. "Whoa, what just happened here?"

"I don't know what to think," Kathy admitted. This was not a typical hospice case, as Timmy's condition did not appear to be clearly terminal—yet it was not difficult to believe that his condition was life-threatening and that he could well die sooner rather than later. The team members agreed that further assessment was needed in order to decide what, if any, role hospice would play in this case.

"I'll look through Timmy's charts and speak with his doctors regarding his recent health problems," Dana said.

"Okay, and I'll see Evelyn, to offer her some support and see if she wants to work on grief issues with me," Kathy volunteered. All four team members agreed to visit Timmy and to attend the upcoming care-planning meeting.

Getting to Know Evelyn

Kathy followed Evelyn into a rather formal and unused-looking living room for her first visit alone with her, with an unfamiliar degree of trepidation about how it would go. As at Pinecrest, Evelyn started talking immediately. It seemed evident from her rather rehearsed tone that she had covered the same topics several times before.

Twice married, Evelyn was facing her second divorce. Her first marriage, to Timmy's father, ended two years after Timmy's birth. Shortly after the divorce, Timmy's father moved out of state. He had since remarried and had only minimal contact with Evelyn and Timmy.

Evelyn directly connected her first divorce to Timmy's birth and subsequent illnesses. However, she believed that the impending second divorce was only tangentially related to Timmy's situation. When Kathy pushed her just a bit, Evelyn acknowledged that she was frequently preoccupied and upset about Timmy and that these feelings perhaps had complicated the other problems in her current marriage.

Evelyn described her relationship with her second son, Ricky, as being "difficult." Several years younger than Timmy, Ricky was approaching adolescence and was becoming rebellious. Evelyn struggled to control his behavior. Although as a younger child Ricky had occasionally accompanied Evelyn on visits to Pinecrest, he now refused to visit Timmy. Kathy had a strong sense that this was only the tip of the iceberg. *Chris is going to really have his work cut out for him with Ricky,* she thought.

Evelyn spoke about her full-time job as a second-grade teacher in an irritated tone that suggested she experienced it as a source of stress, not satisfaction. Kathy winced inwardly at the thought of second graders being exposed to that irritation for hours every day.

With the exception of a few sporadic visits by his father, Evelyn indicated that she was the only family member to visit Timmy. Although she was not responsible for his immediate care (or even the financing of his care), Evelyn clearly conveyed her sense of obligation to make frequent trips to Pinecrest to check on him—even though, she insisted to Kathy, she felt there was "no one there" when she looked at him. Kathy recognized her own discomfort at that but felt uncertain about how to address it at this point.

Kathy had been listening for any mention of a friend, a personal support system, and she still hadn't heard anything, so she asked directly. "Are there any family members or friends—neighbors, co-workers, parents of Ricky's friends, anyone—who give you some support?"

"No, I don't really have time for socializing," Evelyn responded, "and there isn't anyone at work or living around here that I'd care to be friends with anyway."

What a lonely woman, Kathy thought. *But she'd be a hard person to be friends with, if what I'm seeing is how she is with others.*

"I know that Hope will talk about this with you, Evelyn," Kathy acknowledged, "but could I ask if you participate in any church or faith-based group? I'm just wondering if that could be a source of some support for you—I'm concerned about how alone you are in all this."

"No, I've never really been interested in religion," Evelyn replied.

Kathy decided to push just a little further on this first real visit, and then leave it up to Hope. "Do you have personal beliefs that help you make sense of life and all that has happened with Timmy?"

"Do you mean do I think that 'God is with me' or that there's a purpose for Timmy being like he is?" Evelyn asked. "No, I guess you'd call me an agnostic—I've never thought that God is all that interested in my life. At least I hope not—I'd hate to think that Timmy is anything other than an unfortunate accident of nature."

Kathy felt hesitant to probe further into Evelyn's feelings about Timmy and his eventual death. *But I still don't really know who she is, what all this means to her, how she's dealing with it inside herself,* she thought. *I wish I could find a "soft spot" in her, where I could connect with her emotionally—but she's got it well hidden, so far.*

As Kathy left Evelyn's home, she rubbed at her forehead to relieve the tension headache she'd developed during the hour and a half there. *Whew, she's really intense,* Kathy thought, *but this poor woman has been through so much, and she seems so totally alone with it all.*

Back at the office, Kathy confided to Dana, "Evelyn Brampton has been through a lot, I know, but I have to admit I dread seeing her again."

Dana nodded. "I know what you mean. I just have a really uneasy feeling about her."

The Staff Meeting

Two weeks after her initial visit with Timmy, Kathy took a seat next to Dana at the large conference table. Although they were still waiting for everyone to arrive for the quarterly care-planning meeting, the atmosphere in the small room was already tense. As the Pinecrest staff arrived, they quietly took seats next to one another along one side of the long table. Evelyn sat at the end of the table with her arms crossed in front of her. She looked at Kathy and nodded a greeting.

Kathy sensed that the presence of the hospice staff had rattled the Pinecrest employees. She observed the wary glances they exchanged among themselves. During all her visits to Pinecrest subsequent to her initial meeting with Timmy, the primarily Caucasian staff had remained guarded.

Kathy looked up as Hope and Chris entered the room. Chris raised his eyebrows questioningly as he and Hope took the two remaining chairs, adjacent to Evelyn. Kathy and her hospice team members had agreed to limit their participation to observing and taking notes. They had not yet settled on what role hospice would play in the case and saw the meeting as an opportunity to gather more information.

The Pinecrest staff looked at one another anxiously. It was clear to Kathy that none of them was sure how to begin a conversation. After several uncomfortable minutes, a small older woman wearing a nun's blue veil, a white smock, and bright blue running shoes entered hurriedly and began the meeting.

"We are here today to discuss Timmy's progress during the last quarter. As I see we have some visitors, perhaps we should begin by introducing ourselves," the woman suggested. "My name is Sister Anne and I am the nurse responsible for overseeing Timmy's care here at Pinecrest."

Kathy listened as each of the Pinecrest staff introduced themselves and stated their job titles. In total, five staff members were present, each representing a highly specialized field of intervention. There was an education specialist, a physical therapist, an occupational therapist, a speech therapist, and the nurse, Sister Anne. Beverly, the social worker whom Kathy had met once before, was home with a sick child. Kathy thought it was odd to have all these specialists involved in Timmy's care. Timmy was unable to make more than the slightest movements without assistance. He could not walk, stand, sit up, or turn over. *What work could they all possibly be doing with him?* she wondered.

After everyone had introduced themselves, Sister Anne announced that each staff member would provide a verbal report regarding Timmy's progress during the last quarter. The educational specialist was the first.

"Timmy continues to do well with his educational plan," he began. "We are continuing to work with him on responding to stimuli. The goal for this quarter is for Timmy to move his hands toward sounds."

Kathy listened with disbelief as the education specialist enthusiastically described the educational plan for Timmy. She understood that all children with special needs were required by federal law to have an individualized education plan. However, given Timmy's severe deficits and limitations, it seemed unrealistic to believe that he would ever achieve much beyond instinctual reactions. As the education specialist concluded his report, Kathy shifted in her chair and looked toward Evelyn. Her face revealed her utter frustration. She had not spoken a word since the introductions.

"Timmy has made some progress in his work with me this quarter," the speech therapist stated as she began her report.

Progress? Kathy thought. It seemed unlikely to her that Timmy, a child who had never spoken or made any verbal gestures, was making progress in speech therapy. She listened in amazement as first the speech therapist and then the occupational and physical therapists provided stories of Timmy's responsiveness to their interventions. They described slight movements of his arms or eyes that they interpreted to be responses to their interactions with him.

Hope shot Kathy a questioning look, as if to say, *I haven't seen any of that. Have you?* Kathy shrugged slightly. She had seen virtually no evidence of purposeful action during her visits with Timmy. The few incidents of movement she had observed appeared to her to be instinctual.

Kathy watched Sister Anne as she fidgeted with the papers on the table in front of her. As the physical therapist concluded her report, Sister Anne pushed herself to the front of her chair, preparing to speak.

"Within the last quarter, Timmy has had a couple of urinary tract infections, one episode of pneumonia, and was hospitalized on one occasion due to a seizure," Sister Anne began.

"Antibiotics were used to treat the infections. In addition, a catheter was inserted to help Timmy eliminate fluids." Sister Anne directed her attention to the hospice staff members seated across the table. "A catheter is a tube that is inserted into the urethra to help drain the bladder. The urethra is a duct leading from the bladder, which can become inflamed and swollen during infections. This swelling can interfere with normal fluid elimination."

Kathy thought that Sister Anne was rather condescending in her explanation. The use of catheters was common among hospice clients, and she and her colleagues were certainly familiar with them.

Evelyn interrupted Sister Anne. "I don't want Timmy's infections treated with antibiotics. Given his condition, treating him with antibiotics is an extraordinary measure. It is only prolonging his life. That is why hospice is here today," she stated emphatically.

"Well, when a patient has any type of infection, antibiotics are the standard course of treatment," Sister Anne responded. "Antibiotics help the patient fight off infections."

"I realize that antibiotics are used to fight infections. However, I am asking that they no longer be prescribed for Timmy." Evelyn's voice was icy.

"All patients at Pinecrest who are diagnosed with urinary tract infections are prescribed antibiotics. Antibiotics are the primary method used to prevent the infection from intensifying." Sister Anne replied.

Kathy noticed that Sister Anne had failed to respond directly to Evelyn's comments. She seemed to be either completely oblivious to the reasoning behind Evelyn's plea to terminate the use of antibiotics or deliberately ignoring Evelyn's remarks. Sister Anne's responses indicated that she viewed Timmy's infections as routine health problems requiring routine treatment. Conversely, Evelyn was stating that Timmy should be allowed to die. The antibiotics were prolonging his life, the quality of which was highly questionable.

Sister Anne read the remainder of her report to the group. She did not indicate that there had been any increase in infections or seizures during the past quarter. Upon completion of her report, Sister Anne announced that the meeting would be adjourning soon, and asked if Evelyn had anything she would like to add. Evelyn restated her wish for a DNR and for the termination of antibiotic treatment. Making note of Evelyn's request in Timmy's chart, but without acknowledging her, Sister Anne concluded the meeting and began looking through her notes for the staff meeting for another patient.

Prior to this meeting, Evelyn had never discussed terminating antibiotic treatment of Timmy's infections with the hospice team. In addition, it appeared to Kathy that the request had only worsened Evelyn's relations with the Pinecrest staff. She was a bit annoyed with Evelyn for the surprise revelation and for implying, without directly stating it, that hospice was in agreement. She realized that Evelyn's request had complicated hospice's potential role in this case, because the team would need to consider the possible implications of their response for the overall hospice program.

Kathy exited the conference room with her hospice colleagues, Hope and Dana. *So,* she wondered, *what are we going to do with this situation?*

2 | ResponseAbilities

Sarah Cearley and Vicki M. Runnion

"HAVE YOU GOT A MINUTE?" Sharon Taylor looked up from her desk and saw Kathy Holder, a recent addition to the social work staff, looking shyly around the half-open door. Sharon nodded and Kathy stepped into the friendly, light-filled office and sat down. Sharon was the director of social services at Hospice of Bayview, where she had worked for a total of eight years. She liked her job, and was proud of the diversity, collegiality, and strengths of the social work department. Sharon cared about the social workers in the hospice program as peers and friends, having been a colleague to several of them for a number of years before becoming their supervisor two years ago.

Sharon had always seen Kathy as enthusiastic about her work, sometimes thinking of her as "bubbly." Today, however, Kathy seemed tentative. After a few faltering starts, the young woman sputtered that Ms. Altman, a patient in their new Hospice Living Alone Program who was dying of cancer, had fallen the day before. Ms. Altman had been sitting out in her garden on that sunny, warm spring day; when she tried to get up to go inside, she fell and could not get up. She had lain outside for more than two hours before Kathy arrived for

Development of this decision case was supported in part by funding from the Project on Death in America and the University of South Carolina College of Social Work. It was prepared solely to provide material for class discussion and not to suggest either effective or ineffective handling of the situation depicted. Although the case is based on field research regarding an actual situation, names and certain facts may have been disguised to protect confidentiality. The authors wish to thank the anonymous case reporter for cooperation in making this account available for the benefit of social work students and instructors.

her weekly visit. Kathy told Sharon that the older woman had sprained her wrist and had scrapes and bruises, but did not seem seriously hurt. But in the telling, the tears began spilling over, revealing Kathy's warm feelings toward Ms. Altman, fear of something bad happening to the older woman because she was living—and dying—alone, and a shaken commitment to the new program.

Living Alone

In the early 1990s the National Hospice Organization (NHO) (now the National Hospice and Palliative Care Organization) passed a resolution intended to address barriers to hospice care for several underserved populations. As third-party reimbursement for hospice care had become available, hospices had formalized their policies and procedures, shifted toward a paid professional workforce, and become increasingly conscious of potential liability. Many hospices had come to insist that a patient have an identified "primary caregiver" who would, among other things, coordinate care and make decisions if or when the patient became unable to do that. The hospice workers could look to this person to help assure the patient's safety and care, particularly as she or he got weaker and needed more help. But the resolution included a statement that the presence of a primary caregiver should not be a requirement for admission to a hospice program.

The new program in Bayview was launched soon after the resolution passed, affirming the renewed expectation that hospices would care for people who were dying without the support of family members or friends who would assume primary responsibility. Further, this policy was consistent with Hospice of Bayview's ongoing effort to meet the needs of the entire community, thus deterring the emergence of competing programs. As the only hospice serving a large metropolitan area, Hospice of Bayview could afford to subsidize services that were not financially self-supporting. But for many hospice workers, the Living Alone Program signified a major shift in thinking about terminal care.

As director of social services, Sharon had known when the upcoming resolution was about to be adopted and had been preparing policies and procedures to put the program in place immediately. Sharon's belief that this was an important and necessary change for Hospice of Bayview had evolved over her eight years of working with patients. In fact, she had often said, "Dying alone is not necessarily the worst thing that could happen to a person; it should be up to the person to identify his or her own wishes." She delineated this new philosophy and broadened definition in the program policies, stating that if a patient was alert and oriented at the time of admission, could clearly identify the risks involved in staying alone, even when quite ill, and could engage in planning to minimize those risks in a variety of ways, particularly risks that could injure others, then the patient had the right to accept those risks and to ask for hospice's support in staying home to die.

Sharon had had some strong ideas about how to implement the new program. Because it represented a significant departure from recent hospice policies, she had wanted to create a specialized team to handle all of the initial cases and thus "work out the bugs" in the new program. Furthermore, she had wanted the team to be composed of staff members who self-selected to participate. This would help ensure they were personally committed to the change. The executive director had fully supported the new program philosophy but opposed Sharon's implementation approach, basically saying, "The policies are changing, and everyone needs to adapt." He told Sharon to forge ahead.

The New Program

Sharon hired a Living Alone coordinator, Ann Young, to help her develop policies and procedures and work directly with the hospice teams already in place. Ann had volunteered with Hospice of Bayview for a number of years and had a passionate commitment to patients' rights of self-determination concerning their own deaths. She described herself as a mid-life grandmother, and she made up for her own lack of self-confidence by the confidence she had in others. She had been advocating for Hospice of Bayview to accept patients without primary caregivers for a couple of years before the NHO resolution and was eager to get the Living Alone Program started.

The hospice employed nurses, home health aides, chaplains, volunteers, and social workers, and assigned teams to particular geographic areas. From these "overall teams" of professionals and volunteers, different combinations were configured for each new hospice patient. In the new program, the coordinator would work with teams that were assigned to people who had no primary caregiver.

Sharon sensed that the social work staff was on board with the new program, but the nurses seemed more anxious, thinking of patients who were not responsive, who had to be completely cared for and were not able to make decisions or choices. Several on the nursing staff were having a hard time picturing how people could be left alone when they were actively dying, and further, were worried about a possible threat it might present to their licensure. For them, caring for their patients' physical needs took priority over most other concerns. The tension began to be evident in the anxiety expressed in team meetings. The social workers were discovering that it was easy to be committed to the idea of self-determination in dying in the abstract and more difficult when it was a real person who didn't conform exactly to the hypothetical situations they had anticipated.

The Team

Ms. Altman's team had four members—a nurse, a social worker, a chaplain, and a home health aide—in addition to the Living Alone coordinator. She had declined having a volunteer thus far.

Lila Harper was the nurse on the team. Lila had a good sense of humor and was well liked. She had worked with hospice for seven years before this new program, and believed strongly that her ethical obligation as a nurse was to "take care of" her patients. Like some of her nursing colleagues, Lila worried that if something awful happened to a patient who was in her care but left alone, she might lose her license. It was difficult for Lila to listen to this patient who was asking for something very different from what her traditional patients would request. In other words, Ms. Altman wanted less care rather than more. Originally Lila had agreed to go along with the Living Alone Program, but she believed there were limits to what staff could permit. As she said, "If someone wants to do things that are really risky, maybe that means they are *not* sufficiently alert and oriented, not really competent to be making decisions like that."

Kathy Holder, the social worker, a recent MSW graduate, was pregnant during this time. Her manner was vivacious, even cheerleaderlike, and spilled into her work as infectious enthusiasm. She also had an eagerness to learn that influenced a fairly rapid growth in her new profession. Kathy processed new information openly, talking through issues, particularly when taking on new tasks or roles. She listened to Sharon, who was her direct supervisor, and tried always to "see things the way Sharon saw them." She had talked at length with Ms. Altman about her wishes for her care, the plans she had already made for her own funeral and burial, and other matters of importance to her, and conveyed this information to her teammates.

Mark Turner, the chaplain, was assigned as part of the team serving Ms. Altman but was not able to visit her regularly because he was covering the caseload for a sick colleague in addition to his own, and thus had to prioritize his visits to see those patients most specifically in need of spiritual care. Mrs. Altman seemed at peace, so Mark left it up to the team members to alert him if they identified particular spiritual needs during the course of her care.

Karen Goodlett, the home health aide, went to Ms. Altman's home weekly to perform domestic and physical tasks that Ms. Altman could no longer do alone, such as light cleaning and occasional shampoos. She did not always attend team meetings, but was in regular communication with individual team members.

The directors of nursing and social services supervised the team collaboratively: Lila and Karen under nursing and Ann and Kathy under social services. Although Sharon was the lead person in developing the Living Alone Program's policies, the director of nursing had supported the plan too.

Janine Altman

Janine Altman was fifty-nine. She had breast cancer, with widespread metastasis. During the time that she had been in the program, she had talked to Kathy about her life. She told her that she had been a kindergarten teacher for thirty years and had retired two years ago. She was married when she was twenty-one and widowed at twenty-nine. She told of so many losses. Her only child, a daughter, had died in a car accident as a teenager. Both her parents were dead. She had no siblings, no aunts or uncles. She had shared her home for a number of years with a colleague/friend, but her friend had died too, about three years ago. Ms. Altman still seemed to be grieving the loss of her friend as she faced her own mortality.

Ms. Altman said that since her retirement, she had become rather a solitary person, reading extensively, painting, going birding alone, and it was clear that she had enjoyed her life. She lived in a small cottage in the country, with no nearby neighbors. She had two dogs and three cats and said, "They are all the company I need."

Ms. Altman was articulate, composed, and confident about what she wanted when she was admitted to the program, and seemed reasonable and rational about it. "I just want to keep on living my own life, in my own home, with my animals, until the very end. The peacefulness here means everything to me. I'm used to being alone, and I like it that way—I'm not afraid." Both of Ms. Altman's parents and her friend had been in nursing homes prior to their deaths, and she was adamant that she would not go into a nursing home while she was able to have any say in what happened to her. She had said, "Nothing that could happen to me at home could be as bad as that—the noise and the smells and everything on someone else's schedule. I just couldn't bear it." She realized that if she became completely disoriented or was in a coma, there might be no alternative, but she begged the team to promise they'd at least give her a few days to die on her own if the end was near, before they took action to have her moved.

The Reality of Living Alone

As Ms. Altman was one of the first patients accepted into the program, her team was naturally going through its own reactions to this new kind of relationship with the dying person. Essentially, Ms. Altman was retaining more independence and thus faced greater risks than patients who did not live alone. At first, the team found her easy to work with, responsive to their suggestions and support, and they voiced a commitment to respect her wish to die at home. A volunteer was assigned to do some shopping and small chores for her, and a home health aide helped her with household tasks once a week. She accepted a Lifeline with a call button to wear when outside, but rarely wore it. She said she chose to take as little pain medication as possible so she could stay more alert.

Soon she began to get weaker, less steady on her feet. When questioned directly, she admitted that she didn't feel strong enough to do much cooking for herself anymore, but also that she wasn't really very hungry. As she got weaker, the team gradually became less and less comfortable with her being alone, especially because she resisted using the Lifeline call button and her medications, but Ms. Altman gently insisted that she was doing okay and preferred her solitude to the various kinds of assistance the team offered.

Sharon, sitting in on the team meetings, could hear the anxiety beginning to be voiced. Ann, the Living Alone coordinator, held beliefs that mirrored and were as strong as Sharon's about the values upon which the program was founded. To the team Ann said, "Ms. Altman is doing things her own way. She is still clear mentally, still sure about what she wants, and conscientious about safety issues. I think she feels crowded by the team's concerns for her safety, and not so sure that we will help her do this her way." She further suggested, a bit hesitantly, that Ms. Altman might begin to withhold some information from the team to keep them from worrying any more than they already did. Ann told the team that she too worried about how they would respond to certain kinds of information. And then the crisis came.

A Turning Point

The day after Ms. Altman's fall, Kathy came to see Sharon. Kathy told how she had pulled into Ms. Altman's driveway and found her lying in the garden. "At first, I was horrified, scared that she was dead or badly hurt. But then she called out to me, and I ran over to her. She said she was okay and just needed help getting up. I saw she could move her arms and legs, and she seemed clearheaded. So I helped her get up, and we went in the house.

"Once we got in the house, Ms. Altman explained what had happened. It was such a lovely day, and she had made her way out to the chaise lounge in the garden to listen to the birds and soak up the sunshine. Several hours later, as she got up to go back inside, she lost her balance and fell. She said she was kind of rattled by the fall. She made a couple of attempts to get up, but she was too weak. So she decided to wait for me—she said she remembered I was coming at 4:30.

"Once I knew she was okay, I felt so relieved. And she seemed surprisingly calm. But on the way home, the more I thought about what happened, and what might have happened, the more upset I got. What if I hadn't been going to visit her yesterday? I woke up a couple times in the night wondering if she was okay."

Kathy went on to confide how she had already been worried about Ms. Altman before the incident. "Sometimes I wanted to call her at night or on weekends, or even to drive out to her house, to be sure she was okay. When I would go to bed, I wondered whether she had gotten to bed all right. When I had morning sickness, I worried about her nausea. When Rick's out of town on business, I wonder if she's lonely or afraid. I thought I really believed in self-determination, but it feels different when there's a real person, someone I know, at risk."

Kathy confessed, "I'm sorry, Sharon—I feel like a failure, like I'm worrying more than I should, identifying with her too much or something," and she wondered if another social worker should be assigned to the case. Sharon's feelings and thoughts about that were on several levels. She wore two hats, developer and manager of the program and supervisor of the social workers. As program developer, she was concerned with and responsible for the program's and the patients' interests. As supervisor, she was interested in the on-the-job education and growth of her supervisees, including Kathy. Sharon also recognized that she identified with and liked the patient, based on all she had heard about her.

As program manager, she did not want one case to blow the whole thing. She feared that a single failed case and any accompanying negative publicity would undermine board support or prompt more restrictive eligibility criteria. Sharon recognized that she was feeling impatient with the team's and Kathy's anxiety over what seemed to be a fairly innocuous event. She wondered if the Living Alone Program would always make people anxious and wished again that they had designed it with a specialized team approach. However, the program was new and procedures had not been fully tested. Perhaps it could still work as planned.

With a twinge of dread, Sharon realized that she would have to decide between letting the executive director know that the team was struggling and pressuring him to do it the way she had wanted, which involved the risk of a damaging knee-jerk reaction on his part, or letting the team slug it out, to the possible detriment of Ms. Altman and of Kathy, if something traumatic happened.

Because of Sharon's long experience in hospice, she trusted her own assessment skills and recognized the familiar urge to just go talk with Ms. Altman herself. But, as supervisor, she knew that her actions now would affect

Kathy's professional self-confidence, Ms. Altman's safety, the team's ability to work together, and the program's effectiveness down the road. As a relatively new supervisor, Sharon had been learning how to trust her staff and to use second-hand information in making decisions, and she knew she had to continue to do so, for Kathy's good and her own continued growth.

Sharon was concerned about trying to transplant her own assessment into Kathy, knowing that Kathy might not thoroughly internalize it and, in the face of new problems, might lack skills for making subsequent decisions. Further, this might undermine her confidence in her own assessment of Ms. Altman's changing needs. In the supervisor-as-educator role, Sharon enjoyed helping new social workers grow in their profession, and Kathy had great potential. However, she wondered if Ms. Altman had time for Kathy to learn.

Sharon was putting all the pieces together in her own mind when Kathy wondered aloud whether another social worker should be assigned to the case, saying, "I'm not sure I can do this." Sharon needed to act. Which direction should she take?

3 | Family Matters

Terry A. Wolfer

WHEN LOU MONTGOMERY, a social worker with Lutheran Hospice, first met Barbara Reeves at Lexington Hospital in October 1998, she felt both surprised and relieved. The referral form had indicated that Barbara was only eighteen years old; in person, she appeared to be in her mid-forties. Caring for a dying parent was always difficult, but at least this woman would have more life experience than an eighteen-year-old.

Still, something seemed odd about Barbara's relationship with her dying father.

Lutheran Hospice

Founded by Lutheran Homes in 1992, Lutheran Hospice (LH) served South Carolina through local offices in Greer, Columbia, and Charleston. Each of the offices employed a director, three full-time nurses, three certified nursing assistants (CNA), a social worker, a bereavement coordinator, and a chaplain. In addition, numerous volunteers participated in the activities of the local

Development of this decision case was supported in part by the Project on Dying in America and the University of South Carolina College of Social Work. It was prepared solely to provide material for class discussion and not to suggest either effective or ineffective handling of the situation depicted. Although the case is based on field research regarding an actual situation, names and certain facts may have been disguised to protect confidentiality. The author wishes to thank the case reporter for cooperation in making this account available for the benefit of social work students and practitioners.

offices, some assisting with office work but most befriending and supporting dying patients and their families.

The Columbia office was one of five hospice organizations in the midlands of South Carolina. Although LH occasionally served indigent patients, it typically charged $105 per day for in-home hospice care. This funding paid for medications, medical equipment, wheelchairs, hospital beds, and a variety of professional services. Medicare, Medicaid, and private medical insurance covered some of these costs. But, like other hospices, LH relied on memorials (gifts in honor of deceased patients) and voluntary contributions to cover the remaining expenses.

LH staff worked as teams. Social workers provided initial information about hospice, assessed each patient and family's understanding of the patient's condition, emotional well-being, financial situation, caregiving plans, and living environment, and then worked with the team to provide psychosocial support to the patient and the family caregiver. They visited patients and their families at least a couple of times a month but more often as needed (e.g., for emotional support and crisis intervention). Nurses visited patients at least once a week and more often as needed (e.g., for pain management). Both social workers and nurses were continuously available on call. CNAs were optional for patients, typically visiting two to five times per week to bathe and provide other physical care. The chaplain visited patients and families at least once a month, more often if requested. Volunteers, often the family members of former patients, visited to "fill in the gaps." As Lou explained, because these volunteers were assigned to particular patients and had frequent informal contacts (e.g., helping with laundry, sitting with a patient while family members ran errands), they often served as the "ears of the team."

Lou Montgomery

Since earning an M.S.W. degree from Marywood University (PA) in May 1994, Lou had held several different social work positions. First she worked for two years in The Youth Advocate Program, a behavioral health program designed to keep kids out of the juvenile justice system. A grassroots organization, it contracted with schools to provide adult buddies and mobile therapists (MSW-level practitioners) for referred youth.

After moving to South Carolina, she worked for two years with the Sumter Department of Health and Environmental Control as the public health social worker for patients with HIV. As Lou confided to a colleague, "Although I had never had an issue working with the gay community, they had an issue working with me. When they found out my husband was in seminary, they assumed 'You're going to condemn me.' I just said, 'I'm here to take you at face value, the way I hope you take me.'"

Lou began working at the Columbia office of LH in September 1998. The hospice position was not one she sought but an opportunity that fell into her lap. A colleague had told Lou of the opening and encouraged her to apply. For Lou, getting a job nearby would eliminate a daily 120-mile round-trip commute. And working at a hospice was something she wanted to do at some point in her career. She had deeply admired and kept in touch with the field instructor for her BSW internship at Hershey Medical Center's Trauma Unit. When this woman later began working at a hospice, Lou imagined she might do the same. She had just expected to do so after having gained more professional experience.

Leonard Morrison

On a Friday morning in late October, a discharge planner from Lexington Hospital called Lutheran Hospice to refer Leonard Morrison for services. As she reported, Leonard was a sixty-eight-year-old white male in the late stages of lung cancer. He also had diabetes. After retiring from the navy, he had worked as a TV and electronics repairman for Sears. Leonard was married to the mother of his two adult children. Their home was in Blythewood, a small town located about thirty miles from the hospital. At the time, however, Leonard was living with their adult daughter, Barbara Reeves, who had an apartment near the hospital.

Until recently, Leonard had been treated for lung cancer as an outpatient. But increased weakness, vomiting, and pain led to a one-week hospitalization. That enabled doctors to stabilize his condition, but because it was clearly terminal, they recommended that he be discharged to hospice.

Hospice nurse Anne Brown completed the face sheet with information faxed by the hospital's discharge planner. She checked to be sure that the medical information was complete and that the doctor had written an order to admit to hospice.

With the referral information in hand, Lou called the hospital to arrange for an admission visit with Mr. Morrison. These meetings usually lasted thirty to forty-five minutes. Basically, Lou would explain, "This is our philosophy. Here's what we provide." Although she was new, she already knew the first question for many people was, "How much is this going to cost me?" It was her job to reassure them that hospice was often economical because it provided some medications and equipment that insurance didn't cover, but also that Lutheran Hospice was a ministry and wouldn't turn them away for inability to pay. As Lou often told prospective patients, "Signing up for hospice is like buying a new car because there's so much paperwork involved and you go through it so fast. I always say, 'Slow me down.'" To help patients process all the information, she provided them with copies of the documents.

The Intake Visit

When Lou arrived in the hospital room, Leonard's adult daughter, Barbara Reeves, was also present. Leonard seemed to be in a surprisingly light mood. In contrast, Barbara had a serious look on her face.

Lou introduced herself simply. "I'm Lou Montgomery from hospice."

"Hey, Lou, how are you?" Leonard responded, laughing. "Oh, that rhymes!"

Somewhat surprised by his teasing, Lou grinned. "Oh, sounds like you're a poet, and I didn't know it. And I'm fine, thank you, and how are you?"

"Just great, can't you tell?" Leonard responded. "I'm ready to get out of here."

"Then is it okay," Lou asked, "if I tell you a little about why I'm here, and what hospice can do for you?"

With a wave of the hand, he replied, "Let my daughter take care of it. Whatever she says, that'll be okay with me."

At Barbara's request, the two women walked down the hallway and sat together in a waiting area. Away from her father, Barbara burst into tears, saying, "I'm too young for this. . . . My dad is so calm, I don't understand . . . and my mom can't handle it."

After consoling the woman, Lou described hospice services.

Barbara listened quietly and then nodded. "Let's go down and be sure it's okay with my dad."

They returned to the room, and Lou started, "I've explained everything to Barbara. She thinks it sounds fine but since it's you that's involved," Lou grinned, "she wants you to hear it from me yourself." Lou explained to Leonard about the services of the interdisciplinary team, how they would arrange for medications and equipment to be delivered, and that it would all be covered by Medicare.

Tentatively, Barbara encouraged, "Dad, I think this is a good idea. You can have a nurse come out and Lou will come too. Somebody'll help you take a bath."

"Fine with me. Do it."

After gaining Leonard's verbal agreement for services, Lou and Barbara went back down the hall to complete the paperwork. Barbara didn't want to do that in his presence, Lou suspected, because, as one of her first patients had told her, it felt like "signing for the grim reaper to show up at your house."

Hospice Admission

Late that afternoon, Emergency Medical Services (EMS) returned Leonard to Barbara's second-floor apartment. Anne, the nurse, met Leonard, Barbara, and Lou there and completed a nursing admission assessment. She needed to determine that he was comfortable, particularly because this was a Friday afternoon, so the on-call nurse wouldn't have to handle a preventable problem.

Barbara indicated that she would be teaching Monday through Friday but had arranged for several relatives to stay with her father while she was gone.

Lou asked, "Is your mom going to come down from Blythewood?"

Barbara replied, "Mom will come down to see him, but she won't be staying here. She's having a hard time with this." Barbara had said several times that her mother was having a hard time.

At this point, Lou sensed that there was more to the story. But with only a beginning relationship, she could not be sure. It was not surprising to Lou that Barbara was upset. But because Leonard was so seriously ill and clearly had been for some time, it seemed odd that Barbara seemed hardly to have begun to deal with the fact that he was dying. Lou also knew that Barbara was recently divorced, and recognized that her grief could be intertwined with distress related to the divorce.

Finishing the nursing assessment took a while because Barbara was quite emotional, alternately crying and withdrawn. Lou decided that they had been through enough for that afternoon and that she would wait until early next week to do her psychosocial assessment. When they finally left at 5:45 p.m., Lou said, "I'll see you next week. If you need anything, you can call our on call staff."

As they walked to their cars, Lou asked Anne, "So, what do you think?"

"It seems pretty typical to me," Anne responded. "I don't think he has a lot of time left."

"I hope Barbara can get ready for that. I don't think she is now." Shaking her head, Lou added, "I feel like there's something we don't know yet. But it just felt wrong to put them, especially Barbara, through any more assessments this afternoon."

Lou later wrote in her notes for the day: "Patient mental status: alert at this time, does not want to know his prognosis." So, he knew he couldn't be cured but he didn't want to know the time frame for death. Likewise, she recorded: "Caregiver healthy, willing to care for father, emotionally distressed, struggling with his illness, constantly saying, 'too young for this.'"

As she often did on Friday evenings, Lou went out to eat with her husband. Working for hospice, Lou realized that life is too short. She learned to appreciate her family, having fun, and having freedom to do things she wanted to do. Lou only thought briefly about Leonard and his situation: *Something seems a little strange about that family, like maybe there's another piece of the puzzle that we don't have yet.* But she assumed she would have the opportunity to get to know Barbara better next week. Mostly, she felt relief that Barbara was older than originally reported: *She's not eighteen, okay, we can handle this.*

Approaching Death

On Tuesday, Lou called Barbara during her lunch break at school to find out how she was doing and schedule a visit for her assessment. Barbara reported that her father had been experiencing some pain that morning. As a result, Lou and Anne set a late afternoon appointment to check on Leonard.

When they arrived, Barbara, her mother, a niece, and Leonard's co-worker were standing around Leonard's bed. Leonard was considerably pale and extremely restless. While they were watching, he unexpectedly pushed back the covers and, despite his weakness, tried to get out of bed. Flustered, his co-worker and daughter responded by lifting him to his feet. He looked around the room but did not seem to register who was actually present. Soon exhausted, he slumped, and they eased him back into bed. He was still for a few minutes but then began to fidget and mumble again. As Lou explained to the family, "While a person's body may be shutting down, the spirit inside the person may be fighting the dying process."

After Leonard dozed off, the women moved to the kitchen to talk. Barbara did most of the talking, telling Lou and Anne about how the weekend had gone, about changes in her father's condition, and asking one question after another; her mother listened quietly. When either Lou or Anne spoke to Mrs. Morrison, the woman consistently looked to her daughter to answer their questions. It looked to Lou like the reality of her husband's imminent death hadn't really sunk in.

In contrast, Barbara was emotional, tearful, and anxious. Because of Leonard's anxiety and pain, and Barbara's emotional distress and work schedule, Anne suggested that it might be beneficial for Leonard to be admitted to Bernadine House, LH's inpatient hospice facility.

While discussing a possible move, Barbara said, "Mom, I just don't know what to do." Her mother responded with a blank look. Barbara asked Lou, "What would you do?"

Lou responded, "I'm not telling you what to do. Personally, I would think about how you will handle being alone with him when he's not comfortable, and also whether you have enough people to be here while you are at work— he can't be left alone anymore. Given how quickly he has gone downhill, it might be easier for both of you if we move him to Bernadine House."

"Yeah, you're right."

But despite Leonard's significant deterioration over the past four days, he could not be moved to the inpatient facility until he had a TB test. The nurse promptly administered the test, which could be read in forty-eight hours. Pending a negative result, he could be moved to Bernadine House right away.

New Information

About noon on Wednesday, Anne called Lou from the Reeves apartment. Concerned about Leonard's rapid deterioration, Anne had stopped by to assess his condition and encountered new complications.

"Lou," Anne whispered intensely, "the girlfriend's here!"

"What? The 'girlfriend'?" Lou replied, puzzled. "He has a *wife*."

"There's a girlfriend too. You need to come quick," Anne implored.

Arriving at the apartment, Lou saw a woman at Leonard's bedside, crying. She was wearing a red sweater and blue jeans, and appeared to be in her sixties. Anne was in the kitchen, talking with Leonard's niece, Shelley.

When Lou approached, the woman introduced herself simply as Nancy. Through tears, Nancy explained that Leonard had lived with her "off and on" for the past few years. She had retired about the same time as he did in order to spend more time with him but expressed regrets about not accompanying him on a trip to Texas. Nancy acknowledged that she had been struggling with depression since Leonard was diagnosed with cancer. While the two women talked, Leonard lay between them, moaning, restless, and occasionally calling out, but then gradually quieting as the suppository Anne had administered began to take effect. Anne and Shelley came back into the room and interrupted the conversation to discuss Leonard's changing medical condition and specific instructions for his care.

Although she had continued to visit Leonard at his daughter's apartment, while Barbara was at work, Nancy expressed shock at Leonard's present condition and how rapidly he had declined in just the past few days. She asked, "Why isn't he in the hospital?"

As Lou explained that Leonard's death was now imminent, probably no more than a week away, Nancy listened quietly. When Lou mentioned that Leonard had signed a Do Not Resuscitate (DNR) order, Nancy shook her head in opposition: "I'm not ready to give up on him yet. Surely there's something more they could do."

"There isn't anything else that can be done to fight the disease," Lou responded gently. "But there are plenty of things we can do at home, or at our inpatient facility, to keep him comfortable. That's the important thing now."

When Leonard appeared comfortable and the women seemed less anxious, Lou and Anne prepared to leave. Anne said, "Tell Barbara I'll call later this afternoon."

A Turning Point

Late that afternoon, Anne again called Lou from the Reeves apartment. But this time she reported, "He's actively dying. He's not going to live long enough to move to Bernadine House. It looks like Nancy's visit was a turning point for him."

"Is Nancy still there?" Lou asked.

"No, she's gone. But Mrs. Morrison's back. Barbara's still at work but she'll be home soon. A few other relatives have come. I could use some help."

"Sure," Lou responded, "I'm on my way."

Immediately Lou drove to the apartment. On the way, she wondered what Mrs. Morrison and Barbara knew about Nancy, and how to handle all of their relationships with this dying man and with one another.

4 | Drug Interactions

Terry A. Wolfer

IT WAS A THURSDAY in early November 2001, and already past 5:00 p.m. Leaving the nurse to finish up a few last details of the admission process, hospice social worker Cheryl Peak stepped outside Frank Barr's apartment. It was still warm, though the days were getting noticeably shorter.

"Please stop." Frank's roommate, Ted White, had followed Cheryl outside. "I need to tell you something."

"Yes," Cheryl replied, trying to hide her fatigue, "what is it?"

"I'm not sure I should tell you," Ted hesitated.

"It sounds like you want to tell me," Cheryl prodded.

"But I don't know whether to tell you 'cause it's going to cause a huge dilemma."

"How huge? I mean, what's going on here?

"Huge. To the point that I don't know whether you'll keep him as a case, if I tell you."

Development of this decision case was supported in part by the Project on Dying in America and the University of South Carolina College of Social Work. It was prepared solely to provide material for class discussion and not to suggest either effective or ineffective handling of the situation depicted. Although the case is based on field research regarding an actual situation, names and certain facts may have been disguised to protect confidentiality. The author wishes to thank the case reporter for cooperation in making this account available for the benefit of social work students and practitioners.

Coastal Hospice

Founded only five years before, Coastal Hospice (CH) now served a three-county area on the coast of South Carolina. The staff included a director, three full-time nurses, three certified nursing assistants, a social worker, a bereavement coordinator, and a chaplain. In addition, numerous volunteers participated in the activities of the local office, some assisting with office work but most befriending and supporting dying patients and their families.

CH did not bill clients directly for services. The agency received reimbursement from Medicare, Medicaid, and private medical insurance, which covered about 80 percent of expenses. This funding paid for medications, medical equipment, wheelchairs, hospital beds, and a variety of professional services. Like other hospices, CH relied on memorials (gifts in honor of deceased patients) and voluntary contributions to cover the remaining expenses and to provide care to those without heath insurance.

CH staff worked as teams. Usually the social worker and nurse who would be assigned to a patient conducted the intake interview. Following admission, social workers typically visited patients and their families at least two times a month but more often if needed (e.g., for support and emotional crisis intervention). Nurses visited their patients at least once a week and more often as needed (e.g., for pain management). Registered nurses were the case managers and worked in conjunction with the patients' attending physicians. All orders for medication or new equipment had to be authorized by the physician. A social worker and a nurse were on call during the evenings and weekends, to assure that help was readily available for patients and families twenty-four hours a day.

Social Worker

Cheryl Peak had worked for CH for about a year. This was her first position after completing an MSW at the University of South Carolina in May 2000. Although she hadn't planned to seek work in a hospice, the job opening caught her attention soon after graduation. Cheryl hadn't known about hospice services when her mother died of cancer in 1992, but she had requested them for her father during his terminal illness in 1993. However, he died before they were able to get these services established in the home. Her personal experiences helped Cheryl understand some of the challenges families face when a loved one has a terminal illness.

Cheryl began her college career at the age of forty-four, after rearing two children. She received a B.S. in political science with a minor in journalism. After completing this degree, she returned to the workforce at Medical University of South Carolina, a large teaching hospital. In seven years, she had learned a lot about organizational policy and procedures, liability issues, holding people accountable, and overcoming obstacles. As Cheryl explained to a colleague: "Working in administration, I learned how the system worked, and then how to work the system." She resigned this position to attend graduate school full time for two years.

Frank Barr

Frank Barr was forty-five years old in 1995 when he learned he was HIV positive. He had taught eighth-grade history at Grover Middle School for ten years before his health problems forced him to stop at the end of the school year in June 2001. There were a few people at work who knew Frank was HIV positive and who had provided emotional, financial, and practical support for him during his last year there.

Following his diagnosis, Frank had fought the disease by taking antiviral medication. However, he concluded that the medication itself was making him quite sick, and he chose to stop taking it in October 2001. Knowing that Frank's disease progression would accelerate without the antiviral medications, his physician suggested that hospice would be appropriate. Frank had begun to notice increasing symptoms, including the upper respiratory infections that marked the transition from HIV positive to AIDS, headaches, mouth ulcers, stomach problems, insomnia, physical weakness, and general aches and pains. In early November, he asked his doctor to make the referral to hospice.

Hospice Intake Interview

As usual, Cheryl Peak conducted the hospice admission interview in collaboration with hospice nurse Nancy Bailey. When Cheryl and Nancy arrived,

Frank was sleeping. Roused by the doorbell, he sat up in the reclining chair and invited Cheryl and Nancy to take a seat.

At first glance, despite the physician's referral, Cheryl wondered whether Frank was actually "end stage." He was still able to walk and appeared able to care for most of his own physical needs. He was actually slightly overweight, clearly sick but not yet emaciated from the illness like other HIV-positive patients Cheryl had encountered. In response to their questions, he recounted the story of his illness and of making a conscious decision that "trying to extend my life and the consequences of that, the side effects of that, are more miserable to me than just going ahead and letting it go."

Nevertheless, Frank reporting taking a variety of medications. These included: 300 mg. of Neurontin tid (see appendix for abbreviations) for nerve pain; 5 mg. of Ambien PRN for insomnia; 40 mg. of Paxil qd for depression; 350 mg. of Tylenol PRN for pain; 5 CC of Magic Mouthwash q6 hours for thrush; oral rinse for mouth ulcers; and 30 mg. of Prevacid qd for epigastric distress. In short, he was taking "comfort meds" but no antiviral medications.

Cheryl and Nancy were a bit startled when the front door opened and another man walked in. Frank introduced Ted White to Cheryl and Nancy as his "roommate." Frank explained, "Ted is a friend from about ten years ago. I contacted him when I found out that I wasn't going to be able to work anymore, and I asked him to come live with me and help pay for the expenses of the apartment." Ted was in his late thirties, good looking, and well dressed. Cheryl instinctively liked him.

Ted confirmed, "I had just moved back from Tennessee a few weeks ago when we ran across each other. I was looking for a place to live, so we decided to live together and share expenses. I can help with things like medications too."

Though trained as a physical therapist, Ted now sold life insurance. He pointed out that the new job allowed him more flexibility to provide care for Frank.

As Nancy and Cheryl raised questions about his needs, Frank complained of pain and discomfort. Nancy recommended that he begin taking 5 mg. of Percocet every six hours as needed for pain. Nancy contacted the physician to order this medication. Ted volunteered to pick it up. Frank acknowledged that he had trouble remembering when he took his medications. "I don't know when I've taken it and when I haven't." Nancy requested that he and Ted keep track of the medicines in a notebook.

Frank also reported that a long-term problem with depression had recently worsened. Cheryl recognized that the multiple changes caused by AIDS could themselves lead to depression. Frank identified several things that made him sad: he couldn't work anymore, he had "extreme" financial difficulties while waiting for disability payments to begin, his eighty-five-year-old father was terminally ill, and his father, as well as his mother and older brother, all of whom lived in Kentucky, would have absolutely nothing to do with him (but he did not explain why they were estranged).

Fortunately, he had long-term care insurance that would become effective in only three more weeks, six months after his last day of work. The benefit would be paid the first of each month. Frank was unsure of the exact amount but stated, "It should be around $2,000 a month."

Frank expressed interest in completing a Declaration of a Desire for a Natural Death living will and Health Care Surrogate form. He explained that Geneva Jones, one of his co-workers from Grover, had befriended him and eventually had become a surrogate mother. Frank had given her power of attorney, and he asked Cheryl to call Geneva and arrange for her to be at the home when the advance directives were discussed. He told Cheryl that it would be fine for Geneva to talk with anyone from hospice. "She's like family," he said. Cheryl planned to visit again the following Monday.

Ted's Disclosure

Leaving Nancy to complete a few last details of the admission interview, Cheryl stepped outside the apartment. That was when, walking out with her, Ted said, "Please stop. I need to tell you something."

Ted's suggestion that his information might change her mind about keeping Frank as a case put Cheryl on alert. His further revelations caused even greater concern.

"I suspect that Frank is abusing drugs. I suspect that he is leaving home to *get* drugs, that he is taking illegal drugs. He got a check yesterday, and I saw him with $800 cash. He was gone all day yesterday and came home in the middle of the night. That's why he's just now waking up. I know he took that money and bought drugs, illegal drugs."

"What kind of drugs?" Cheryl queried. "Are you talking about marijuana, heroin, cocaine?"

"Probably all of the above." Ted paused. "So now what?"

"Oh, my gosh! Well, I'll tell you what. Here's what we're going to do: nothing, right now. I'm going to tell the nurse case manager when she finishes up."

Ted interrupted, "I don't want Frank to know that I told you. Please don't tell him that I told you."

"You might want to think about what your responsibility is and whether you want to stay here. Because if drugs come, somehow, to this home—say, he goes out and buys stuff and brings it back and you're here, don't you think the authorities are going to question you too? You probably need to confront him about this."

Cheryl continued, "I won't tell Frank what you told me, but I've got to share this with my team. I will discuss it with Nancy tonight and then we will take it to the team on Monday. But for right now, for all you know, we're going to follow him and it's not going to be a problem." At the same time, Cheryl thought, *Great, this is going to really complicate things. It might be easier at this point not to tell anyone. Maybe this guy is exaggerating.*

Cheryl waited for Nancy at the car. When Cheryl related what she had just learned, Nancy replied, "Oh God, what are we going to do?" Nancy was not sure the agency should keep the case; she wanted to call the director immediately.

At the end of that long day, Cheryl was exhausted. She suggested, "Let's keep him for now and wait until morning to discuss it with Janie [Miller, the executive director], and then take it to the entire team on Monday. We need to at least figure out what's going on here."

Nancy persisted, "I think we need to call Janie now."

"Nancy, we'll see her tomorrow, and we can talk about it then. Then we can discuss it with the team on Monday."

Reluctantly, Nancy agreed. "Maybe we can go ahead and keep him. He does need medication for comfort and pain. If we don't help him, who will?"

Checking in with the Director

When Cheryl arrived at work the next morning, Janie Miller, the director, immediately asked, "Why didn't you call me about that patient you had last night?"

"I didn't see that it would matter last night," Cheryl countered, swallowing her irritation with Nancy. "I figured it could wait until today, and that we would discuss it with the team on Monday."

"Well, Nancy called me, and we're not sure that we can keep him."

Cheryl responded, "We don't have a whole lot to go on right now. All we have is this guy's word, and we don't know these people. Can't we just monitor the situation and try to figure out what's going on?"

The director asked, "What about our responsibility as an agency?"

Cheryl continued, "We really don't know what is going on in that house. Ted just moved in and hasn't been around Frank for the past ten years. We should at least try to check things out for ourselves, not just take his word for it. How do other hospice agencies handle these types of problems?"

Ending a phone call and joining the conversation, Nancy volunteered, "We can monitor the medications closely. I'll go by the house two or three times a week until we get a handle on things. We need to give this guy a chance, because he doesn't have anybody to provide care."

"You're right," Janie conceded, "we don't really have enough information. The doctor has referred him, and we should give it a few days, at least try it out. But we need to take some precautions. We need to monitor this situation tightly, and if it looks like there is any drug abuse, then we need to consider discharging him." She concluded, "This plan is going to be on a trial basis. We'll discuss it with the entire team on Monday."

Week One

On Monday morning, the team met and discussed Frank's situation. Holly Reed, the nurse who had been on call Friday night, reported, "Ted called Friday evening at 10:00 p.m. He said Frank had experienced a headache and sore throat all day and mentioned that he stopped by the doctor's office to pick up some free samples of Zithromax for Frank's cold symptoms. He was calling to see what else could be done. I noticed in the chart that the doctor prescribed Percocet and asked Ted about that. Ted said that he hadn't picked it up yet, so I encouraged him to do that first thing Saturday morning."

The team also reviewed Frank's physical history, which had been faxed from the doctor's office since the intake visit. The records clearly stated that Frank had been a "polydrug abuser" in the past. After a lengthy discussion, the team decided that with Ted in the home to assist with monitoring medications, they should give it a try. Janie insisted that Cheryl and Nancy visit frequently and monitor the situation closely. The team recommended that Cheryl try to "raise the question with Frank, of his using illegal drugs outside the home, without implicating Ted."

Late Monday afternoon, Cheryl visited Frank to discuss the advance directives that he had requested and the importance of taking his medication exactly as instructed. The appointment was scheduled for 5:30 p.m. to allow Ted and Geneva to be at the home to witness the documents. When Cheryl arrived, Frank appeared agitated and restless and complained of a severe headache, so Cheryl contacted the nurse on call. After further inquiry, they discovered that Ted had still not picked up the Percocet that had been prescribed at the time of admission. Cheryl remained with Frank and Geneva while Ted went to pick up the prescription.

Ted later explained to Cheryl that he didn't want to set a precedent of paying for Frank's medications. Cheryl reassured him that the insurance company would cover all prescribed meds.

While Ted was gone, Cheryl brought up the issue of drug abuse. "Frank, we've reviewed some of your medical history, and your records state that in the past you have abused drugs. Can you tell me about that?"

"Dr. Simpson is exaggerating about that," Frank responded. "Since my HIV diagnosis I've taken medication for depression, but I've never really abused it. He really doesn't like me."

Because Frank was so uncomfortable with his headache, he requested that the advance care documents be completed at a later date. After Ted returned with the medication and Geneva started to cook supper, Cheryl left.

Nancy visited Frank by herself on Tuesday and later told Cheryl that Frank was less agitated and more comfortable. He had started using the Percocet and reported to Nancy that, on a scale of one to ten, his pain was now a two.

Tuesday afternoon, Ted called Cheryl to report that he had confronted Frank about taking "illegal" drugs. "I told him," Ted reported, "'I'm going to tell Nancy if I suspect you're taking any drugs.' He said he won't. I told him, 'I don't want any illegal drugs in this house. I don't want any of this going on.' And he promised that he wouldn't have anything in the house."

Ted also explained to Cheryl that Frank was very needy. "I didn't know what I was getting myself into when I moved in here." Cheryl recommended that Ted encourage Frank to take care of his own needs and promote as much independence as possible.

When the full team met again on Wednesday, their discussion centered on Frank's apparent inability to follow instructions. They were also puzzled about why Ted had not picked up the prescription. Considering all the events that had transpired since his hospice admission six days ago, team members were beginning to wonder aloud whether Frank was manipulative and had surrounded himself with enablers. During the discussion, Cheryl wondered, *Am I falling into the enabling role too?*

On Friday, prior to the weekend, Nancy called to check on Frank. As she told Cheryl, "He said he was feeling much better and didn't need anything."

Week Two

At the Monday staff meeting, Helen Domino, the nurse who had been on call over the weekend, said that Ted had contacted her on Sunday evening to report that Frank was in distress. Helen visited their apartment and found Frank to be short of breath and highly anxious. He also complained of a sore throat and esophageal pain. Helen activated the physician's standing order for Nystatin "swish and swallow." While she was there, Ted went to pick up the prescription from the drugstore. Helen emphasized to Frank how important it was that he notify hospice of any changes in his condition and not wait until problems became severe. Helen said she promised to call his physician on Monday and request changes in his medications. She instructed Frank to continue with the Percocet for pain until the physician wrote new prescriptions.

At the staff meeting, Helen agreed to contact the physician's office to update him about the changes in Frank's condition and to request Ativan for anxiety, Diflucan for oral fungal infection, and Oxycontin for pain.

That afternoon, when Cheryl and Nancy stopped by Frank's apartment for a weekly assessment, Frank said that he was "doing much better." Cheryl tried to reinforce the importance of taking medications as prescribed rather than waiting and calling hospice in a crisis.

On Wednesday afternoon, Cheryl checked in with Nancy.

Nancy explained, "I still had not received a call from the doctor's office about the new medications that Helen requested on Monday, so I stopped in. I told the office nurse about Frank's condition, especially that the Percocet was not relieving his pain. She talked to the doctor and got me the prescriptions for Ativan, Oxycontin, and Ambien. She also said the doctor wanted to remind me that 'the Percocet and Oxycontin should not be taken together,' as if he hasn't known me since he first started practicing medicine! Anyway, I dropped off the prescriptions at the pharmacy on my way to see Frank.

"When I got to the apartment, Frank said he was 'feeling much better today.' Ted was home for lunch, so I went over the medication schedule with both of them. I wrote out a schedule for all of Frank's current medicines and told Ted that the prescriptions were at the pharmacy."

About 4:00 p.m. that afternoon Frank's friend, Geneva, called Cheryl. "Frank has been picked up by the highway patrol and detained at the Northwoods Mall," she said. "Someone saw him weaving all over the road and reported him."

"You sound pretty upset," Cheryl commented.

"I'm very angry with him," Geneva responded. "Why is he acting so selfish? He's not considering how his behavior affects so many other people. Another friend of ours, Susan, is on the way to get him from the mall and bring him home."

"We're concerned about possible drug abuse," Cheryl probed. "Can you enlighten me about this? What's going on here?"

"He has had problems with drug abuse for years," Geneva acknowledged. "Frankly, if he hadn't had to quit work because of his health, he might have lost his job. I don't know what we're going to do. But you're our last-ditch effort. Nobody else will take care of him. They've all had it. He's abused drugs in the past, and you're our only hope. If you don't take care of him, I don't know what's going to happen."

"We're trying," Cheryl responded, "but he must not abuse the drugs we're providing."

After getting off the phone with Geneva, Cheryl called Nancy to report the latest developments.

At the Friday team meeting, Nancy reported, "I made three calls to Frank's home yesterday but got no answer. So before I went home I stopped by his apartment. I was determined to set him up on a medication schedule he could follow. The notebook didn't seem to work, so I took a medicine box to organize the medicines for each day. When I got there, he was just getting out of bed. After he let me in, he asked, 'What day is this? And what time is it?' When I told him, 'Five o'clock,' he asked, 'Is that a.m. or p.m.?'"

Nancy couldn't find the Oxycontin, and noted that all of Frank's Paxil and Neurontin were gone. She called the pharmacy and discovered that the Oxycontin had not been picked up yet. The pharmacist stated that Frank should not yet be out of the other medicines but she would give him a few to carry him until his next refill. Nancy went to the drugstore to pick up the medications.

While Nancy was at the pharmacy, a call came in for the pharmacist from someone who also wanted to pick up the prescriptions for Frank. It turned out to be Susan, Frank's friend. When the pharmacist handed the phone to Nancy, Susan explained, "Frank asked me for $150 for medications. I told him that instead I would pick the medicine up for him." To save herself a trip, Susan agreed that Nancy could pick up the meds.

"While I've got you on the phone," Susan added, "please don't tell anyone, but I highly suspect that Frank was using illegal drugs yesterday."

Oh great, Nancy thought, but to Susan she just said, "Oh dear—well, thanks for telling me."

Later Thursday evening, Nancy called Geneva to discuss the latest problems. Geneva told Nancy how thankful she was that hospice was providing service to Frank. She also acknowledged, "Frank has abused drugs in the past." Nancy explained that she had set up a schedule for Frank's medications and that she would be visiting three times a week to monitor the medicine box.

Week Three

On Monday, Nancy reported to the team that after their Friday meeting, she received a call from Ted saying that Frank had fallen out of bed Thursday night but appeared to be uninjured. When Nancy arrived at the home, Frank was in the hospital bed and very groggy. In response to her questions, both Frank and Ted denied any illegal drug use. Nancy and Ted reviewed all the medications and noted that there were approximately fourteen Ativan missing from her last count the day before, as well as five Neurotin and several Paxil. But Frank insisted, "I haven't taken any Ativan for two summers."

Nancy told Frank, "Don't take any more medication today, start with the box tomorrow."

Ted confirmed that he would start with the scheduled meds the next day. Nancy set up the medicine box for two days only, enough to get Frank through Saturday and Sunday. Ted agreed to administer the medications and hide the remainder in a location of his choosing. Nancy told Frank of this arrangement, but she was not sure he was coherent enough to remember it.

"I was on call over the weekend," Nancy continued, "and I got a call from Ted Saturday morning about eight o'clock. 'Frank is yelling and in pain,' he said. 'He's been a handful since the drugs started wearing off. He wants something for pain.' I reminded him that Frank could start taking the meds again that day, and to give him the scheduled doses in the medicine box.

"Saturday noon, I got a call from the answering service: 'Mr. Frank Barr called and told us he's calling the FBI because hospice won't give him what he needs.'

"I immediately called Frank. He just said, 'I had a bad night and called the FBI this morning because you won't give me what I need for pain. I also told them that I want to find a place where I could stay to end my life because I'm tired of it all.'"

"He thinks he's tired of it all!" Holly Reed quipped. "He has no idea how tired *you* are."

"Then he handed the phone to Ted," Nancy continued, "who told me that Frank had taken one of the Oxycontin that morning. I told him to give Frank one Percocet to work quickly in his system because the Oxycontin was time-released and it would take several hours for it to begin working. That seemed to satisfy them."

After the Monday team meeting, Cheryl and Nancy visited the home together as previously scheduled. When they arrived, no one answered the door. Cheryl called Frank's number on her cell phone but received no answer. Cheryl imagined, *Maybe he's really done it this time and overdosed.*

Cheryl called Ted at work to learn Frank's whereabouts.

"Frank is probably gone," Ted speculated, "because I heard him on the phone with someone this morning arranging a meeting."

As Cheryl and Nancy were leaving the home, Frank and his friend Susan came walking up the sidewalk.

"I took today off to spend with Frank," Susan explained. "It's such a beautiful day that we went to the park and walked around." Frank was walking slowly without assistance but appeared short of breath.

As they entered the apartment, Nancy briefly explained the medication schedule again and said that she was going to fill the medicine box while Cheryl sat with Frank and Susan. Frank began by telling Cheryl, "I'm searching for a dying center where someone can perform physician-assisted suicide."

Is he being melodramatic, Cheryl wondered, *or is he for real?* But she asked, "Frank, will you tell me why you feel this way?"

"I just don't want to be in pain. I'm afraid I'll die in pain."

"Frank, have you ever thought about speeding this process along yourself?"

"No, and I don't plan to, now or in the future. I'm too chicken to do myself in."

"Physician-assisted suicide is not something that we can help you with as an agency. As a matter of fact, it's illegal in all states but Oregon. Our goal," Cheryl explained, "is to help provide you with comfort care and symptom management so that you aren't in pain. Research has shown that when patients' symptoms are managed, they aren't so likely to want to end their lives early. That's why we're trying to monitor your medicines and ensure that you're taking the proper doses."

"I understand," he responded.

"Frank, have you ever seen a counselor at any time in the past?"

"No, I got some names from John Palmer, a social worker at the AIDS Society, but I never called anyone."

"Do you mind if I follow up on that while I'm here today?"

"Nah, go ahead."

Cheryl called John and scheduled an appointment for him to visit Frank's home the next day and discuss services provided by the AIDS Society, which included referral to psychiatric services and transportation to the appointment.

After Nancy finished refilling the medicine box for three days, she reviewed the medication schedule with Frank again. Then she put the medicine back in Ted's bedroom in the designated hiding spot. Nancy reminded Frank that Ted would assist with administering the medications.

Frank asked, "Why can't I take my own medications? Where is the rest of the medicine anyway?"

Nancy explained, "We've asked Ted to help you with this since you don't always remember when you have taken the medicine."

"Well, Ted takes some of my medicine anyway," Frank replied.

"I believe Frank," Susan blurted out. "Frank told me that his roommate takes some of his medications. They just swap medications back and forth, so it's possible that that's why they keep being missing."

Nevertheless, Cheryl insisted, "The only way that we can track the medicine and make sure you are getting the proper doses is to come three times per week to fill up the box. If Ted is stealing the medicine, this will assist us in tracking that down also." *Now who's lying?* Cheryl wondered. *It's two against Ted. But Susan fits nicely into the enabling role.*

Late the next day, Cheryl returned to the apartment to discuss the legal documents Frank had requested. Frank said that he was feeling better, less nervous and with less pain. While waiting for Geneva and Ted to arrive for the meeting, Cheryl asked, "Did John come today from the AIDS Society?"

"Yes! He will schedule an appointment for me to see a psychiatrist, arrange transportation, and he said he would help me with the rent this month too."

"That's fantastic," Cheryl stated, relieved that he was going to get some counseling soon.

"I called the FBI," Frank stated. "I told them that my physician was not working with hospice to provide adequate medication to control my pain."

"But Frank, your doctor has called in all of the medication that has been requested for pain and you have it," Cheryl reminded him. Trying to remain calm, she asked, "How are you doing with having the medication in a dosage box? How's that working for you?

"Well, I spilled all my meds and I can't find them. I guess they're all lost somewhere." Frank showed Cheryl the medicine box; there was only one Neurotin left. "What day is it anyway? Is it Wednesday?"

Alarmed and frustrated, Cheryl blurted out, "It's just Tuesday! We were here yesterday, and we put enough meds in there for three days. There should be enough of all your medicine left to last until Thursday morning!"

"I know I didn't take that many. I thought it was Wednesday and I must have taken those too."

"But Frank, we put enough meds in there to last until Thursday morning. There should be some left. Do you understand the problem? You're taking all these medications and you could overdose. We don't know what you're using. You could be taking other drugs along with these. If you are, you need to understand that those could interact with what we're giving you and that could present some serious medical problems. That's why it's so important for you to be honest with us about your meds. If you're doing drugs, just tell us. It's okay, we just need to know what interacts with what. We had a patient who smoked marijuana, and we all knew it. Nobody told, but we knew it when we requested drugs from the doctor. We can work around these things if we need to, but you have to be honest with us."

"Ted probably took some of them. I told you he takes them when he needs them."

Concerned that Frank might die from an overdose of medications provided by hospice, Cheryl called Nancy to check on this.

Nancy replied, "Nah, he'll be fine. He's probably so used to it that it won't even faze him. He's still talking, isn't he? Is he coherent?"

After the call, Cheryl told Frank that he would simply have to wait for more medication on Thursday. She explained, "If you're not going to use the drugs as they are ordered, we're not going to be able to continue to work with you. You have to do your part. If you won't do that, then we are not going to be able to work with you. We're doing everything we can to help."

"Well," he responded, "I know my roommate steals some of my medicine. I'm sure he's the one that took it."

As Cheryl left the home, her thoughts and feelings were churning. *What else can we do for this guy? He has a master's in education and can't figure out when to take his medicines? Ted is becoming less and less available; he's obviously had it with Frank. Who's going to take care of him? Tomorrow at team is going to be awful. They're not going to want to keep him after this. But what if he really is suicidal? Who will follow up and make sure that he sees the psychiatrist? We can't just dump him. How will he obtain comfort meds? Obviously, his physician is done with him too. That's probably why Frank was referred to us in the first place, to place the liability on someone else. And what about Geneva? She practically begged us to care for him.*

Normally, Cheryl tried to leave work at the office and spend her evenings reading, relaxing, or walking on the beach. Tonight, she was consumed with thoughts about what to do with this patient. *Should I continue to advocate for him or just be thankful to get rid of this mess of a case?*

Appendix

Medical Abbreviations

bid:	abbreviation for Latin phrase *bis in die;* twice a day
CC:	abbreviation for cubic centimeters; 5 CC equals 1 teaspoon
PRN (or prn):	abbreviation for Latin phrase *pro re nata;* for the emergency, as needed
q:	every
QD (or qd):	abbreviation for Latin phrase *quaque die;* daily
QID:	abbreviation for Latin phrase *quater in die;* four times a day
QM:	abbreviation for Latin *quoque matutino;* every morning
qod:	every other day
qp (or q pl):	abbreviation for Latin phrase *quantum placet;* as much as you please
tid:	abbreviation for Latin phrase *ter in die;* three times a day

5 | Whose Will When?

Vicki M. Runnion

SOCIAL WORKER MARIANNE THORNWELL came out of Mr. Robinson's room at Holly Hills Nursing Home ready to blast someone. His bright blue eyes had burned right into her heart. On her way to get his chart to try to sort out what had happened, and why, she was fuming: *This isn't right! Why in the world do we have living wills and health care powers of attorney if people aren't going to respect them?!* Her instincts to advocate for this worn-out family were at war with her usual inclination to give the nursing home staff the benefit of the doubt. Furthermore, her own personal struggle with the issue of discontinuing artificial nutrition and hydration demanded attention. *What do I do now?*

Marianne Thornwell

A young-looking woman in her late forties, Marianne Thornwell had decided to go back to school and get her M.S.W. after working for several years in administrative positions in various health care settings. She had graduated

Development of this decision case was supported in part by the Project on Dying in America and the University of South Carolina College of Social Work. It was prepared solely to provide material for class discussion and not to suggest either effective or ineffective handling of the situation depicted. Although the case is based on field research regarding an actual situation, names and certain facts may have been disguised to protect confidentiality. The author wishes to thank the case reporter for cooperation in making this account available for the benefit of social work students and practitioners.

only six months before and been thrilled to find a job with a hospice, since her mother's terminal illness had been part of her motivation for turning to social work. Marianne found it interesting to be "on the other side of the desk," and she was still sorting out how her personal experience should or shouldn't affect her work. It was only since she had come to work at hospice that she had begun to hear information counter to her long-held assumption that providing hydration and nutrition via feeding tube was always appropriate. She'd heard more than one minister insist that to discontinue such care was tantamount to starving a person to death, so hearing from hospice colleagues that sometimes it was *in*appropriate to continue tube feedings for a terminally ill person had precipitated something of a spiritual crisis for her.

Charity Hospice

Charity Hospice was one of three hospice programs in Macon, Georgia—the oldest, the largest, and the only religiously affiliated one. As a component of a large Catholic health care network, in many ways Charity operated very much like a business. Staff were expected always to be conscious of the financial implications of decisions they made regarding services to patients and families. Along with the talk about regulations and contracts and average daily census, there was also talk about the mission and values of the organization. But Marianne wasn't confident about which would win out if there were a contest between the mission statement and the bank statement. Sometimes she felt she was walking a tightrope between meeting an individual patient's or family's needs and focusing on the well-being of the overall organization—which of course made it possible to care for the individual patients and families in the first place.

The Robinson Family

Allen Robinson, an 82-year-old retired engineer, had been on a slow decline for 6 months or more, following the first of several strokes. The first had left him unable to speak, but he was still able to read and to walk, and had remained engaged in the life he shared with Alma, his wife of

57 years—gardening, crossword puzzles, watching TV with their old golden retriever. A second stroke had made it quite difficult for him to eat. After a lot of soul-searching, they had agreed to have a feeding tube placed, because he was still alert and able to enjoy many of the long-standing pleasures in his life. Then, a little over three months ago, he had fallen and broken his hip, probably as a result of yet another stroke. Alma, healthy but just 5 feet tall and barely 100 pounds, in contrast to Allen's more than 6 feet and 200 pounds, was not able to manage caring for him at home—but she had visited him every day since his admission to Holly Hills Nursing Home. She was a strong-minded woman, even at 80, but witnessing her husband's steadily diminishing responsiveness and weight loss in spite of the tube feedings had taxed Alma's emotional reserves.

The three Robinson children—John, fifty-three; Ben, fifty-one; and Corinne Corley, forty-seven—were supportive and concerned, though only Corinne lived close enough to visit regularly and offer practical help. A third-grade teacher, Corinne was thankful to have had the summer free to be with her parents but was dreading the start of school in only two weeks. Her own children had been much more independent that summer, with sixteen-year-old Tommy driving the others to swimming and the library, and her husband Frank had been a source of steadiness and comfort for her.

Holly Hills Nursing Home

Holly Hills was a relatively new, attractive facility on the outskirts of Macon. It had sixty beds certified by Medicare to provide skilled nursing care and had just opened an ambitious forty-bed special unit for patients with Alzheimer's disease and other forms of dementia. Marianne had enjoyed the other cases she had had there since starting with Charity Hospice. She had found that the staff was conscientious and she didn't have to overcome much resistance in getting them to shift to a hospice plan of care. When Charity Hospice became involved in a nursing home case, they took on a case management role, as federal regulations required—and although that could be a challenge in some facilities, the teamwork had always seemed a bit more cohesive with the Holly Hills staff. She particularly enjoyed working with Marty Taylor, the supervisor on Mr. Robinson's unit, and was pleased to know that she would be on duty for this visit.

The Hospice Visit

A Holly Hills nurse had called Charity Hospice on Friday afternoon with Mr. Robinson's physician's order for hospice services. She indicated that there was some urgency, because Mr. Robinson was receiving tube feedings and the family wanted them discontinued in accordance with his living will, so Marianne scheduled an unusual Saturday admission visit with her colleague, Bonnie Freeman, a nurse who usually worked on call for hospice on the weekends. Little did they know what was in store for them.

Marianne and Bonnie met Mrs. Robinson, Corinne, and Marty in the lobby, and Marty led them to a small conference room. Marianne was curious that Marty wouldn't make eye contact as she left the room, but she got the answers to her questions as Mrs. Robinson and Corinne spilled out what had happened.

"When my husband was planning his retirement," Mrs. Robinson began, "we consulted with an attorney to be sure all our affairs were in order. Both of us were in good health and looking forward to traveling and more time for our rose garden, but Allen thought it was a good time to plan for the future. We both completed living wills, to make it completely clear about our wishes not to have our lives prolonged artificially if or when either one of us had a terminal illness. Corrine was given power of attorney for health care decisions for both of us, because we knew she shared and would respect our beliefs." (See appendices for sample forms.)

Corinne added, "My brothers would respect their wishes too, but they live out of state. I would be the one who could get there first in a crisis, but we're all basically in agreement about this."

Taking turns with the story and with the box of tissues, Mrs. Robinson and Corinne tried to make Marianne and Bonnie understand the situation. "When Allen had his first stroke, he couldn't speak anymore, and that was hard, but he could still do most things for himself. After the second one, he couldn't swallow, but even then he was really alert and able to enjoy TV and being out in the garden with me. We decided together that he would have a feeding tube placed—I just wasn't ready to let go of him, and I guess he felt the same about me." Her chin trembled, and she bit her lower lip.

"It was hard," Corinne took over. "I never thought he would agree to a feeding tube, but I guess you just don't know till you're in the situation. But then he fell and broke his hip, and Mom just couldn't take care of him at home after that. You'll understand when you see him—he'd make two of Mom. He's never been really alert since then, either—they thought he had had another stroke and that's what made him fall. He never was able to participate in any physical therapy to get him walking again."

Mrs. Robinson was ready to pick it up. "So he came here, and they've been very good to us, but he's just been going downhill ever since, especially in the last—what, Corinne—three or four weeks?"

"Then, just over a week ago," Corinne said, looking at her mom, "we were here together, and we looked at each other and said it at the exact same time: 'Do you think it's time to stop this?'" Tearfully, Corinne turned back to Marianne and continued, "Dad couldn't tell us what he wanted anymore. It was so much harder to decide for him than we'd expected. We wondered how it would be for him, whether he would feel hungry or thirsty, whether he would realize that he wasn't being fed anymore and wonder why—whether he would still make the same choice today." Up to this point, Marianne hadn't heard anything that particularly surprised her. Making this decision had been difficult for many of the families she'd met in her few months as a hospice social worker. But she wasn't expecting what came next.

Her lips trembling, Mrs. Robinson said, "But that was what he wanted, so we talked to the doctor, and he agreed that Allen's condition could be considered terminal, and stopped his feedings last Thursday, a week ago. It was so hard to keep coming each day, wondering each morning if that day would be the last. We were really getting worn out. Then when we got here Thursday morning this week and saw him hooked up to the feedings again, we just couldn't believe it. No one had asked us or told us anything about it."

Corinne nodded, and added, "Ever since then we've been trying to get them to stop, but they just say it's their policy not to let patients go more than seven days without eating and, frankly, we've been made to feel like we are in the wrong, like we're wanting him to starve. This decision was hard enough to make the first time—it's just *awful,* and *wrong,* to have to make it again—but to the best of our knowledge, it's what he would have wanted. We thought about contacting a lawyer, but finally we found out that if hospice was involved, then they wouldn't insist on the feedings. Can you get them stopped today?"

Marianne and Bonnie exchanged looks. Marianne said, "Let us tell you about what's involved in getting him admitted to hospice, and if you want to go ahead with that we will do everything we can to get this straightened out." Mrs. Robinson and Corinne nodded, and Bonnie started the standard explanation of hospice care, assuring them that Medicare would cover hospice services if they wanted that benefit for him.

Looking on, Marianne had the distinct feeling that they weren't hearing much of it, were just going through the motions so that hospice would become their advocate. Further, she was a bit perplexed by Bonnie's demeanor—Marianne sensed that Bonnie wasn't fully engaged, and she didn't sound completely confident in explaining hospice policies to the Robinsons.

Once the initial paperwork was completed, Corinne led them all to Mr. Robinson's room so that Bonnie could complete a physical assessment and start a hospice plan of care. Marianne sat quietly, observing, thinking about what she had heard, and she was gripped by the way this emaciated man's eyes drifted toward his wife's voice—unfocused, probably unseeing, but still somehow seeking her.

Realizing she was more than a little agitated, Marianne knew she needed to sort out her thoughts and feelings—her own beliefs about stopping nutrition, about whether a person could really make a choice about something like that so long before the situation actually arose, her understanding of the living will legislation, her memories of her mother's last illness and the apparent insensitivity of medical personnel to her values and her wishes. In her gut she felt conflict between pushing the nursing home staff to respect this family's wishes and the need not to alienate them, for the sake of future patients. And that conflict was complicated by her own uncertainty about the right time in a terminal illness to stop feedings and fluids, and by her anger on behalf of this family, their grief, and their desire to respect Mr. Robinson's intentions. She knew she needed to move, to get out of the room for a few minutes.

As Bonnie was completing her assessment, Marianne said, "I'm going to go get the chart and see if I can figure out what happened, okay?" Corinne nodded.

As Marianne approached the nurses' station, she was telling herself, *Calm down, slow down, take a deep breath. If you jump right into this, you'll make them defensive and that won't help anything.* She asked Marty for Mr. Robinson's chart, and turned first to his living will. There it was: "If at any time I should have a terminal condition . . . I direct that the application of life-sustaining procedures to my body . . . including nourishment and hydration . . . be withheld or withdrawn and that I be permitted to die."

Marianne looked up at Marty and, pointing to the document, asked, "What happened?"

Marty came closer and spoke softly, "Janet, our new assistant director of nursing [ADON], came in here Thursday and said that Mr. Robinson had been off his feedings for a week, and that we have a policy that patients can't be left without feedings for more than seven days. I questioned her about hospice patients, and she said if they are in hospice, that's different. But Mr. Robinson isn't in hospice. And she called Dr. Lander, the patient's long-time attending physician, told him about the policy, and he gave her the order to restart the feedings."

Marianne asked, "Do you have a copy of that policy?"

"No," Marty responded.

"Have you ever seen the policy?"

"No."

"Is it written or verbal?"

"I have no idea."

"Is it available here on the unit?"

"No."

To buy some time to think, and wanting to be sure she'd covered all the bases, Marianne turned to walk back to Mr. Robinson's room, but Mrs. Robinson, Corinne, and Bonnie were already coming down the hall toward her.

As they approached, Marianne asked, "Mrs. Robinson, when you talked with Dr. Lander about stopping the feedings the first time, were the words 'terminal state' used?"

"Yes—but it was Dr. Merrick who stopped them." Marianne knew Dr. Merrick was the medical director for the nursing home. Holly Hills allowed a patient to keep his or her own physician if the doctor was willing to continue, with the understanding that the medical director would step in whenever an immediate order was needed. The two physicians would be expected to work out any differences of opinion.

Confused, Marianne turned to Bonnie, and they stepped toward the nurses' desk and talked quietly with each other. Marianne repeated what Marty had said, that the new ADON had called Mr. Robinson's attending physician and that Dr. Lander had restarted the feedings. "So," she concluded, "we've got two different doctors messed up in this. What should we do now, do you think?"

Bonnie favored asking the facility nurse to call the doctors and let them know that hospice was now involved, and ask for the feedings to be stopped again. Marianne was accustomed to the nurses being the ones to communicate with patients' physicians, but she wasn't comfortable with that in this situation. What if the nurse didn't follow through or the ADON interfered again? If they hadn't gotten it straightened out in forty-eight hours, she wasn't sure about trusting them to do it now—and she'd seen more than one nurse hesitate to call doctors over the weekend, thinking it could wait until Monday or, in facilities, until the doctor came in for rounds. Marianne preferred that Bonnie call instead. But she wasn't sure about pushing Bonnie to be more assertive, given the tentativeness she had noticed earlier. Meanwhile, Marianne sensed Mrs. Robinson and Corrine awaiting her response. Feeling in way over her head, she wondered, *What do I do now?*

Appendix A

Living Will

Living will made this _____ day of _____ (month, year).

I, _____, being of sound mind, willfully and voluntarily make known my desire that my life shall not be prolonged under the circumstances set forth below and do declare:

1.   If at any time I should (check each option desired):

     ( ) have a terminal condition,
     ( ) become in a coma with no reasonable expectation of regaining consciousness, or
     ( ) become in a persistent vegetative state with no reasonable expectation of regaining significant cognitive function,

     as defined in and established in accordance with the procedures set forth in paragraphs (2), (9), and (13) of Code Section 31–32–2 of the Official Code of Georgia Annotated, I direct that the application of life-sustaining procedures to my body (check the option desired):

     ( ) including nourishment and hydration,
     ( ) including nourishment but not hydration, or
     ( ) excluding nourishment and hydration,

     be withheld or withdrawn and that I be permitted to die;

2.   In the absence of my ability to give directions regarding the use of such life-sustaining procedures, it is my intention that this living will shall be honored by my family and physician(s) as the final expression of my legal right to refuse medical or surgical treatment and accept the consequences from such refusal;

3.   I understand that I may revoke this living will at any time;

4.   I understand the full import of this living will, and I am at least 18 years of age and am emotionally and mentally competent to make this living will; and

5.   If I am a female and I have been diagnosed as pregnant, this living will shall have no force and effect unless the fetus is not viable and I indicate by initialing after this sentence that I want this living will to be carried out. _____ (Initial)

Signed _____

_____ (City), _____ (County), and _____ (State of Residence).

I hereby witness this living will and attest that:

1.   The declarant is personally known to me and I believe the declarant to be at least 18 years of age and of sound mind;

2.   I am at least 18 years of age;

3.   To the best of my knowledge, at the time of the execution of this living will, I:

   (A)   Am not related to the declarant by blood or marriage;
   (B)   Would not be entitled to any portion of the declarant's estate by any will or by operation of law under the rules of descent and distribution of this state;
   (C)   Am not the attending physician of declarant or an employee of the attending physician or an employee of the hospital or skilled nursing facility in which declarant is a patient;
   (D)   Am not directly financially responsible for the declarant's medical care; and
   (E)   Have no present claim against any portion of the estate of the declarant.

4.   Declarant has signed this document in my presence as above instructed, on the date above first shown.

Witness _____   Address _____

Witness _____   Address _____

(Additional witness required when living will is signed in a hospital or skilled nursing facility.)

I hereby witness this living will and attest that I believe the declarant to be of sound mind and to have made this living will willingly and voluntarily.

Witness: _____

(Medical director of skilled nursing facility or staff physician not participating in care of the patient or chief of the hospital medical staff or staff physician or hospital designee not participating in care of the patient.)

Appendix B

Georgia Statutory Short Form
Durable Power of Attorney for Health Care

NOTICE: THE PURPOSE OF THIS POWER OF ATTORNEY IS TO GIVE THE PERSON YOU DESIGNATE (YOUR AGENT) BROAD POWERS TO MAKE HEALTH CARE DECISIONS FOR YOU, INCLUDING POWER TO REQUIRE, CONSENT TO, OR WITHDRAW ANY TYPE OF PERSONAL CARE OR MEDICAL TREATMENT FOR ANY PHYSICAL OR MENTAL CONDITION AND TO ADMIT YOU TO OR DISCHARGE YOU FROM ANY HOSPITAL, HOME, OR OTHER INSTITUTION; BUT NOT INCLUDING PSYCHOSURGERY, STERILIZATION, OR INVOLUNTARY HOSPITALIZATION OR TREATMENT COVERED BY TITLE 37 OF THE OFFICIAL CODE OF GEORGIA ANNOTATED. THIS FORM DOES NOT IMPOSE A DUTY ON YOUR AGENT TO EXERCISE GRANTED POWERS; BUT, WHEN A POWER IS EXERCISED, YOUR AGENT WILL HAVE TO USE DUE CARE TO ACT FOR YOUR BENEFIT AND IN ACCORDANCE WITH THIS FORM. A COURT CAN TAKE AWAY THE POWERS OF YOUR AGENT IF IT FINDS THE AGENT IS NOT ACTING PROPERLY. YOU MAY NAME COAGENTS AND SUCCESSOR AGENTS UNDER THIS FORM, BUT YOU MAY NOT NAME A HEALTH CARE PROVIDER WHO MAY BE DIRECTLY OR INDIRECTLY INVOLVED IN RENDERING HEALTH CARE TO YOU UNDER THIS POWER. UNLESS YOU EXPRESSLY LIMIT THE DURATION OF THIS POWER IN THE MANNER PROVIDED BELOW OR UNTIL YOU REVOKE THIS POWER OR A COURT ACTING ON YOUR BEHALF TERMINATES IT, YOUR AGENT MAY EXERCISE THE POWERS GIVEN IN THIS POWER THROUGHOUT YOUR LIFETIME, EVEN AFTER YOU BECOME DISABLED, INCAPACITATED, OR INCOMPETENT. THE POWERS YOU GIVE YOUR AGENT, YOUR RIGHT TO REVOKE THOSE POWERS, AND THE PENALTIES FOR VIOLATING THE LAW ARE EXPLAINED MORE FULLY IN CODE SECTIONS 31–36–6, 31–36–9, AND 31–36–10 OF THE GEORGIA "DURABLE POWER OF ATTORNEY FOR HEALTH CARE ACT" OF WHICH THIS FORM IS A PART (SEE THE BACK OF THIS FORM). THAT ACT EXPRESSLY PERMITS THE USE OF ANY DIFFERENT FORM OF POWER OF ATTORNEY YOU MAY DESIRE. IF THERE IS ANYTHING ABOUT THIS FORM THAT YOU DO NOT UNDERSTAND, YOU SHOULD ASK A LAWYER TO EXPLAIN IT TO YOU.

DURABLE POWER OF ATTORNEY made this _____ day of _____, _____.

1. I, _____ (insert name and address of principal) hereby appoint _____ (insert name and address of agent) as my attorney in fact (my agent) to act for me and in my name in any way I could act in person to make any and all decisions for me concerning my personal care, medical treatment, hospitalization, and health care and to require, withhold, or withdraw any type of medical treatment or procedure, even though my death may ensue. My agent shall have the same access to my medical records that I have, including the right to disclose the contents to others. My agent shall also have full power to make a disposition of any part or all of my body for medical purposes, authorize an autopsy of my body, and direct the disposition of my remains.

THE ABOVE GRANT OF POWER IS INTENDED TO BE AS BROAD AS POSSIBLE SO THAT YOUR AGENT WILL HAVE AUTHORITY TO MAKE ANY DECISION YOU COULD MAKE TO OBTAIN OR TERMINATE ANY TYPE OF HEALTH CARE, INCLUDING WITHDRAWAL OF NOURISHMENT AND FLUIDS AND OTHER LIFE-SUSTAINING OR DEATH-DELAYING MEASURES, IF YOUR AGENT BELIEVES SUCH ACTION WOULD BE CONSISTENT WITH YOUR INTENT AND DESIRES. IF YOU WISH TO LIMIT THE SCOPE OF YOUR AGENT'S POWERS OR PRESCRIBE SPECIAL RULES TO

LIMIT THE POWER TO MAKE AN ANATOMICAL GIFT, AUTHORIZE AUTOPSY, OR DISPOSE OF REMAINS, YOU MAY DO SO IN THE FOLLOWING PARAGRAPHS.

2. The powers granted above shall not include the following powers or shall be subject to the following rules or limitations (here you may include any specific limitations you deem appropriate, such as your own definition of when life-sustaining or death-delaying measures should be withheld; a direction to continue nourishment and fluids or other life-sustaining or death-delaying treatment in all events; or instructions to refuse any specific types of treatment that are inconsistent with your religious beliefs or unacceptable to you for any other reason, such as blood transfusion, electroconvulsive therapy, or amputation):

_____

_____

_____

THE SUBJECT OF LIFE-SUSTAINING OR DEATH-DELAYING TREATMENT IS OF PARTICULAR IMPORTANCE. FOR YOUR CONVENIENCE IN DEALING WITH THAT SUBJECT, SOME GENERAL STATEMENTS CONCERNING THE WITHHOLDING OR REMOVAL OF LIFE-SUSTAINING OR DEATH-DELAYING TREATMENT ARE SET FORTH BELOW. IF YOU AGREE WITH ONE OF THESE STATEMENTS, YOU MAY INITIAL THAT STATEMENT, BUT DO NOT INITIAL MORE THAN ONE:

I do not want my life to be prolonged nor do I want life-sustaining or death-delaying treatment to be provided or continued if my agent believes the burdens of the treatment outweigh the expected benefits. I want my agent to consider the relief of suffering, the expense involved, and the quality as well as the possible extension of my life in making decisions concerning life-sustaining or death-delaying treatment.

Initialed _____

I want my life to be prolonged and I want life-sustaining or death-delaying treatment to be provided or continued unless I am in a coma, including a persistent vegetative state, which my attending physician believes to be irreversible, in accordance with reasonable medical standards at the time of reference. If and when I have suffered such an irreversible coma, I want life-sustaining or death-delaying treatment to be withheld or discontinued.

Initialed _____

I want my life to be prolonged to the greatest extent possible without regard to my condition, the chances I have for recovery, or the cost of the procedures.

Initialed _____

THIS POWER OF ATTORNEY MAY BE AMENDED OR REVOKED BY YOU AT ANY TIME AND IN ANY MANNER WHILE YOU ARE ABLE TO DO SO. IN THE ABSENCE OF AN AMENDMENT OR REVOCATION, THE AUTHORITY GRANTED IN THIS POWER OF ATTORNEY WILL BECOME EFFECTIVE AT THE TIME THIS POWER IS SIGNED AND WILL CONTINUE UNTIL YOUR DEATH AND WILL CONTINUE BEYOND YOUR DEATH IF ANATOMICAL GIFT, AUTOPSY, OR DISPOSITION OF REMAINS IS AUTHORIZED, UNLESS A LIMITATION ON THE BEGINNING DATE OR DURATION IS MADE BY INITIALING AND COMPLETING EITHER OR BOTH OF THE FOLLOWING:

3. ( ) This power of attorney shall become effective on _____ (insert a future date or event during your lifetime, such as court determination of your disability, incapacity, or incompetency, when you want this power to first take effect.

4. ( ) This power of attorney shall terminate on _____ (insert a future date or event, such as court determination of your disability, incapacity, or incompetency, when you want this power to terminate prior to your death).

IF YOU WISH TO NAME SUCCESSOR AGENTS, INSERT THE NAMES AND AD-DRESSES OF SUCH SUCCESSORS IN THE FOLLOWING PARAGRAPH:

5. If any agent named by me shall die, become legally disabled, incapacitated, or incompetent, or resign, refuse to act, or be unavailable, I name the following (each to act successively in the order named) as successors to such agent:

_____

IF YOU WISH TO NAME A GUARDIAN OF YOUR PERSON IN THE EVENT A COURT DECIDES THAT ONE SHOULD BE APPOINTED, YOU MAY, BUT ARE NOT RE-QUIRED TO, DO SO BY INSERTING THE NAME OF SUCH GUARDIAN IN THE FOL-LOWING PARAGRAPH. THE COURT WILL APPOINT THE PERSON NOMINATED BY YOU IF THE COURT FINDS THAT SUCH APPOINTMENT WILL SERVE YOUR BEST INTERESTS AND WELFARE. YOU MAY, BUT ARE NOT REQUIRED TO, NOMINATE AS YOUR GUARDIAN THE SAME PERSON NAMED IN THIS FORM AS YOUR AGENT.

6. If a guardian of my person is to be appointed, I nominate the following to serve as such guardian:

_____ (insert name and address of nominated guardian of the person)

7. I am fully informed as to all the contents of this form and understand the full import of this grant of powers to my agent.

Signed _____
        (Principal)

The principal has had an opportunity to read the above form and has signed the above form in our presence. We, the undersigned, each being over 18 years of age, witness the principal's signature at the request and in the presence of the principal, and in the presence of each other, on the day and year above set out.

Witnesses: Addresses:

_____   _____

_____   _____

_____   _____

Additional witness required when health care agency is signed in a hospital or skilled nursing facility.

I hereby witness this health care agency and attest that I believe the principal to be of sound mind and to have made this health care agency willingly and voluntarily.

Witness: Addresses:

_____   _____

Attending Physician:

_____

YOU MAY, BUT ARE NOT REQUIRED TO, REQUEST YOUR AGENT AND SUC-
CESSOR AGENTS TO PROVIDE SPECIMEN SIGNATURES BELOW. IF YOU INCLUDE
SPECIMEN SIGNATURES IN THIS POWER OF ATTORNEY, YOU MUST COMPLETE
THE CERTIFICATION OPPOSITE THE SIGNATURES OF THE AGENTS.

Specimen signatures of agent
and successor(s)

I certify that the signature of my agent
successor(s) is correct.

_____

_____

(Agent)

(Principal)

_____

_____

(Successor agent)

(Principal)

_____

_____

(Successor agent)

(Principal)

6 | Unusual Appeal

Rachel C. Parker and Terry A. Wolfer

"YOU KNOW, I do sign your paycheck."

Cynthia Sanders was taken aback. She knew she was a good mitigation investigator. But had Diane Epps, her boss, a dedicated and talented lawyer, just threatened her job? Diane often joked around, but this time Cynthia sensed anger as well.

Diane adamantly believed that the death penalty was wrong and had dedicated her career to preventing executions. Cynthia also opposed the death penalty, but she argued that their client might have a right to self-determination.

Their client, a death row inmate named José Aranda, wanted to waive his right to appeal his death sentence. He preferred to die. But Diane didn't want to allow it; she planned to do everything in her power to keep José alive. Diane not only vehemently opposed the death penalty but also believed that José was innocent.

Development of this decision case was supported in part by the Project on Death in America and the University of South Carolina College of Social Work. It was prepared solely to provide material for class discussion and not to suggest either effective or ineffective handling of the situation depicted. Although the case is based on field research regarding an actual situation, names and certain facts may have been disguised to protect confidentiality. The authors wish to thank the case reporter for cooperation in making this account available for the benefit of social work students and practitioners.

Florida Project for Human Justice

Cynthia worked at the Florida Project for Human Justice, a nonprofit agency in downtown Tallahassee that provided legal services to inmates pro bono. The agency's primary mission was to represent death-sentenced inmates across the state who were appealing their sentences. It also advocated for life sentences for clients and for a change in state law to end the death penalty. The ultimate mission was to protect and sustain the lives of those on death row. The agency received funding through the federal Indigent Defense Fund, court allocations, and donations from a large private law firm.

Seven employees staffed the agency, including Diane Epps, executive director; Joe Moran, the other lead attorney (and the only African American on staff); a legal fellow and two other lawyers; Cynthia, the mitigation investigator; and an accountant. However, the employees were constantly changing. The work was stressful, staff turnover was high, and the agency operated on a shoestring budget.

The agency was primarily devoted to appellate work. As Diane explained during the hiring interview, "Appellate work involves appealing death sentences. When a person is sentenced to death, he has three appeals. The first is a direct appeal, which is filed immediately after the sentencing. This occurs automatically, and the inmate doesn't need a private lawyer because the state appellate defense division automatically pursues it. The second appeal is post-conviction review, which is where we come in. We look at three things: first, did the client's attorneys neglect something or do something they shouldn't have that caused their client to lose the case? Second, was there juror misconduct, such as watching news about the case on TV, drinking, or feeling pressured to make a certain decision? Third, are there psychosocial mitigating factors that precipitated the crime, something in the person's background that helps to explain why they did what they did? The third appeal, which our agency also works on, goes to the supreme court."

Diane Epps

Diane Epps, a fifty-five-year-old Caucasian woman, had dedicated twenty-five years of her career to the agency. Diane was no-nonsense and shot straight from the hip. She was fair, intelligent, and had a great wit. She was immaculately dressed and always appeared professional, whether meeting a death row inmate or a supreme court judge. Raised in the hills of central Alabama, she was a true Southerner. She was sharp as a tack and smarter than many of her colleagues, but would defer to them and let them take credit. When she did take a stand, it was for either her beliefs or her clients' well-being; then she could be hard-nosed and inflexible. Years ago, she had believed in executions, but during law school, her sense of justice broadened and deepened. She changed her mind and had not looked back. At the time of José Aranda's case, she was known nationally for her work; the media often called her regarding death row stories.

Cynthia Sanders

Cynthia Sanders was a petite twenty-eight-year-old Caucasian woman. She had an intense presence about her; she talked with great energy and confidence. With a sharp, active mind, she was always questioning and, seemingly at the same time, answering herself. Feisty and self-assured, she could hold her own with lawyers, even the long-timers.

Cynthia knew the job was made for her the moment she interviewed for it. Although fresh out of an M.S.W. program in 1998, she had significant life and work experience. She had worked as a waitress and a mental health aide, and met countless characters in the process. As a result, she was somewhat fearless. She had also worked in a mental health hospital, where she gained important knowledge about mental illness, and a correctional institution, where she learned to work with disenfranchised and stigmatized males. These experiences had helped to clarify her values and ethics regarding self-determination, mental competence, and execution. She had also developed empathy for inmates. As Cynthia liked to say, "Many death row inmates have a lot stacked against them. You have to consider their experiences with poverty, education, abuse, and mental health issues when making judgments about their character." Diane saw that Cynthia was perfect for the position; she hired her on the spot.

A Troubling Case

One Monday evening after a long work day, Diane, Joe, and Cynthia sat discussing cases over dinner. Diane began telling Cynthia about an especially troubling case, that of José Aranda, a thirty-four-year-old Mexican American man.

"Five years ago," Diane recounted, "José walked into a pawn shop. His timing couldn't have been worse. Jewelry was stolen, a gun fired, and the clerk killed. Everyone inside ran. Because of his mental health history, the police were familiar with José. They had picked him up often. So he made an easy target for them. He was arrested, eventually convicted for the murder, and sentenced to death. The thing is, I don't think he really committed the murder. He was probably there, though.

"Not only does he claim that he didn't do it," Diane continued, "we have a track record here in Florida of granting death row inmates new trials if prosecutors withheld evidence suggesting innocence or knowingly used false evidence. We think it's likely that José is yet another innocent victim of our wonderful court system."

"Of course," Joe cut in, "here in Florida, just because you murder someone doesn't mean you get death. There have to be aggravating circumstances—rape, robbery, kidnapping, or some other crime, along with the murder—to get the death penalty. Since José was convicted of robbing *and* murdering a man, he got sentenced to death. If he had just killed him, he wouldn't have gotten such a harsh sentence. But, of course, I agree with Diane. I don't think he did it either."

"Unfortunately," Diane resumed, "since he's been in prison, he's been extremely violent. He's gotten into several knife fights; one guy he fought almost died. So the guards consider him extremely dangerous. He lives on the Q wing of the Florida State Prison in Starke, which is reserved for the most violent criminals in Florida. Living conditions are pretty rough in there; the guards usually don't allow him clothes, blankets, pillowcases, or anything else he could use to harm himself or other prisoners. There are no windows, and the noise of the buzzing doors keeps him awake. Sometimes he sleeps under his mattress because the noise grates on his nerves. He doesn't see many people, only the guards who bring his food and check on him. And it's really hard to get him things, like books. You should have seen the hassle we had to go through to get José a picture of his mother. The guards really hate the prisoners."

This information reminded Cynthia of how such conditions affected prisoners. Life was difficult for all inmates, but for those with mental illness, prison conditions could exacerbate their psychotic symptoms. She knew, for example, it could worsen hallucinations, delusions, and inability to think or concentrate.

Diane's voice interrupted Cynthia's thoughts. "And that brings us to what makes this case so difficult for us. Because his living conditions are so inhumane, he doesn't want us to appeal his death sentence. We don't think he's competent to make that decision because he's been diagnosed with paranoid schizophrenia. Our main focus is to show he's not competent to waive his appeal."

"Cynthia, maybe you ought to come out and meet him," Joe suggested. "He's really interesting. When you're with him, it feels like his eyes are boring holes into you. He's intense."

"He's not a very big man," Diana added, "but his demeanor makes him seem much larger than he is."

"Sure! I'd like to meet him," Cynthia responded. "I've worked with a lot of people with schizophrenia, so I might be able to offer some insight."

"Well," Diane offered, "we're going tomorrow; you're welcome to come along. We'll leave early, because it takes more than two hours to drive over to Starke."

"I'd love to," Cynthia replied.

The Meeting

The next day, in the car on the way to the prison, Diane and Joe told Cynthia more about José to prepare her for her first visit.

Diane began. "José has been diagnosed with paranoid schizophrenia. He thinks he's Chac, a Mayan god. According to ancient Mayan religion, Chac is the rain god. José believes that when he dies, he will fall on the whole world as rain and bring peace and prosperity. He thinks that this heroic act will cause everyone to worship him, and he will no longer be the long-forgotten god that he is now. Because he's paranoid, he doesn't trust professionals, and he tests them. When you meet him, be sure to maintain eye contact. If you don't, he won't trust you. He'll also test you by putting his leg against yours under the table. Don't move. If you do, he won't trust you."

"Yeah, and remember," Joe joked, "don't flirt with him, because he thinks he's a Casanova."

Cynthia tried to digest all this information. She was determined not to undermine the rapport Diane and Joe had worked so hard to build with José, especially because trust was hard to rebuild with people who had paranoid schizophrenia.

Inside the prison, the guard led them to a dusty room furnished with a battered table, mismatched chairs, and old odds and ends. Two small windows placed high in a concrete wall provided the only connection to the outside world. José was brought in, dressed in pajamas and slippers. Shackles were clasped around his ankles and chains ran up the sides of his legs, then attached to the shackles on his wrists. Although, as she had acknowledged previously, Diane did not feel comfortable being alone with José, she felt sufficiently safe with Joe and Cynthia present to ask the guard to take a shackle off one of José's wrists.

What first struck Cynthia was José's regal demeanor. After they had settled into their chairs and greeted one another, José looked intently into Cynthia's eyes and, with a dignified air, asked, "So, Cynthia, how did you come to be a social worker?"

As José looked intently at her, waiting for her answer, his back straight and hands folded, Cynthia felt as though she was being interrogated. Then she felt something more physical. He had leaned his leg against hers. His movements had been slow and deliberate, and he continued to hold her gaze, as if waiting for her next move. Careful not to flinch, she tried to respond as if nothing was awry.

"I have always enjoyed working with people. I like talking to them, and learning from them," Cynthia answered evenly, wondering whether she had passed his test.

Diane and Joe allowed José to control the session. They knew if they didn't, he might lose trust in them, something they needed desperately and worked hard to maintain. Any information they needed from him had to be extracted from whatever he wanted to talk about.

When Joe asked José if he had any issues he wanted to discuss, José's countenance changed. A shadow fell over his face and he began to fidget in his seat.

"Yeah, I have something to discuss, all right. This morning, they busted into my cell, threw me on the bed, yanked my pants down, and shot me in the ass. It really pissed me off."

Cynthia felt a pang of empathy for José; it was clear he felt violated. She shared his anger with the prison system that treated people like animals. She had seen it fail so many. The rest of the meeting, he voiced other nagging concerns: he was cold, he wanted a book on Mayan gods, and he wanted to discuss his art. Joe offered to post José's art in a prison newsletter for other inmates to see. Cynthia noted that José seemed very intelligent. She couldn't imagine the double frustration of being cooped up in a small cell and trapped in his own psychosis. She knew that it was going to be hard for Joe to get José a book.

An Informal Staff Discussion

During the car ride back to the office, Diane steamed. "We had a court order that José was not to be medicated against his will. Who ordered this, right before the competency hearing on Thursday? We need to find out what that shot was and how it will affect him. We may need to seek a postponement until the meds clear his system."

Cynthia offered, "I could look into that for you. From what I know, I bet it was a long-acting, time-released Haldol shot, an antipsychotic drug. The guards were probably just afraid of him. It's easier to give him a shot than to have to deal with him. It will probably take a month for it to wear off."

Joe replied, "That would be great, Cynthia. I think you should get more involved in this case. Your psychiatric background sure would be helpful."

Diane added, "Actually, I think we *need* you on this case. Why don't you plan on coming to the competency hearing on Thursday?"

"Sure, but how can we have a competency hearing now, if he's been drugged?"

Diane replied, "Well, we probably won't complete the hearing now. I'll request that we postpone it for a month or so. But I'm sure the judge will still want to meet with José."

The Hearing

The following Thursday, Cynthia accompanied Joe and Diane to court. The judge began by asking José, "Is it true you don't want to appeal?"

José replied, "Yes, sir, that is true. I would rather die than live like an animal."

"For you, what does it mean to die?" the judge asked.

José replied, "I would be strapped into a machine, and be given three injections." José explained each of these injections, what they were for, and how long it would take him to die.

The judge then asked, "What happens when someone dies?"

José said, "When you die you are buried, and your family has a funeral. If you believe in God you may go to heaven or hell, and if you don't you just get buried."

The judge then asked, "Mr. Aranda, your doctors said that you have some beliefs about Mayan gods. Would you mind telling me about those?"

José straightened his back and held his head high. "Those are my personal beliefs and I don't want to discuss them."

As the judge continued his questioning, Cynthia wondered whether José really believed what he was saying about death. He could just be repeating what he knew others believed. It was clear that José knew he had to seem as rational as possible. From the judge's reaction, José had accomplished this; the judge was impressed. Still, he agreed with Joe and Diane to allow a month and a half for the shot to wear off, and then hold another competency hearing.

A Month and a Half Later

After the medication had worn off, Cynthia and Joe visited José again. Now familiar with Cynthia, José was more personal, even flirtatious. He talked more freely about Mayan culture and, without pause, reminded Joe that he wanted to waive his appeal.

Joe tried to talk him out of it by asking questions. "You're not going to let the state government fry another innocent person in Old Sparky, are you? You aren't going to let them get away with that, are you? Aren't you going to stand up to them?"

José responded, "Look, man, I already told you, I'm living in a cell, and those door buzzers keep me awake. Half the time I'm naked, and the guards walk by staring at me. It's like being an animal. I'm sick of it. If I could have the drugs I need, I might be able to muddle through it. But they won't give those to me. They say it's too expensive. They don't think I'm worth it. All they give me is that poison, and I know it's all part of their plot. I hate Haldol! It makes me stiff, and I drool like a damn mad dog. I can't have anything to read. I can't even get a damn photo. I don't want to live like this anymore, man."

José was so adamant, so sincere, that Cynthia began to wonder about his right to self-determination, and basic human dignity. She wanted to tell Joe to just stop pressuring José. It made her stomach twist to hear him have to argue about why he wanted to die.

The Argument

Back at the office, Cynthia brought up her concerns. "Maybe we should let José waive his appeal." Diane and Joe looked at her incredulously.

"But he doesn't think he will die," Diane insisted. "He thinks he's going to fall as rain on the whole world and reinvigorate the world's worship of him."

Cynthia replied, "I agree. He might not know what will really happen to him when he dies, but he does understand that his life will continue to be hell if he lives. He doesn't want to live like that anymore, Diane. He feels degraded, he is degraded, and he knows he's degraded. I'm not sure I would want to live like that either."

Diane's voice began to rise. "I don't think he is competent enough to make that decision. Plus, I think he's innocent."

Cynthia could feel her own adrenaline kicking in. "Still, doesn't he have a right to have a voice in the matter and have his reasons considered? He's obviously miserable in that cell. He could live like that for another thirty years or more. I'm not sure that we have a right to make that decision for him."

Diane's face was red. "Cynthia, we have *got* to present a united front to that judge next week." She paused briefly. "You know, I do sign your paycheck."

Cynthia felt confused and frustrated. She knew Diane and Joe believed they had José's best interests at heart. She had seen their dedication over the past year; they often visited former clients, even when their professional work was done. They would put a few dollars into inmates' accounts so they could buy cigarettes. They had made huge sacrifices in their personal relationships. They got to know their clients and developed compassion for them. They held scrupulously to their own ethics.

But would she be able to reconcile her ethics with theirs? They believed José was not competent to make the decision to waive his appeal. *But,* she wondered, *how competent is competent enough? Shouldn't he have a right to have his wishes seriously considered? What if it'ss not just a decision about life but a decision about quality of life? What is my responsibility as a social worker to this client?*

7 | The Last Dose

Georgianne Thornburgh

LISA PARKER'S THOUGHTS were racing. Jason Jones had just stopped breathing, and Lisa was acutely aware that she would never see the twinkle in the twelve-year-old's eyes again.

In her years of hospice social work with adults, Lisa had never experienced anything quite like this. *What just happened here? Did I really see what I think I saw? Why isn't anybody saying anything about it? There are three other people in the room; did anybody else see? Maybe not—maybe everything is just fine, and I'm reading things into it because of Janie.*

Children's Hospital and Dr. Mazzoni

Children's Hospital was part of a large teaching hospital complex in Indianapolis, connected to the university. The hospital was new and well funded. The rooms were spacious, with window seats that could be converted to a comfortable bed for family members. When the patients felt well enough,

Development of this decision case was supported in part by the Project on Dying in America and the University of South Carolina College of Social Work. It was prepared solely to provide material for class discussion and not to suggest either effective or ineffective handling of the situation depicted. Although the case is based on field research regarding an actual situation, names and certain facts may have been disguised to protect confidentiality. The author wishes to thank the case reporter for cooperation in making this account available for the benefit of social work students and practitioners.

they could hang out in one of the large, light-filled playrooms on each floor, or around the huge aquariums.

Dr. Mazzoni, head of the pediatric oncologists on staff, was well known around the hospital and in the community. Dark, wavy hair, an enviable tan from time spent on his boat, a flashing smile, and a vigorous ego all were put to maximum use in his infamous flirtations—with nurses, children, moms, medical students, and anyone else who seemed susceptible, according to the hospital grapevine. But to Lisa, his genuine concern for "his" kids was always right up front. He would go out of his way to alleviate pain, and he never seemed to let hospital routines get in the way of making something positive happen for a child whose spirits needed a lift. And unlike some of his colleagues, he seemed to be willing to acknowledge when "enough is enough"— when medicine wasn't going to be able to save a child's life.

Shepherd Hills Children's Hospice and Home Care

Shepherd Hills Children's Hospice and Home Care worked only with pediatric patients. It was well funded and followed patients from diagnosis with a life-threatening or terminal illness until death. Most of the services provided were free to the patients, thanks to the endowment established by its founders, a wealthy couple whose child had died of a rare brain tumor in 1967, prior to the emergence of hospices in the United States. Shepherd Hills staff supported the children in their care wherever they were—at home, in clinics, or in any of the hospitals in the region. It was not unusual for them to work closely with Dr. Mazzoni's patients, even those who lived outside the usual service area, following them through their outpatient treatments and hospitalizations. Dr. Mazzoni sat on the board of Shepherd Hills and was actively involved in raising both community awareness and significant amounts of money for the organization.

The Shepherd Hills Team

Janie Lanham, the hospice R.N., had worked with Dr. Mazzoni on the oncology unit at Children's Hospital for nine years before coming to work for Shepherd Hills seven years ago. She had maintained close relationships with him and the hospital nurses , and was still treated as an "insider." She was more fanatical than some of her colleagues about keeping up with the latest research on pediatric cancers, drugs, and related nursing care, which made her a valuable resource for them. Janie's child had died of cancer, and Dr. Mazzoni had been his physician. After his death, she had entered nursing school, determined to work with children like her son. Janie was in her early fifties, petite and cute. She related well to the kids and often wore fashionable clothes. Today she was wearing plaid wool shorts, oxford cloth shirt, sweater, loafers, and knee socks. She always dressed for special occasions, so today she had on Halloween socks.

Janie was totally devoted to the families she served. It was not unusual for her to stay with a patient for twenty-four hours at a time. She gave families her home phone number and pager number so she could be reached at any time of the day or night. The hospice team complained and argued with her about this practice and the several other ways that Janie operated more as a "Lone Ranger" than as a team member, but their frustration didn't seem to register. Occasionally, Lisa suspected Janie was holding back information—for example, the time she had evidently stayed for more than twenty-four hours at the home of a family while their child was dying but never mentioned it to the team—but it was never something she could confirm without questioning the families, and it had never seemed right, or necessary, to ask. Lisa had to give her credit—she brought a seemingly bottomless supply of positive energy and compassion to her work. Janie had known Jason and his family since the time of his diagnosis.

Ken Barry was a gifted art therapist whose position was endowed by a local foundation, a fact that made many other hospices in the state more than a little envious. He was in his mid-twenties, fresh out of grad school, but he seemed to Lisa to be a natural at hospice work. His ability to connect with kids through specially constructed activities allowed them to address some of the feelings that were too overwhelming or confusing to talk about readily. And his wacky sense of humor and easy laugh made him popular both with kids and their families for bringing some levity into a situation that was often no fun.

Lisa Parker was a relative newcomer to Shepherd Hills and pediatrics, but not to hospice work. She had spent twelve years getting a small hospice program up and running, working directly with patients and their families as social worker, and establishing guidelines and procedures. She'd served only five dying children during those years, but had found it rewarding enough to jump at the chance, four months previously, to accept the position at Shepherd Hills and work with children and their families full time. Recently turned thirty-six, Lisa still entertained occasional thoughts of having children but focused most of her energy on her work, friends, and dogs. She was on the quiet side, and sometimes envied Janie the bubbly, outgoing personality that made it so easy for kids to relate to her. But there'd been no problem connecting with Jason—he'd felt like an old friend from the time she first met him.

The Jones Family

Jason Jones had been diagnosed with acute leukemia at the age of eight. He lived with his mother and ten-year-old sister in rural Indiana, about sixty miles from Indianapolis. For the past four years Jason had traveled those sixty miles at least once a month, to the pediatric oncology clinic adjacent to Children's Hospital for outpatient care. Occasionally he would land in the hospital with complications from the chemotherapy or an infection. The hospice team at Shepherd Hills had followed Jason since his first relapse, a little over three years ago. He was amiable and possessed an irrepressible sense of mischief, and his nurses and other caregivers had become attached to him rather quickly.

Jason's mother, Susan, was in her early forties and very level-headed—someone people often described as "a really strong woman"—although Lisa suspected that she just kept her feelings well hidden. She clearly enjoyed her children, and somehow managed to keep their shared sense of fun and playfulness alive even during difficult times. Susan was divorced from Jason's father, who had been largely absent during Jason's illness. Occasionally Susan would acknowledge her fatigue at handling everything by herself, and one time recently had let it slip to Lisa that a part of her would be relieved when everything was over. Susan did not want Jason to die at home because they lived in such an isolated area. "I don't want to be out there by myself," she admitted, "but I don't want anyone coming to stay for a long time, either."

The Last Hospital Stay

Jason's current hospitalization was due to an infection. After a few days, it had become apparent that this crisis was not like earlier ones. Jason was very

sick and not rebounding as he had in the past. His condition had deteriorated during his hospital stay, and it had become apparent to Lisa and her
teammates that he was in the last days of his illness. Jason had been sleeping
deeply for the past forty-eight hours, not eating or drinking. Occasionally
he would rouse to speak or acknowledge a conversation, but mostly he was
nonresponsive.

Lisa stopped by the hospital on a rainy fall afternoon just to sit with Jason
and his mother for a while. When she walked into the room, it was obvious
that the vigil had begun. Jason's mother, Susan, was sitting on the window
seat with Janie. Susan was tearful and Janie was listening intently. She had
walked with Jason and Susan through almost Jason's entire illness. She knew
firsthand the pain of losing a child to cancer, and mothers seemed to bond
quickly with her, reassured by her obvious competence and ready empathy.
Ken, the art therapist, was sitting quietly on the floor near the foot of Jason's
bed, just watching the boy, lost in thought. Lisa sat on the floor next to Ken,
wanting to be able to reach him for a hug if either of them needed that. *Jason
is really special to him—this is going to be tough,* she realized.

Jason appeared to be resting comfortably. Lisa wondered how long he
would last. She didn't note any signs of imminent death such as apnea or labored breathing. *This could go on for hours,* Lisa thought, *or days.*

Even when things were rough, Susan would occasionally share a story with
whoever was around. The one she told this day, tears spilling down her face,
was that Jason had awakened earlier that morning and told her that he had
seen his friend Robby and Robby's new puppy in heaven. Jason and Robby
had developed a friendship over the years during their visits to the clinic.
Jason was supposedly unaware that Robby had died just before his own hospitalization, and the puppy had been killed by a car a few days later. Not
wanting to upset Jason, Susan had not shared this information with him. Lisa
had heard quite a few stories like this one, making explicit a continuation of
life beyond death, but, because it was Jason, Lisa found herself laughing and
crying at the same time. It was impossible not to smile at the thought of Jason
and Robby stirring things up in heaven.

Lisa had been at the hospital for about two hours when Cindy Holt, one
of the oncology unit nurses, entered the room. She mumbled something
about the oxygen. She turned off the oxygen, unscrewed the water bottle,
fiddled with it briefly, and replaced it on the oxygen valve. Then she left the

room without turning the oxygen back on. Lisa looked around the room to see if anyone else had noticed this, but she didn't say anything. *That's odd. I wonder what she's doing. Is she going to get something? Should I say anything to Janie?* Janie was so engrossed with Susan that she didn't even look up, and Lisa hesitated to interrupt them. *Surely she will be back and check on the oxygen,* Lisa told herself. About fifteen minutes went by before Cindy returned to the room. *Now she'll turn the oxygen back on.* Instead, Cindy administered some medication into Jason's IV tube and left the room again. *She seems really quiet today,* Lisa thought, *even given what's going on. I haven't had many patients with her, but when I've seen her, she has almost always explained what she was doing and why.*

A few minutes after Jason received the medication, his breathing changed—it was noticeably slower and seemed labored. After about ten more minutes, he took a couple of ragged breaths, then just didn't take another one. Although she was expecting Jason to die, Lisa felt a sense of surprise when she looked at her watch and realized how quickly it had happened after the last dose of medication. Looking around to see her colleagues' reaction, Lisa felt a growing sense of unease. *Was that a scheduled dose of medicine or an extra dose? And what was it for? He seemed so easy and peaceful, really comfortable. Something about all this feels so . . . peculiar. Cindy has been so quiet today, just slipping in and out. But Janie's a nurse—why didn't she say something about the oxygen, or ask about the medication, the way she usually does? Is it my place to question the nursing care? Surely Janie would have spoken up if she'd seen anything out of the ordinary. Should I call her out of the room and ask her about it?*

Or—Lisa's stomach began to hurt as she recalled Janie's report of a little girl's somewhat unanticipated death, right after Lisa had joined the team— *maybe Janie is in on it and that's why she was keeping so close to Susan, distracting her.*

Aware that one of the few, if any, opportunities to gather evidence would be gone once Jason's body was removed, Lisa hesitated. But, uncertain how to raise these questions, she thought, *I better not say anything right now. I'm just not sure enough. I need to think about it, and right now there are other things to do.*

8 | No Place for Grief (A)

Rachel C. Parker and Terry A. Wolfer

THE ROOM WAS SILENT. The wide eyes of seven middle school students were riveted on Deb Weston, their mouths agape. A tear slipped down Deb's face, too late for her to wipe away undetected.

As a social worker for School District 4 in Fort Mill, South Carolina, Deb was responsible for providing grief counseling in the aftermath of a school tragedy. She had just told the group she was working with that Shane McKinsey, their fellow student, who had died in a four-wheeler accident over the weekend, was her nephew-in-law. The words had slipped out of her mouth, and as the tear ran its course, she wondered whether she should have revealed her feelings.

School District 4 and the Social Work Program

On the outskirts of the Charlotte metro area, School District 4 included 5 elementary schools, 3 middle schools, and 1 high school, and served more than

Development of this decision case was supported in part by the Project on Dying in America and the University of South Carolina College of Social Work. It was prepared solely to provide material for class discussion and not to suggest either effective or ineffective handling of the situation depicted. Although the case is based on field research regarding an actual situation, names and certain facts may have been disguised to protect confidentiality. As indicated by the (A), the instructor's manual provides a continuation of the case. The authors wish to thank the case reporters for cooperation in making this account available for the benefit of social work students and practitioners.

7,000 students. In 1991, the district hired Marilyn Corley to start a school social work program. Under her leadership and with grant money, the program soon expanded with several innovative initiatives. The social workers served as liaisons between students and their homes, teachers, the community, administrators, and the schools. The program focused on prevention and family or group intervention, but the social workers sometimes provided individual treatment if such services were not available in the community. The program now employed 3 social workers besides Marilyn, including Deb Weston.

Deb Weston

Deb Weston was a short, energetic woman in her early forties. She had many ties to the district in which she worked: her children attended school there, and she was good friends with several teachers and professionals, including Christie Fleming, the mother of Josh Fleming. Josh had been with Shane when he was involved in the fatal accident.

Prior to her current position, Deb had worked eleven years for the York County Department of Social Services, first in foster care and abuse and neglect and then as a foster care manager. Subsequently, she worked in a hospital, and then as a bereavement coordinator for a hospice agency. School District 4 hired her as the second social worker, following Marilyn, to work on a three-year violence prevention grant.

Divorced after a ten-year marriage, Deb had remarried in 1997. Her second husband, Mike, had two children, thirteen-year-old Shannon and ten-year-old David, from his own previous marriage. Deb had quickly grown to love her new family.

The Day of the Accident

On a bright Saturday afternoon in late August 2000, Deb was up on a ladder, painting a friend's house with her father. Her daughter, Shannon, was at another friend's house around the corner, and Deb was enjoying a quiet day outside. When Shannon came running across the lawn with a worried look on her face, Deb knew something was wrong.

"Mom! Della's mom heard that Shane's been in an accident. She said he's dead."

Stunned, Deb slowly put down her paintbrush and turned to her father. "Dad, I have to go check this out. Would you mind staying here with Shannon?"

"Of course not, and please call me as soon as you know what's going on."

Without a thought of the paint spattered on her face and in her hair, Deb sped to the hospital. She thought about Shane, a bright, vivacious twelve-year-old who was always planning his next "adventure." *There's no way this boy could be dead.* Deb suddenly wished her husband was not out of town on a business trip. Once she arrived at the hospital, she became increasingly flustered. She had to drive around the complex several times because the emergency room had been moved. She finally found her way and ran breathlessly through the matrix of hospital halls to the emergency room. Rounding a corner, she saw Shane's grief-stricken family. So it was true. Shane was dead.

Joy, Shane's mother, was in agony. Deb walked over and embraced her, and they sobbed together.

"Joy, what happened?" Deb asked after several minutes.

In a trembling voice, Joy explained. "Last night, Shane spent the night at his best friend Josh's house. I had warned him not to ride the four-wheelers the kids ride near Josh's house. Shane was always talking about them. So I guess they went over there to watch, and Shane talked one of the boys into letting him ride. Well, Shane doesn't know how to control one of those things. He hit something and it threw him and his chest was crushed." She started sobbing uncontrollably, and Deb hugged her. Deb thought about her own son. She couldn't imagine this happening to him. She needed to call her husband, Mike, and let him know what had happened.

Later that evening, as she drove to Joy's house, Deb called her colleague and supervisor, Marilyn Corley.

"Marilyn, you're not going to believe this, but Shane McKinsey was in an accident and he died."

"Oh, Deb, how terrible! Are you okay?"

"Yeah, I'm fine," she said calmly, "but Joy and her family are a wreck. I just can't believe this has happened. I don't think it's sunk in."

"Well, I don't want you to worry about anything as far as going to Shane's school tomorrow. We'll get it covered." Normally, it would have been Deb's responsibility to provide Shane's schoolmates with grief counseling because she was responsible for that middle school.

"Actually, Marilyn, I think I'm okay. I can handle it."

"Well, then I won't cancel my meeting Monday morning, but I'm still going to meet you there afterward. Please be sure to let me know if you change your mind."

"I will, but it'll be fine." After all, she thought, Shane was her nephew through her husband's family. She had only known Shane for three years, since her marriage to Mike. She felt fine, and thought her personal attachments would not get in the way of her professional role on Monday.

Monday at Springfield Middle School

Deb arrived at Springfield Middle School at 8:30 a.m. Ann Marie Younguist, one of the two guidance counselors, saw her come in the door and walked over to give her a hug. Besides being colleagues, they were good friends.

"Are you okay?" Ann Marie asked, her face showing concern.

"Yeah, I think so," Deb replied.

"I think the principal wants to see you. He's trying to figure out what to say over the intercom to inform the students."

They walked down the hall to Principal Graham Hutchinson's office. After making sure Deb was okay, he asked, "What should I tell the kids?"

"Just give the details, that he was on a four-wheeler, and was . . ." All of a sudden, Deb choked up. She couldn't say the word *killed*. Her emotions came like a flood, unexpectedly. *What am I doing?* she thought. *I need to calm down, but I feel like I'm losing control.*

Ann Marie saw the tears welling up in Deb's eyes and motioned for her to come into her office.

"Go on, Deb. I can handle this," Graham assured her.

"I thought I could do this. But I think I'm in way over my head. What am I going to do?" Tears were streaming down her face.

Ann Marie handed her some tissues and rubbed her back. "You don't have to do it, Deb."

Moments later, the announcement came over the intercom. "Students, this is Principal Hutchinson. I have some sad news. Last Saturday, Shane McKinsey was in a four-wheeler accident. He died from his injuries. If you feel like you need to talk, counselors are available in the counseling center. Teachers, please allow your students to leave class if they want to."

"I don't know if I can handle this," Deb said as the tears came faster, despite her struggles to stop crying. "I can't handle it."

Kids were already walking into the counseling center, with shocked looks on their faces. She knew they would soon rely on her to help them sort out their feelings. But she hadn't processed her own. She realized she had been in shock, and now the reality of Shane's death was hitting her full force.

"I think I better call Marilyn right now," she told Ann Marie. She dialed Marilyn's cell phone, but Marilyn didn't answer. Deb figured she was probably in the meeting and had turned her cell phone off. So Deb steeled herself and determined to forge ahead. She reminded herself that Marilyn would be there later that morning, and decided that she had to manage things until then. She pulled herself together and went in to introduce herself to the first group of students who had assembled. Shane had had a lot of friends, and the group was a mixture of Caucasians and African Americans, both girls and boys. The first two groups went smoothly, and Deb was able to concentrate on the needs of the kids and her role as group facilitator. But then, in her third group, the kids were sharing memories of Shane, and something one of them said triggered a memory for Deb. Instantly, her throat constricted. She felt her eyes filling with tears.

Without thinking, she said softly, "You know, your memory just sparked a memory for me." She felt a warm tear glide down her cheek. "I have not shared this with you before, but Shane was my nephew."

There was a stunned silence in the room. All eyes were on her, and Deb wondered whether she had made a mistake.

She continued, "At Christmas, I remember Shane coming in dragging all the presents and I remember how he lit up the whole room because he was so loud and goofy."

The students broke out in giggles and the tension in the room lifted. They related to her memory; Shane had been a class clown, so everyone knew his impulsive, fun-loving personality. But Deb pulled back inside herself, wondering, *Oh, what have I done? I don't think this was supposed to go this way. Have I made a mistake? Should I continue on a personal level or put my professional face back on? And should I . . . Is it too early to be laughing about our memories of Shane? Should I push them to focus more on the reality of his death?*

9 | Right Before Their Eyes

Rachel C. Parker and Terry A. Wolfer

ONE MONDAY IN SEPTEMBER 2002, school social worker Caroline Eastman was sitting at her desk in the school district office, finishing paperwork, when her phone rang. The agitated voice of Don Osmar, the principal of Goldsboro High School, implied something was seriously wrong.

"Caroline, we have a situation over here. This morning, we had a bus full of students coming to school and when they stopped to pick up Marie Boswell, Marie's ex-boyfriend, Joe Shipley, stepped in front of the bus and blew his brains out. A lot of the kids saw it happen."

Principal Osmar's words set Caroline's heart pounding. After asking a few more questions, she hung up the phone, rubbed her temples, and took a moment to gather her thoughts. In her thirteen years as a school social worker, she had never had a case in which students had actually witnessed a traumatic event. She had no idea how she was going to handle this one. Little did she know, it would become even more complicated.

Development of this decision case was supported in part by funding from the Project on Death in America and the University of South Carolina College of Social Work. It was prepared solely to provide material for class discussion and not to suggest either effective or ineffective handling of the situation depicted. Although the case is based on field research regarding an actual situation, names and certain facts may have been disguised to protect confidentiality. The authors and editors wish to thank the anonymous case reporter for cooperation in making this account available for the benefit of social work students and instructors.

Goldsboro, North Carolina

Located in eastern North Carolina, Goldsboro was founded on the banks of the Neuse River. As the county seat of Wayne County, it was originally named Wayneborough but was later renamed after an official with the railroad. Over time it became an agricultural and transportation center for the surrounding region. Goldsboro was also the site of Seymour Johnson Air Force Base, home of the 4th Fighter Wing. According to Census 2000, Wayne County's total population of more than 113,000 included nearly 40,000 residents of Goldsboro. The county population was about 60 percent white and 33 percent black, but the residents of Goldsboro were about 52 percent black, 42 percent white, and 6 percent other minorities.

Goldsboro High School

One of four public high schools serving the city, Goldsboro High School was an institutional-looking place. It reminded Caroline of a prison with its cement block walls and barbed-wire fence along the periphery of the large campus. Don Osmar was the principal, and Jeff Carnes was the assistant principal. Despite the generally middle-class composition of the greater community, more than 70 percent of Goldsboro High's students qualified for free or reduced lunches.

The Wayne County School District, of which Goldsboro High was a part, had policies for dealing with the event of a student death. The responding police officers were to report to the school district's public information officer, who was to report to the superintendent, who then reported to the principal of the school affected.

The Social Work Program

The district had hired Caroline in 1989 to start a districtwide social work program that employed three additional M.S.W.s. Although initially designed to serve disabled preschool children, as funds shifted, the social work program began to focus on providing services to all of the district's students. Caroline and the social workers she supervised helped to connect parents, children, school, and community. School-based prevention and intervention activities were their primary responsibilities, although they also provided other services not available elsewhere in the community. Each social worker was assigned to certain schools. Caroline's office was located in the school district headquarters, and the other social workers had offices in the particular schools they served.

Caroline Eastman

Caroline Eastman was a veteran social worker. She spent the first two years after earning her M.S.W. as a student counselor at a community college. Next, she worked as a caseworker for the South Carolina Department of Social Services (DSS) in adult and child protective services. After six years, she was promoted to assistant director for the human services programs in Goldsboro. In that position, she participated on a community task force and developed many relationships with local community leaders. She was also responsible for case reviews, development of local policy, training, community relations, and budgeting. This position gave her the administrative skills she subsequently needed to start the school social work program for the Wayne County schools. She also developed many valuable relationships with people in the community that she would later depend on as a school social worker. Also, she worked with a client population similar to that at DSS, and was familiar with their life skills.

On the morning of the shooting, Caroline was in her thirteenth year as director of social work for the Wayne County School District. Now in her early fifties, she still enjoyed the challenging work.

The Shooting Incident

During the initial telephone call, after Principal Osmar told her about the shooting, Caroline took a second to think, and then asked, "Isn't there another Shipley at the high school?"

"Yeah, Joe's sister, Gail Ann, is a junior here," Principal Osmar replied.

"And didn't Joe used to go to school there?"

"Yeah, that's right," he replied. "He graduated a year ago."

"Okay, I'll be right there," Caroline said, her stomach already knotting from the shock of what she'd just heard. "Please call Gail Ann's parents, or has someone already called them?"

After gathering her thoughts and letting her heart slow down, she picked the phone back up and called Joanne Kimball, one of the three social workers she supervised.

"Joanne, drop whatever you're doing and meet me at Goldsboro. The ex-boyfriend of a student just shot himself in front of a busload of kids. They need us at the high school right away."

Once she arrived at the high school, Caroline went straight to the principal's office. "So are the kids on their way?" she asked Principal Osmar.

"I don't know. They're not here," he replied.

"What do you mean, they're not here?" she asked.

"I don't know where they are. Go ask Mr. Carnes. He's the one dealing with this now."

Wondering about the principal's avoidance, Caroline went to find the assistant principal. He was in his office.

"Mr. Carnes, where are the kids who saw the shooting this morning?"

"The bus driver sent them all to class," he said, and shrugged.

"You mean the kids are here?" Caroline asked, incredulous. She had assumed that since the students were not waiting for her in the guidance office, they were still en route to school.

"Yeah, the bus driver, Hal, was pretty upset. After the shooting, he drove the bus a ways away from the scene, then stopped and said a prayer with the students. Then he picked up the rest of the kids, brought them to school, and sent them to class. He was really upset. He didn't know what to do."

Caroline was stunned. What if Gail Ann found out about the shooting from another classmate? Plus, she thought, the students who had witnessed the shooting were probably in no shape to attend class. "Mr. Carnes, we've got to get those kids down here."

"How are we going to do that?" Mr. Carnes looked puzzled. "We don't know who was on that bus. The bus driver doesn't take attendance." Pausing, he added, "There is a bus roster, though. Maybe the transportation director would have it."

Caroline immediately got on the phone and asked Emma Kizer, the transportation director, to bring the bus roster to her at the principal's office.

"I don't know which of these kids were actually on the bus," Emma informed Caroline, "but I'll send the roster of kids on that route." Right before they hung up, Emma made a request: "You know, Hal is pretty shook up. Do you think you could talk to him?"

"Sure," Caroline responded, sighing, and added the request to a growing list of high-priority tasks. Caroline had another concern about Hal. *He shouldn't have gone on to pick up the rest of the kids on the route, much less released them to class,* she thought. *Something needs to be done to make sure that doesn't happen again.*

Getting off the phone, Caroline noted that the guidance counselors were busy doing something else in their offices. *I'm sure they know what happened. What could they be doing that's more important than this?* she wondered, with more than a little irritation.

Caroline turned to Joanne, who had arrived while she was on the phone. "There are so many traumatized people involved. At least Victim's Assistance will take care of Marie once the court gets involved. But that doesn't help right now. Should we call parents first and then work with the kids, or vice versa? We need to think about Hal too. I know he didn't know any better—he must have been pretty rattled—but he should not have picked up the rest of the kids on the route. I don't know where to start, Joanne."

10 | Private Charity (A)

Miriam McNown Johnson and Karen A. Gray

"THIS IS BILL. Can you come see me in my office?"

"Sure, how about in twenty minutes?" Her boss's unexpected call caught Melissa Sinclair by surprise, and she hoped to get through the first draft of a quarterly report before taking a break.

"How about *now?*" Bill insisted.

"Okay."

She walked briskly down the hall and into Executive Director Bill Cannon's corner office. He motioned for her to take a seat across from him at his conference table.

"How are you?" he asked.

"I'm fine," she said, knowing that her health certainly was not what he wanted to talk about.

Lowering his head slightly so he could look over the top of his glasses, Bill peered intently into her eyes. "I need to ask you something. Have you loaned Hao money?"

Development of this decision case was supported in part by funding from the University of South Carolina College of Social Work. It was prepared solely to provide material for class discussion and not to suggest either effective or ineffective handling of the situation depicted. Although the case is based on field research regarding an actual situation, names and certain facts may have been disguised to protect confidentiality. As indicated by the (A), the instructor's manual provides a continuation of the case. The author and editors wish to thank the anonymous case reporter for cooperation in making this account available for the benefit of social work students and instructors.

The question caught her off guard. Melissa couldn't gauge what was going on. *Am I in trouble here?* Melissa wondered. Hao Tran worked for her, and she worked for Bill, but at first she thought, *That's none of your business. It was a transaction between friends, outside of our work relationship.* But then she thought, *There's no reason not to tell you.*

"Yes."

"How much?"

"Umm, five hundred dollars." Melissa searched his face for an expression that might help her guess where this conversation was going.

A First Management Position

Melissa had thoroughly enjoyed almost every aspect of her middle-management position over the last three and a half years. She interviewed for the job the same day she defended her master's thesis in December 1979, after a long five years of mostly part-time graduate study. She was a little surprised to be hired. Although she had ten years of social work experience with her undergraduate degree, all of it was with county departments of social services. She had only limited experience in actual supervision and no experience working with refugees or other international clients of any kind.

It had taken a while, but Melissa gradually became accustomed to her role as a mid-level manager. At first, when Bill came past her office and announced, "Come on, management team meeting time," she had to remind herself, *Oh yeah, I'm a manager now. He's talking to me.*

The Programs and Employees

In January 1980, Melissa was hired to be the first director of the Unaccompanied Refugee Minor (URM) Program at Lutheran Social Services (LSS) in Cedar Rapids, Iowa. Through arrangements with the United Nations High Commissioner for Refugees, the U.S. Department of State, and the Immigration and Naturalization Service of the U.S. Department of Justice (which has since been replaced by the U.S. Citizenship and Immigration Services within the U.S. Department of Homeland Security), young refugees who had been separated from their parents were arriving from refugee camps in Southeast Asia to be resettled with foster families in the United States. LSS had received a contract from the Iowa Department of Health and Human Services to establish a receiving group home for up to ten youths, who would be assessed and then placed with foster families in four cities across the state.

The majority of their clients were males in their late teens but less than eighteen years old, mostly Vietnamese or ethnic Chinese from Vietnam, with a handful of Laotians who had fled with other "boat people" to refugee camps in Indonesia. Others had fled overland from Laos to refugee camps in Thailand. Usually their desperate families had made arrangements for the youths to flee the country, knowing that if they were resettled in America, the rest of the family would be given the opportunity for reunification there at a later time. After a dangerous, often life-threatening escape experience, these young people had lived in the refugee camps for at least several months, waiting to be cleared for resettlement. While in the camps they were screened and treated for chronic and contagious health problems, such as hepatitis B and tuberculosis. Once matched and "assured" by a program in the United States, they were flown first to the West Coast and then to their final destination. Generally a public welfare agency assumed legal custody while a Volag (voluntary agency) provided foster care placement and supervision services.

Melissa's first assignment was to hire the group home staff and a Vietnamese interpreter to work with both the home and the foster families. For the group home she hired a diverse mix of enthusiastic people who had a broad range of experience working with youths. The staff amazed her—dealing masterfully with adolescents who were homesick and in culture shock and who rarely spoke more than a few words of English.

In addition, there were social workers who worked with the foster families. Melissa saw these social workers as totally competent and dedicated. She knew that they gave their home phone numbers to all of the families and encouraged them to call at any time. She was very excited about all her staff, but she felt her best "catch" was the man she hired to interpret, Hao Tran.

Hao was the core of the program. He had a postsecondary degree in pedagogy, had been a classroom teacher in Vietnam, and had come to the United States in the first wave of refugees after Saigon fell in 1975. Besides his native Vietnamese, Hao could speak English and Laotian. He had been an interpreter with the welfare department in Cedar Rapids and was delighted to leave it for a new job at LSS. He was in his fifties, with graying hair that he dyed solid black. He lived with his wife, who earned some money as a seamstress but didn't speak much English. "She will make you a beautiful *ao dai* [traditional Vietnamese outfit]," Hao offered Melissa.

"Doesn't she need a pattern?"

"No, she never needs a pattern. She can measure you and make it. You choose the colors."

Because none of the other staff could speak Vietnamese and most of the youth were just beginning to learn English, Hao was on call 24/7 for new arrivals, court hearings, registration at school, doctor appointments, transfers to family foster homes, and crises of every kind.

The staff learned that even though most Southeast Asian refugees had experienced significant losses, they were hesitant to discuss their problems outside of their own families. Melissa had a visual image—the clients she was used to counseling were like small planes with engine trouble, alternately sputtering and gliding to a rough landing. The Southeast Asians were more like a helicopter with a broken blade—they went as far as they could manage on their own and then suddenly dropped like a stone.

Melissa struggled with getting her social work staff to actively recruit and license foster homes although the client arrivals were largely unpredictable, and the program's contact person in the state office was often impatient with both the slow rate of arrivals and the lack of places for them. But the URM youth trickled in over the next several months, the staff matched them with foster homes, and the program slowly grew to capacity, more than forty youths total.

After less than a year, Bill asked Melissa to also serve as manager of the resettlement program for refugee families. Volunteers from co-sponsoring churches did most of the ground work with the refugees—locating housing and household goods, arranging clinic appointments, enrolling the younger ones in school, matching the older ones with jobs in the community, and getting everyone to ESL (English as a Second Language) classes. There were no volunteers to interpret, though, so the agency employed three bilingual interpreters—Bin Mey, a Cambodian man; Teng Chu, a Hmong man; and Ly Thanh, a Vietnamese woman—who also filled the role of paraprofessional human service workers. There were no Cambodian or Hmong youth in the URM program, but sometimes Teng Chu, who spoke some Laotian, and Ly Thanh could help out with the youth when Hao needed to be elsewhere.

One of the major highlights of the refugee program was the regular ethnic celebrations. Melissa bragged to her friends that she celebrated at least four or five "new years" every year. The festivities always included fabulous ethnic clothing and music, and potluck dinners with ground beef and noodle casseroles and Jell-O salads (brought by the co-sponsoring American families) and delicious, exotic, difficult-to-pronounce dishes that the refugees prepared.

After three years, the URM program had begun to slowly wind down. With no new arrivals, LSS closed the group home, laid off several staff, and retained others to work as counselors and case managers for the youth moving into independent living situations. Hao continued in his role as interpreter.

Money, Money, Money, Money

Hao bought a new home in a nice west side neighborhood and invited everyone to a housewarming. But all was not well. Soon after, one of the program staffers confided in Melissa, "I helped Hao understand the closing process, but I really tried to persuade him not to go through with it. He can't afford this house. Other staff told him the same thing, but he won't listen to us. He's caught up in the American dream, I guess."

Then one day Hao asked to see Melissa in her office. In a quiet voice he asked, "Mrs. Sinclair, can I borrow some money until payday?"

"How much do you need?"

"Five hundred dollars, just for two weeks, or maybe three weeks."

"Let me think about it a minute," Melissa hesitated.

Five hundred dollars was a lot of money, even on a middle manager's salary, but just for a few weeks wasn't asking much. Melissa knew she had to be objective about her decision and that her first consideration must be whether she could afford to lose that much if Hao couldn't pay her back. *I don't give much to charity,* she thought. *This could be my charity project. What good is having money if you can't help worthy people in need?* She was surprised, but not shocked, that Hao was asking her for money. After all, they really trusted each other. She knew Hao would use the loan for his mortgage or utilities; he didn't have a gambling or drug problem.

"I'll have to take some funds out of my savings, Hao, but I'll do it. I'd like to ask you why you need it, but I guess it's really not my business."

"Thank you," Hao replied. "I promise I will pay you back."

Trouble

It was about ten days after that, on a Thursday afternoon, when Bill called Melissa into his office. "I need to ask you something. Have you loaned Hao money?"

"Yes."

"How much?"

"Umm, five hundred dollars. What's going on?"

"Hao bought a new house—I think you knew that—and I guess he's gotten in over his head." Bill shifted his gaze for a moment, then looked her straight in the eyes again. "Did you know he also has borrowed money from four or five other refugee program employees?"

Surprised, Melissa said, "No, no, I didn't know that." Immediately, she thought, *Uh oh. This is trouble. This is more than a loan between two friends.*

"Are you going to do something about it?"

Melissa knew that "No" was not an acceptable response. She respected Bill and his administrative abilities. His background was in business rather than social work, but he had a strong commitment to human services. Melissa liked the way he said he wanted to hear the "bad news" as well as the "good news." His management style was not to rescue employees when things got sticky but to insist that they take care of their responsibilities. He didn't tell people how to do their jobs.

"Yes." Melissa paused, thoughtfully. "I'm not sure just what, but yes, I will."

Like a Stone

Friday morning, Melissa caught Hao before he left the office for his first appointment with one of the URM youths. "Hao, I found out you've been borrowing money from a number of people. I'm not concerned about the money I gave you, but I'm concerned that you're in over your head and you need someone to help you get control of your financial situation. I'd like you to see someone at the Consumer Credit Counseling program at the United Way Office. I know the director, Margo Rock. She'll take good care of you. Consumer Credit Counseling can talk to your creditors and work out payment arrangements that you can manage. Does this sound okay with you?"

Hao nodded silently.

"I don't need to know what you talk about or what you decide to do," Melissa continued. "I just want to know that you're actually attending sessions there."

"Yes, fine, I'll go." Hao appeared docile, with no affect. He seemed neither ashamed nor resistant, but he also did not seem eager to seek out the help.

"Good. I'll call Margo now and tell her I'm sending over a very special person—one of my best employees."

Hao left quickly and quietly.

Melissa felt relieved. *Hao is going to get help, good help. The staff at the Consumer Credit Counseling program are excellent.*

The following Tuesday afternoon, Melissa's secretary buzzed her in her office. "It's Margo Rock. She needs to talk to you right now."

"Hi, Margo. What's up?"

"Your employee, Hao, is here."

"Good."

"No, not good. The counselor said she can't work with him—he's suicidal. She persuaded him to agree to a no suicide contract, but only for twenty-four hours, until he can see you tomorrow. Can I tell him you'll talk to him tomorrow?"

"Sure." Melissa's thoughts raced. "Tell him I'll be in my office all day." As she hung up the phone, Melissa's heart sank. She had hoped the counseling would be a turning point and would get Hao back on track with his finances. *He must be in worse shape than I thought. It sounds like he's coming apart at the seams.*

Melissa thought about how to handle the next day's meeting. She reflected on what she'd learned in class about suicide. She knew the bottom-line game plan was a no suicide contract. She hoped that the Consumer Credit counselor had misread Hao or overreacted; after all, they were financial counselors, not psychotherapists.

Hao appeared at her office door at mid-morning Wednesday.

"Come in."

Hao took a seat across from Melissa's desk.

She looked at him earnestly. "Hao, Margo tells me you're thinking of killing yourself. You know I can't let that happen. Are you really feeling that bad?"

They talked a long time. Melissa tried to get Hao to put his present troubles into perspective. She knew that all refugees had lost a lot: homeland, relatives, career, credentials, culture, and language. They certainly had good reason to be grief-stricken. But Hao had come a long way since leaving Vietnam. "Look at all you've been through. You lost everything when you had to flee your homeland. You started from scratch here. That must have been really hard, but you managed it."

"It was manageable. I was coping," Hao responded. "Except when they killed my son."

Surprised that she had never heard this before, Melissa probed, "They killed your son?"

"The Communist troops took my village and they shot him. Killed him." Without expressing any emotion, Hao continued. "They left his body in the street. I couldn't leave my house or I would have been shot too. His body was there in the street for three days. Three days. I couldn't do anything."

Melissa pictured a muddy street in a small Vietnamese village, and she could feel her eyes tearing up as Hao spoke. But his face showed no emotion. *How can he just sit there like that?* she wondered.

After more conversation, Melissa tried to gauge Hao's risk of suicide. "Do you have a plan about how you would kill yourself?"

"I have a gun, a hunting rifle."

"I don't want you to kill yourself. Can you get rid of it?"

"I have a friend I could give it to. He would keep it for me. I could put it in a box and not even tell him what it is."

"Would you do that, Hao? Would you do that and promise me you won't do anything to hurt yourself without contacting me first?"

"Okay. I'll take it to my friend tonight."

Melissa felt satisfied that she could trust Hao to give the gun away and call her if he was having thoughts of suicide. Since he'd told the credit counselor—a total stranger—that he was suicidal, maybe he wanted help and wouldn't actually hurt himself. Melissa wasn't certain that he wanted to live, but she knew he wasn't going to kill himself that night.

Melissa addressed another matter. "Hao, I can't be your therapist and your supervisor too. You need to be seeing someone." Melissa knew that Vietnamese people don't like talking to strangers about their personal problems because it brings shame on their families; everything is dealt with within the family. She also knew that Hao, like most Southeast Asians, tended to defer to authorities and would be reluctant to openly disagree with her. Melissa often thought that the refugee staff she supervised were physically incapable of saying no. *Asians want to please, they want things to be harmonious, and they do not like arguments.*

"I'll think about it," Hao said.

This was the best response Melissa knew she could get—she couldn't call to make the appointment yet because he would need to think it over. She thought he had a better idea than most refugees of the purpose of therapy because he took kids there—actually interpreted in therapy assessments. She had hope that he'd agree to counseling.

Reassured by Hao's responses, Melissa ended the conversation with a request: "Tell me if anything changes."

More Trouble

Although Melissa believed that Hao was truthful and hoped he would agree to therapy, her sense of relief was short-lived. Late that day Eva Black, one of the URM foster mothers, called her. Mr. and Mrs. Black had two boys in their home. "We have a crisis here," Mrs. Black confided. "We can't really understand what the boys are saying, but I think . . ."

Melissa interrupted her. "I think Hao is at the health clinic with another kid, but I can try to track him down for you."

"I'm afraid Hao may be the problem."

"Oh." *Oh no!* Melissa thought. *How can things get any worse?!*

"I think there is money missing from the boys' bank accounts," Mrs. Black continued. "There should be several hundred dollars in each one, and there's almost nothing. Hao opened a joint account for each boy with himself as a co-signer."

"Will you be there for a while? Let me get right back to you."

Melissa went straight to Bill's office. "We've got a problem. A big problem." She filled him in on her conversation with Mrs. Black.

"What do you plan to do?"

"If Ly Thanh is free tomorrow, I'll ask if she can go with me to talk to the boys and maybe go to the bank. Do you think it's okay to get her involved in this?"

"I don't think you have any other choice," Bill responded. "Keep me posted."

Melissa checked with the other interpreter and then called Mrs. Black. "Can you and the boys meet us at the bank tomorrow at 3:00 p.m.?"

On a hunch, Melissa decided to take a look at the program's petty cash box. The account balanced, but she was surprised to find there were several large IOUs filled out by Hao. It wasn't unusual for staff to put in an IOU if they borrowed cash to take a client out to lunch or for other small bills, but these weren't client-related expenses and the sums were much larger than a lunch. However, the fact that Hao was putting in IOUs was reassuring. He wasn't stealing and was trying to be accountable. But to Melissa it seemed a disturbing indicator of a broader problem.

The visit to the bank the next day confirmed Melissa's worst fears. It was clear that Hao had withdrawn funds from the boys' accounts. Melissa started to feel nauseated. *What about Hao's fragile mental health? If I have to confront him and maybe even fire him, it might push him over the edge. If I don't handle this right, and he kills himself, is his blood on my hands?*

11 | Suicidal Co-ed

Jeanette Ucci and Terry A. Wolfer

SILENCE HUNG IN THE AIR as social worker Lisa Conway tried to decide whether Mary Williams, her client on the other end of the telephone crisis hotline, was in imminent danger of hurting herself. Lisa sensed that Mary was hesitating in responding to her inquiries; she had been avoiding questions with either silence or vague "mmm-hmms." She did speak about a letter that she was composing, yet she would not say directly whether or not it was a suicide letter.

"Is it a suicide letter?"

No answer.

"Do you feel like you're going to hurt yourself?"

No answer.

"By not answering, I feel like you're giving me an answer. Am I interpreting this correctly, that you're planning to hurt yourself tonight? If you don't answer me, I'm going to interpret that as a yes."

No answer.

Development of this decision case was supported in part by funding from the Project on Death in America and the University of South Carolina College of Social Work. It was prepared solely to provide material for class discussion and not to suggest either effective or ineffective handling of the situation depicted. Although the case is based on field research regarding an actual situation, names and certain facts may have been disguised to protect confidentiality. The authors wish to thank the anonymous case reporter for cooperation in making this account available for the benefit of social work students and instructors.

Although Mary seemed more distant during this conversation than she had in previous crisis calls during the past couple of weeks, she did not reveal any direct information upon which Lisa could base a clear decision.

The University of Georgia

Founded in 1785, the University of Georgia (UGA) was established as the flagship institution for the University System of Georgia. The main campus, located in Athens, enrolled close to 33,000 students, including nearly 25,000 undergraduates. The student body was composed of 43 percent men and 57 percent women, and approximately 43 percent of the students were from Georgia. Nearly 20 percent of the students resided on campus, including 85 percent of all freshmen.

Office of Relationship/Sexual Violence Prevention

The Office of Relationship/Sexual Violence Prevention (RSVP) at UGA was formed in 1992 in recognition that there was a need for improved services to assist survivors of sexual assault on campus. This office was part of the larger Health Promotion Department, which also included the Office of Preventive Health Programs. That office provided students with information about subjects such as nutrition counseling, smoking cessation, cholesterol screening, and fitness. According to the university Web site, the programs offered through RSVP "provide a range of services for UGA students on issues surrounding sexual health, sexual assault, and relationship violence." This included education on sexual health as well as crisis intervention and counseling for survivors of relationship violence and sexual assault.

The RSVP staff included Alicia Porterfield, the office director; Lisa Conway, the program director of Relationship Violence Services; and Sarah Spencer, the program director of Sexual Health and Violence Prevention. Both program directors and the office director served as client advocates and counselors. In addition, the staff supervised UGA graduate interns who helped provide services. RSVP was housed in the University Health Center.

Interoffice Relations

As a campus office at UGA, RSVP worked closely with other departments of the university, particularly the Department of Student Housing and Residence Life and the University Police Department (UPD). RSVP had written and distributed detailed protocol for each department regarding how to deal with sexual assault and relationship violence in both emergency and nonemergency situations. The advocates at RSVP also conducted training sessions for housing staff members, including resident assistants (RAs), prior to the beginning of each academic year.

When speaking about her job, Lisa often said, "Being housed in a university is both positive and negative." Employees and clients at RSVP had access to a wide range of campus resources. However, the missions and policies governing the different departments varied greatly, and this sometimes caused difficult situations. A further complication was that RSVP, under the Health Promotion Department, considered its records to be medical information, and thus held to the strictest standards regarding confidentiality. Housing did not have the same standards for student records. For example, if a student had to be taken to the hospital for any reason, housing notified the student's parents. However, RSVP policy considered student hospitalizations confidential medical information and did not release it.

These differences in philosophy could lead to tension between the offices on campus. For instance, before this case, Lisa had been mandated to provide officials in housing with updates on her clients who resided on campus. However, she disagreed with this policy and chose not to comply. Furthermore, if a RSVP advocate and a housing employee, such as a RA, responded to an emergency call at the same time, the advocate was bound by confidentiality regarding whatever ensued, but the housing employee was not. Students were not always aware of these differences in policies. Lisa believed that she had an ethical responsibility to inform clients in crisis that, unlike advocates from RSVP, housing staff would not keep information told to them confidential. This was not something that Lisa particularly liked doing, because housing employees were potential supports for clients as well. According to Lisa, the advocates were "caught in the middle." Similar situations could occur with RSVP and the Office of Student Affairs, between which there were also policy differences. For example, while staff at RSVP viewed their clients as independent adults, staff at student affairs recognized the importance of family relationships, especially for traditional college students, and sought to keep parents informed of emergencies. In contrast, RSVP had a close working relationship with the Student Health Center (SHC), whose staff better understood mental health issues and the need for confidentiality.

Lisa Conway

When she accepted the position of program director of Relationship Violence Services in May 2000, Lisa was already familiar with serving survivors of domestic violence and sexual assault from two field placements in her M.S.W. program. The first had been an internship at the Department of Social Services in the Working Together program. There, she had worked with women who were HIV positive and at risk for drug abuse or actively using drugs. All of these women were either pregnant or had very young children, and all were at high risk for domestic violence. During this time, Lisa had become much more aware of the connections between social problems (particularly drug abuse, HIV, and domestic violence) and social policy.

Lisa's second field placement in the macro concentration, which focused on social work practice at the organizational or community level, was an internship at the Georgia Coalition Against Relationship and Sexual Violence. At the same time, with passion sparked by her field experience, she volunteered at Sexual Assault Emergency Services, which operated on a feminist model, working with survivors of sexual assault and domestic violence. This volunteer situation allowed her to gain further experience working with individuals while learning about social policy issues in the field agency. Lisa had increased her understanding of and appreciation for the reciprocal relationship between private troubles and public issues.

Believing that she needed more education about and experience with the feminist model, she accepted a position with The University of Georgia Department of Women's Studies immediately following her graduation from the M.S.W. program in 1999. She served as an instructor and a research assistant for one year. Her experiences in field placements and in Women's Studies profoundly shaped her views of social work practice. Lisa considered herself an "integrator" and emphasized the connections between micro and macro practice.

Such connections were evident in Lisa's work at RSVP, her first postgraduate position as a social worker. Lisa provided crisis intervention as well as long-term counseling for survivors of sexual assault, relationship violence, and stalking. The position was funded through a series of two-year grants from the U.S. Department of Justice intended to combat violence against women on university campuses. Because RSVP provided twenty-four-hour emergency services, Lisa's job duties included carrying the agency beeper for two or three nights per week. While on call, she might be awakened at any hour to respond to a crisis. Such calls came once or twice a week.

A Freshman Client

During mid-August 2002, as a new academic year began, the staff members at RSVP resumed their weekly Wednesday staff meetings. During these meetings, they discussed recent events of general interest and consulted with one another on any particularly difficult cases. At the first meeting, Sarah Spencer mentioned an unusually early referral of an incoming freshman. According to Sarah, this student's RA brought her to RSVP for help related to "emotional problems and drug use." In a subsequent individual session, she reported long-term physical and sexual abuse by her father. Sarah had initiated ongoing services to help her heal from this trauma.

Two days later, Lisa was covering the twenty-four-hour emergency beeper when a ringing telephone awakened her at 4:00 a.m.

"Rise and shine, Lisa!" Lisa immediately recognized the voice of Jamie Kee, a dispatcher from the University Police Department. "We have a sexual assault case," Jamie began. "A young female student was assaulted on campus. She's on the way to the emergency room, along with her RA. Officers Jones and Schumacher are on the way to the hospital, and I've paged Calvin," the victim-witness coordinator for the police department.

"Thanks," Lisa responded. "I'll head right over."

Lisa took a few minutes to wash her face and brush her teeth before driving to the emergency room. From previous experience she knew that these visits could last for hours. As usual with crisis calls, she was unsure what the situation might hold.

Arriving at the hospital about 4:30, Lisa reported to triage, where she typically met survivors of sexual assault. Waiting outside the door of a triage room were several UPD officers. One directed Lisa to enter the room. She went in and saw two young women sitting in the only chairs under the bright fluorescent lights. Neither woman had obvious physical injuries, but one was staring down to the right, looking at the floor, and did not look up when Lisa entered. The other immediately introduced herself.

"I'm Claire, Mary's RA," she said, sounding anxious.

"My name is Lisa, and I'm a survivor advocate from the Office of Relationship/Sexual Violence Prevention on campus," Lisa began.

"Yeah," Claire interrupted, nodding in recognition, "I think I remember you from a training session you did for the RAs a few weeks ago." She hurried on, gesturing toward the other woman. "Mary and I have gotten to know each other pretty well during the past couple weeks. She's been through so much. I really want to help," Claire stated, reaching over to give Mary a hug.

In keeping with her training for working with survivors of sexual assault, Lisa asked Mary, "Is it okay for me to be in the room?" When Mary nodded, Lisa squatted low so that her head was below Mary's. "Is there something that you need right now?"

"Yes," Mary replied, "I have to go to the bathroom."

Lisa was not surprised because clients she met post-trauma in emergency rooms often voiced this immediate need. Survivors of a sexual assault were sometimes unsure what they could and could not do following an assault. Specifically, they often believed that they were not allowed to use the bathroom at the hospital because they would be required to provide a urine sample. After checking with a nurse outside the room, Lisa confirmed that Mary could provide the urine sample at this time if she were willing to do so.

While Mary used the restroom, Lisa had a few moments to collect her thoughts and consider what to do next. She tried to get acclimated to the setting, something she did not have to do when seeing clients at her office. Meanwhile, Claire provided some basic information about the assault.

"Mary was walking home late last night, and was really on a lot of drugs and alcohol," Claire explained, anxiety obvious in her voice, "and someone literally grabbed her on the street on the way to our residence hall and assaulted her. I don't know how, but she managed to make it back to our dorm." She shook her head in amazement. "But Mary lost her keys and couldn't get back into her room, so she called me from the front desk of the dorm."

Lisa nodded, and Claire continued rapidly.

"When I met her at the front desk, she looked really upset, and then she told me about the assault. I knew that I had to get help for her right away, so I let Mary into her room, then called the University Police Department.

"This is so terrible," Claire continued. "Mary and I had already become pretty good friends. You know, she'd even confided in me that her father had sexually abused her in the past. Mary's just been through so much."

By this point, it was evident that Claire herself felt quite shaken by the events of the night. Lisa reassured her. "It's really important that you're here, Claire, and it's obvious that Mary trusts you."

"Yeah," Claire nodded, "but I have to leave for work pretty soon."

"That's okay if you need to leave," Lisa replied. But she felt concerned about what would happen if Claire left the hospital. *I haven't made any real connection with Mary,* she thought. *I'm afraid that she won't be able to connect while she's in the middle of a crisis.*

Mary returned from the bathroom, and a nurse informed them that they would be moved to a different room.

"Is it okay if I come with the two of you to the other room?" Lisa asked.

Mary nodded.

After they entered the other room, Claire turned to Mary. "Mary, I hate to have to say this, but I have to leave soon. I've got to be at work this morning on campus. I wish I didn't, but . . ." her voice trailed off uncertainly.

"Don't leave me here, Claire," Mary answered, her voice rising. "I don't want to be here by myself. If—if you leave, then I think I might go back too!"

Lisa stepped in. "Mary, it really is your decision whether or not you want to remain here. Being at the hospital is completely voluntary. It's a good idea to have a medical exam, but that is entirely up to you."

"But won't I get in trouble if I leave?" Mary asked nervously.

"Definitely not," Lisa replied. "Your being here is completely your decision. I'm just here for support if you want me to be. I don't represent any kind of authority, and you will not be in any trouble if you do opt to leave."

"Well, as long as it won't cause problems, I guess it's okay to stay," Mary answered uncertainly.

Lisa began to wonder whether Mary was the same student that Sarah had mentioned in the staff meeting several days before. Claire had said that Mary had been sexually abused by her father, just like Sarah's client. Lisa remembered the description Sarah had given and connected this to Mary's present behavior. *Mary seems to be completely despondent and "spilling," emotionally spilling out of her own body and not yet able to reclaim it.* Lisa thought. She recognized this as particularly indicative of people who had been repeatedly traumatized.

I know that trauma survivors frequently seem to be emotionally bleeding and not really there, Lisa reasoned. *And Mary really does seem to be like that now. She is totally vulnerable, totally exposed, and seems not connected to her body anymore, probably as a result of the chronic sexual abuse, and then of being raped again. She has this blank stare on her face, almost like she's watching herself and trying to negotiate some boundaries.* Lisa had seen similar conditions in working with survivors of trauma, who were experiencing a temporary time of acute stress following their horrific experiences. She was now fairly certain that Mary and Sarah's new client were one and the same person.

But, Lisa wondered, *how much is she still under the influence of drugs or alcohol? How much of her behavior comes from dissociation and how much from intoxication?*

Because it now appeared that Mary was going to remain at the hospital, Lisa began options counseling. Knowing Mary's uncertainty, Lisa repeated, "This is completely voluntary, and you do not have to stay." Claire and Mary started to ask questions about the medical procedures that Mary could choose to have performed at the hospital. Lisa described the rape protocol exam, a series of voluntary procedures to collect forensic evidence from the survivor's body. A Sexual Assault Nurse Examiner (SANE), a specially trained nurse, would perform the exam if Mary wanted to have it.

"The rape protocol exam is to collect evidence," Lisa explained. "Part of it is a medical exam to look internally."

"I—I don't want that part done, definitely not," Mary said, shaking her head. "That's really disgusting . . . no way."

Sensing Mary's nervousness about this part of the exam, Lisa did not talk about it any further. Instead, she described some of the other procedures that the SANE would perform if Mary consented. "The nurse would also shave behind your fingernails," Lisa continued, "take clippings, and take samples of head and pubic hair to differentiate between your hair and the perpetrator's hair. She would also take blood. The evidence would go into a box that would be analyzed by the police. That doesn't mean that you have to press charges, provided they catch the person. If you want to, that evidence will be there, and if you don't it will just sit in that box on a shelf. But if you decide tomorrow that you do want to press charges, we'll have that evidence and be able to go forward. So it's a good idea to just get it, and you can take as much time as you need to think about whether to press charges."

Like many other survivors with whom Lisa had worked, Mary immediately responded that she did not want to press charges. Lisa explained potential judicial and medical benefits of having the exam but assured Mary, "It's your choice."

After Claire left the hospital at 5:30 a.m., Lisa continued to sit with Mary as they waited for the SANE. Mary had agreed to wait with Lisa to ask about the other options for medical treatment. Because no SANE was available at the time, Mary and Lisa waited nearly ninety minutes until one arrived.

Several times while waiting, Mary turned to Lisa and asked, "What would happen if I just walked out of here?"

"Nothing. It's your choice," Lisa repeated.

Each time, Mary giggled nervously but chose to stay.

At one point, Mary blacked out and fell toward Lisa. Lisa reacted quickly, catching Mary under both arms to prevent her from hitting the ground. Lisa was shocked by the strong odor that hit her as she laid the young woman on the hospital bed. *Ugh. I will never forget this awful smell! It's like wet ground, and she was assaulted outside . . . and dirt, and alcohol, and cigarette smoke all mixed.*

As Mary lay on the bed, she apparently drifted in and out of consciousness. Lisa left the room to find a nurse to check on her. She found one several moments later, and the nurse entered the room, turned on the fluorescent lights, and began to snap her fingers at Mary.

"Why are you here?" the nurse questioned. "Why are you here?"

"She was assaulted," Lisa volunteered.

"Oh. Well, okay, I didn't know." As the nurse exited the room, she added, to no one in particular, "You look fine to me."

At this point, Mary regained consciousness. She looked at Lisa and began to laugh, and Lisa laughed in response. "That was our first connection," she recalled later.

The SANE arrived at 7:00 a.m. Mary adhered to her original decision, choosing not to have the nurse perform the rape protocol exam. However, she opted for emergency contraceptives and antibiotics to treat any possible STDs, and she did participate in an interview with the SANE and the university police.

Lisa assured Mary that no one would find out about the assault unless Mary wanted them to. This seemed to deepen the sense of connection between them.

"I just don't want my father to find out," Mary repeated.

"He won't," Lisa replied.

After the interview with the SANE and the university police, Mary told Lisa that she had had an appointment scheduled with Sarah at RSVP for that morning, and that she still wanted to go to it. She did not want to wait for a taxi to transport her back to campus and insisted she could walk there. The hospital was a good distance from the campus, and Mary, assaulted only hours before, would have had to walk alone through some potentially dangerous sections of the city. Ultimately, Lisa decided to take Mary to RSVP in her own car, because "Otherwise, she would have put herself in another high-risk situation."

Follow-Up

Following the sexual assault, both Lisa and Sarah provided services for Mary at RSVP. Mary continued meeting with Sarah to address her history of sexual abuse perpetrated by her father, and Lisa began helping her to address the recent sexual assault. Mary was especially concerned that her father not learn about it, and Lisa assured her that the information was confidential. Thus, they gradually established rapport and trust. It was becoming evident that Mary had great difficulty when someone she considered close to her attempted to leave her, even for a short time. For instance, she resisted Lisa's efforts to terminate counseling sessions. As the end of a session approached, Mary would appear to "pass out," slumping over in her chair and becoming unresponsive. When Lisa would inform Mary that she was calling a nurse to look after her, Mary would "recover" from her faint state, and sometimes giggle at her own behavior. As Lisa recalled, "Mary would play the other advocate and me off of each other. If one of us tried to set up a boundary, she would go to the other one."

In addition, Mary began calling the emergency crisis hotline, and Lisa fielded several of these calls. Mary often sounded despondent and at times spoke of harming herself. Lisa was typically able to get her to contract for safety for the night and to promise to report to RSVP the next morning.

This happened several times. Each time, during subsequent evaluations by a psychologist or psychiatrist, Mary denied suicidal thoughts or intentions. As a result, the mental health professionals could not involuntarily commit her to an inpatient facility for services.

During the month following the sexual assault, Mary continued to make regular late-night phone calls to the crisis line while Lisa was on call. Lisa had given Mary her pager number for use in emergencies. One night, Lisa was at home when the pager rang. She quickly returned the phone call.

"Lisa, it's Mary." Lisa recognized her voice from the numerous calls to the crisis phone line. "You've gotta help me! I'm really scared. Somebody must've told my father. He's here on campus, in my dorm! They let him in! I can't see him, Lisa, I'm so afraid of him. I managed to run out the back door just before he got to my floor!"

Lisa's mind raced. By this time, she had begun to grow weary of all the late-night calls and lack of sleep resulting from Mary's case. Nonetheless, she believed that she had a responsibility to respond and to protect her from danger. "Where are you now, Mary?"

"I'm hiding from him, out back behind my dorm." Mary's voice was full of panic. "You've got to help me! I can't see him!"

Lisa quickly thought through her options. *I really do need to protect my client here. Mary could be in real danger if her father comes in contact with her.* "Mary, we'll work to make sure that your father doesn't find you, but you have to listen carefully. I'm going to call the university police to come to the back of your dorm and pick you up in a car. They will take you immediately to some confidential housing that we have here on campus. Your father won't be able to find you there. You'll be safe. I'm going to make the call right away, and the police will be right over."

"Okay, but hurry!" Mary responded. "He just can't find me!"

"We'll make sure he won't."

Lisa hung up the phone and immediately called the university police. The dispatcher indicated that an officer would report immediately to Mary's dorm. Approximately fifteen minutes later, the dispatcher phoned Lisa, reporting that Mary was on the way to confidential housing.

Lisa figured that Mary was safe for the night, so she could follow up on this case in the morning. Later that night, however, her pager rang again. When she returned the call, it was Mary on the other end of the line.

"Lisa, I'm still scared. I think my father could find me here! I mean, I can't even go outside or he might find me!"

"Mary, I understand your concern, but I assure you that your father will not be able to find you there." Lisa tried to reassure her, "You're safe," but Mary still sounded upset.

Although Mary had certainly expressed fear of her father before, this time Lisa sensed something different. In particular, Mary did not speak in the same way she had in the previous calls to the crisis line. However, she had been in such a pattern of thinking about suicide that Lisa felt she had to ask about it. As she attempted to ascertain whether Mary was in imminent danger of harming herself, Mary avoided her questions with either silence or vague "mmm-hmms." After several unsuccessful attempts and nearly twenty minutes of asking Mary to promise that she would not harm herself, Lisa worried that her time was running short.

I know we've discussed that if I think she's in serious danger of harming herself, I have to call campus police and they'll take her to the hospital, she thought. *And Mary knows that if she's hospitalized by the police, the housing office will notify her parents.* Lisa shook her head, exasperated.

Her mind racing, Lisa weighed her options. *If I have Mary hospitalized, her father will find out soon, so I would be sending her into the hands of someone who could be dangerous!* Another thought crossed her mind. *If I hospitalize her, the relationship and the trust that we've built these last two weeks will be broken. But if I don't call the police tonight, I risk Mary seriously harming herself. She sounds more distant, and something about her is different. She won't tell me whether she's thinking of hurting herself or writing a suicide note. Not doing something seems pretty risky.*

Lisa knew that, regardless of her decision, her actions would have a significant impact on Mary. She struggled to compose her next response.

12 | What Can I Tell? (A)

Rachel C. Parker and Terry A. Wolfer

CAROLYN JOHNSON, a case manager for Augusta Primary Care, was at her desk filling out paperwork when she heard loud footsteps in the hall. When she looked up, Karen White, a homeless client, was standing in the doorway, an angry look on her face.

"Hi, Karen, why don't you come in?" Carolyn offered.

"Look, I need to know what's up with Mark. What's wrong with him?"

Carolyn could smell the alcohol on Karen's breath. She knew that Karen would not like what she had to say.

"Karen, client medical information is confidential. You know I can't tell you anything."

"But I'm his wife, for God's sake. I have a right to know."

Carolyn was not sure what to say. She wanted to tell Karen, but Mark, Karen's common-law husband, had made it clear that he did not want her to know his condition.

Development of this decision case was supported in part by funding from the Project on Death in America and the University of South Carolina College of Social Work. It was prepared solely to provide material for class discussion and not to suggest either effective or ineffective handling of the situation depicted. Although the case is based on field research regarding an actual situation, names and certain facts may have been disguised to protect confidentiality. As indicated by the (A), the instructor's manual provides a continuation of the case. The authors wish to thank the anonymous case reporter for cooperation in making this account available for the benefit of social work students and instructors.

Augusta, Georgia

Augusta, Georgia's second-largest city, is about 150 miles east of Atlanta. It has long been known as the home of the Masters Golf Tournament. In 1993, the Augusta–Aiken (SC) metropolitan area had a population of more than 400,000. Though a majority was white, African Americans made up more than one third. Sparked by the Medical College of Georgia and Augusta State University, Augusta was one of the fastest-growing communities in the state. Despite the growth and increasing prosperity, a significant number of residents, both white and African American, remained impoverished. And it was still a conservative Southern community: homosexuality was not accepted by many.

Homebase and Augusta Primary Care

Volunteers of America started Homebase in 1988. The founder had originally envisioned a small business at the center, such as a bakery, to simultaneously create jobs for indigent clients and revenue to sustain the agency. Although this idea never came to fruition, Homebase maintained a centrally located office that housed multiple services for Augusta's homeless. It had an executive director, a volunteer coordinator, a finance manager, and a director of volunteer services. There were also two volunteer administrative assistants. Indigent clients filled custodial and secretarial positions. Homebase provided clients with a mailing address, lunch, and a snack each day. There was a living area where they could relax on the couches, watch TV, and socialize.

Homebase had evolved into a one-stop, umbrella agency. Several agencies operated satellite offices on the premises, including the county's Department of Social Services, Department of Mental Health, and Department of Health and Human Services, Augusta Housing Authority, and the federal Veteran's Administration. The employees of each agency were supervised by their home offices.

Homebase also housed the only office of Augusta Primary Care (APC), which provided medical services. Medical staff often saw homeless clients with hepatitis, STDs, nutritional deficiencies, skin diseases, and dental problems. This agency employed two part-time doctors, a nurse, and a case manager. One of the doctors, Dr. Juanita Morales, was known throughout the region as the doctor for poor people with HIV. Her practice grew rapidly as more and more poor HIV-positive clients sought her services.

On the one day Dr. Morales was in the clinic, there was much speculation in the waiting room about who was going to see her. However, APC had a strict policy protecting client confidentiality, never disclosing client information unless the client signed a consent form releasing the information to specific entities, or the agency was forced to do so by subpoena or court order. Because HIV infection was so highly stigmatized, staff members knew they had to be extra careful. Clients known or rumored to have HIV could become victims of hate crimes. APC itself sometimes received threatening phone messages.

Carolyn Johnson

Carolyn Johnson was an African American in her early thirties. She had a friendly and light-spirited demeanor, but she took her work seriously. She always dressed professionally and made sure that she referred to her clients as "Mr." and "Ms.," which often seemed to take them aback. Most were not accustomed to and did not expect common courtesy from professionals.

After Carolyn received her bachelor's degree with double majors in social work and rehabilitation counseling, she worked with youth services in Kansas City for several years. When her husband got a job with the Department of Juvenile Justice in Augusta, Georgia, she moved to an administrative position at Paine College, a historically black college in Augusta. But her passion had always been social services, and five years later, in 1990, she took a volunteer coordinator position with Homebase. Six months after that, she moved into a case manager position with Augusta Primary Care.

When she first took the job, Carolyn knew little about medicine and health; her only training was a medical terminology class for her rehabilitation counseling degree. So she had a steep learning curve, especially when it came to HIV. Initially, Carolyn thought she would be working mostly with clients who had nutrition problems and poor dental health. She didn't realize there would be so many with HIV. She had to catch up, and fast. The local infection rate was three times higher than the national average for communities of the same size. As a result, Carolyn's HIV-positive caseload of seventy clients was large, and it continued to grow rapidly. This surprised her, because she had thought that HIV was only a problem in larger cities.

Carolyn's work became more of a personal mission than a job when her nephew died from complications related to HIV in 1992. He was only twenty-six years old. Her family took the news hard. Her sister-in-law begged Carolyn to help change the cause of death on the death certificate from HIV to heart attack. She didn't want people to see her son as a bad person.

HIV in the Early 1990s

Her sister-in-law's reaction illustrated the prevailing attitude toward HIV in Augusta at that time. The diagnosis was to be kept silent, something to be ashamed of, something to fear. That HIV was connected to drug use or homosexuality only increased the stigma. People didn't even like to say "HIV"—they called it "the trace" or "the bug." It was the leprosy of the twentieth century; those infected were often shunned. In a state where prejudice against both African Americans and gays was strong, people were reluctant to acknowledge their membership in yet another stigmatized group, as carriers of a misunderstood and feared disease.

HIV was a terrible disease to have, and not just because of stigma. Despite increased understanding of its transmission, researchers had developed few treatment options. AZT, the most widely accepted and successful drug at the time, cost $400 a bottle. It was common to see wasting from the disease, and for death to follow soon after diagnosis. The general population misunderstood it. Some feared that slapping a mosquito with HIV-infected blood could spell doom. Some thought that dirty clothes had to be put in plastic bags until laundered, and that HIV-positive people had to use disposable plates and utensils to avoid spreading the virus to others.

The battle against HIV faced unique barriers in Georgia. In 1993, the state was twenty-fourth in the nation for AIDS infection rates. Outside Atlanta, Georgia was primarily rural, so most people assumed that AIDS rates would be low. In this morally and politically conservative state, it was against the law to discuss homosexuality in schools unless disease was being addressed. Also, Georgia was the midpoint of an I-75 Detroit–Miami drug trail, and a popular market for crack, and high rates of poverty, illiteracy, and early onset sexual activity helped spread HIV rapidly.

African Americans, who made up one third of the population but represented 60 percent of the AIDS cases, tended to be suspicious of government help. Much of this had to do with word-of-mouth knowledge of the infamous Tuskegee experiments conducted on African Americans from the 1930s to the 1970s. Government officials lied to 400 black men who were infected with syphilis, telling them that they had "bad blood" and were being treated for it. Only they weren't; the government wanted to observe the progress of the disease. Many patients went blind, went insane, or died. Now, in 1993, some African Americans felt that AIDS was a government attempt to wipe out undesirables, such as African Americans and gays. Their distrust probably contributed to HIV's rapid spread in Georgia.

Mark and Karen White

Mark and Karen, who referred to each other as husband and wife, were homeless. They were both African American and in their mid-thirties. Addicted to crack, they chose to spend Karen's monthly veteran's check on drugs instead of rent. Although they were companions and depended on each other, their arguments could get violent. But they always settled their arguments, and one was rarely seen without the other, whether at the Gospel Mission homeless shelter, at Homebase, or on the streets. Both had volatile personalities, charming one minute and mean the next. Despite their life on the streets, they always tried to keep themselves neat. Mark had family in Mississippi, and he would periodically call and even go visit them. Karen was from the Caribbean and had an accent. She had been in the military ten years and had served in Korea.

First Contact

Carolyn knew that Dr. Morales was seeing Mark, which could mean only one thing: Mark had HIV. Before the day of his appointment, Carolyn had often seen Mark and Karen hanging around at Homebase. But this was the first time she had met him as a client. As case manager for Augusta Primary Care, it was her responsibility to help him get prescriptions filled, talk to him about how to manage his health, and provide support when and if he chose to tell his friends and family about his diagnosis. She always talked with clients after they met with Dr. Morales.

When the doctor was done with Mark, she came to Carolyn's office. "That poor woman," she said, referring to Karen, "he doesn't want to tell her that he's HIV positive. You know he's going to end up infecting her. Why don't you try to talk to him? I'll send him over."

When Dr. Morales brought Mark to Carolyn's office, he kept his eyes averted and his shoulders slumped, and shuffled his feet as he came in.

"Hello, Mr. White, why don't you come in and have a seat?" Carolyn offered.

Mark came in and sat down in the chair across from Carolyn.

Dr. Morales introduced them and mentioned that Carolyn knew his diagnosis. "Ms. Johnson will talk to you about everything, and help you get your prescriptions filled," she said, before going back to her office to see the next patient.

"Look, I just want to get out of here," Mark replied, keeping his eyes on the floor.

"Well, it'll just take a few minutes. There are a few things we need to go over."

Mark sat motionless.

"Okay, we need to go over your prescriptions." Scanning Dr. Morales's notes, Carolyn added, "Looks like you have six here. I'm not sure that we'll be able to get them all filled. But I'll call around and see what pharmacies would be willing to give you a month's supply of the AZT, just to get started. How's that sound?"

Mark responded with a barely audible, "Mmhm."

"Look, I can tell you really don't want to be here, but have you thought at all about Karen? HIV is a serious disease, and Karen needs to know you are positive. I would be happy to sit with you when you tell her, or I could go with you to the shelter to tell her. Whatever would help make it easier. I would like you to sign a consent form to allow me to talk to her about . . ."

"No way, I'm not gonna tell her. I can't. I just want to get out of here," Mark answered. He sat up straighter in his chair and looked Carolyn in the eye. "Don't tell her."

"Well, that's up to you, Mr. White. I can't make you tell her anything, and I can't make you sign a consent form. But I hope you change your mind. If you do," Carolyn offered, "I'll be glad to meet with both of you."

"Can I go now?"

After Mark left, Carolyn thought about what he'd just said. She knew that he was probably ashamed and scared, and was going through the normal stage of denial about the seriousness of HIV. But Karen was in real danger of getting the virus, if she had not already. Carolyn wanted to tell Karen; that was one more life she might be able to save. She decided to talk to Dr. Morales about it.

When Dr. Morales came out of her office to get a patient's file, Carolyn approached her.

"Dr. Morales, may I speak to you for a second?"

"Sure, what's up?" she responded, as they both stepped inside Carolyn's office.

"I need to talk to you about Mark White. I know we have a policy against sharing medical information without consent, but I think in this case, Karen needs to know," Carolyn said.

"Look, Carolyn, I know where you're coming from, but we have to respect his wishes. Unless he signs a consent form, you can't tell Karen anything."

"What did Karen's last HIV test come up with?"

"It was negative," replied Dr. Morales.

So maybe she still has a chance, Carolyn thought. "Well, maybe I'll just talk to her about HIV and how to protect herself."

"I wouldn't say anything specific, though, Carolyn, because she'll pick up on that. You can talk to her about STDs in general and include HIV, but if you get too specific she's going to know why you are bringing it up."

Carolyn took a deep breath. She felt frustrated that she could only tell Karen so little.

A Visit from Karen

"Ms. White, please calm down," Carolyn said. The day after Mark had come in for his first appointment, Karen demanded to know what was wrong.

"I know it must be something pretty bad. He was gone to the hospital for six weeks, for God's sake, but he's not talkin'. Please tell me. You gotta tell me!"

Despite the fact that Karen had obviously been drinking, her pleas tugged at Carolyn's heart. Karen's desperation was heartbreaking.

"Why don't you come in and have a check-up? It would be really . . ."

"Do I need to?" Carolyn cut in. "Do I? Why don't you just tell me? Something must be wrong since you want me to come in. There must be something you need to tell me. Just tell me! I'm his wife. I have a right to know!"

"Why don't you come in and sit down, Ms. White. We could . . ."

"NO!" Karen refused to budge from the doorway. Her voice resonated down the hall, and Carolyn knew everyone in the agency could hear. "I'm not moving 'til you tell me what's wrong. All I know is Mark not getting better, he getting worse."

"I'm sorry, Ms. White, but we have a policy that medical information is confidential. I can't share that with you." It tore at Carolyn's heart to say these words. However, she suspected that Karen already knew Mark had HIV, but just needed to hear it confirmed.

During the next few weeks, Carolyn periodically saw Karen in the center. As soon as Karen would see Carolyn, she would start talking loudly: "They back there and they know things and they won't tell you. Mark's sick and they won't tell me what's going on with him." Carolyn recognized this attempt to provoke a disclosure, but Karen's words stung her conscience nevertheless.

13 | Grief at Work

Laura Cox and Terry A. Wolfer

MIKE OWENS SAT in the Franklin Center conference room, drumming his fingers on the table as he waited for his supervisee, Brian Stanfield, and his program supervisor, Brenda Shelley, to join him. He could feel the heat from the strong rays of the October sun filtering through the window. Feeling like he had been "punched in the stomach," Mike tried to make sense of the two-month blur that led up to this point.

As a new supervisor giving his first formal disciplinary action, Mike felt that his abilities were being tested. What began with an effort to accommodate a bereaved supervisee had seemingly spun out of control.

Gastonia, North Carolina

By the late 1990s, the small town of Gastonia had developed into a bustling suburb of Charlotte, North Carolina, one of the fastest-growing cities in the United States. As the town grew, a variety of new companies replaced the textile mills as a major source of employment. With a population of more than

Development of this decision case was supported in part by the Project on Dying in America and the University of South Carolina College of Social Work. It was prepared solely to provide material for class discussion and not to suggest either effective or ineffective handling of the situation depicted. Although the case is based on field research regarding an actual situation, names and certain facts may have been disguised to protect confidentiality. The authors wish to thank the case reporter for cooperation in making this account available for the benefit of social work students and practitioners.

50,000, Gastonia was increasingly middle class. About three fourths of the residents were white and most of the remainder were African American.

Franklin Center

The Franklin Center (FC) had operated in Gastonia for 30 years—29 of them as a home for children whose parents were deceased or unable to provide for them, and the past year as a residential center for emotionally disturbed children. Of the residents, 30 percent were wards of the state, case managed by staff from the North Carolina Department of Social Services. The other 70 percent were placed voluntarily by their parents, usually via referrals from a local mental health center following an assessment and recommendation for placement.

The Franklin Center consisted of six residential units (cottages). In the North Carolina child welfare system, out-of-home placements differed by intensity of treatment services and reimbursement rates, with higher levels indicating more intensive services. The Franklin Center's four group homes were considered Level III and the two therapeutic foster homes were considered Level II. The residential group homes each housed six to nine children, while the therapeutic foster homes housed two to three children and served as a "step-down" program for those who had made significant progress in residential treatment but were not yet ready for discharge. For example, a client was typically admitted to FC with presenting problems such as severe behavior issues and placed in a group home. The group home staff would work toward eliminating or significantly reducing these behaviors. Once they were addressed, the client might still benefit from being in a structured environment like that provided by the therapeutic foster homes. This setting could help clients step down or transition from the FC back into their own homes by focusing on consistency, structure, natural/logical consequences, and positive reinforcement. The step down was a way to ensure that clients were ready for reunification with their families by addressing issues other than their original presenting problems.

The group homes had most of the amenities of a private residence. Each was staffed with approximately 14 professionals, including 2 supervisors and 12 residential counselors. There were separate supervisors for the weekday and the weekend shifts. The weekend shift was tough, consisting of 8 hours on Fridays and 16 hours each on Saturdays and Sundays (7 a.m. to 11 p.m.), with 2 or 3 residential counselors and 1 supervisor per shift.

All of the group homes used a token economy based on behavior modification principles. Behavior was rated on a scale of 1 to 4, with the higher levels indicating greater success in achieving behavior modification goals. Clients gained points for positive behavior and lost points for negative behavior. Privileges and freedoms directly correlated to the points that were tallied at the end of each week.

Each individual client had a treatment team that included a consulting psychiatrist, an individual therapist, and a coordinator. The psychiatrist prescribed and managed medications. All of the individual therapists were master's level clinicians who provided individual, group, and family therapy services. These services were scheduled during the week, but the therapists were also on call for weekend crisis intervention. The client's participation in therapeutic services and response to behavior modification were the most important components of their treatment at the Franklin Center.

Each group home had a name and a specific population. For example, the Kennedy Group Home typically housed eight or nine children from six to fourteen years of age. Like other residents at the center, these children had extreme behavior problems that made them unsafe in their own homes. The range of problems included severe aggression as well as suicidal and/or homicidal behaviors. Placements ranged on average from twelve to eighteen months in length. The treatment provided at the Franklin Center was comprehensive and intensive, but one of the biggest challenges was getting families involved.

Brenda Shelley

In 1999, Brenda Shelley was hired as director of clinical programs for the Franklin Center, as part of a major restructuring. The center was transitioning from an older orphanage model to one with greater emphasis on professionalism and clinical interventions. Brenda supervised twelve cottage supervisors and several support staff members. With ten years of practice experience in mental health settings, Brenda brought strong clinical skills to the position. But with all the restructuring going on, only crisis situations seemed to get her attention. She spent most of her time "putting out fires" and did not schedule time for regular supervision of staff.

Mike Owens

Mike Owens was an undergraduate social work student intern when he began his career with the Franklin Center. He was a nontraditional student, having entered college at age twenty-three. Previously, Mike had pursued a childhood dream and played music professionally. He had briefly attended the Juilliard School, where he studied saxophone with some of the world's top jazz, rock, and Latin musicians. Eventually opting for a career with more financial stability, Mike decided to work toward a degree in human services.

After completing his internship at the center, Mike was offered a position as a residential counselor. He held that position for two years, then was promoted to supervisor of the weekend shift in the Kennedy Group Home. He was one of the first people promoted under Brenda's new leadership. After the restructuring, the Franklin Center wanted supervisory staff to have bachelor's degrees in psychology or social work. Although he did not yet have a degree, Mike had several years of good performance with the agency, was just a semester away from graduation, and fit the new model.

As weekend supervisor, Mike had a regular work week that included some additional meetings and paperwork to be attended to during weekdays, in addition to working the weekend shift itself. As he soon learned, that schedule was enough to wear on anyone.

When Mike became weekend supervisor, at the age of twenty-seven, there was much chaos within the group home. As he recalled later, "I had staff who were unmotivated. They didn't want to be there and didn't really respond to me in my new role as supervisor." Within one month of his starting in the new position, one staff member quit and another transferred to a different group home, leaving him to build a new weekend group home staff. "I wanted a lot of structure, but I wanted incentives for the kids." The setting needed to be therapeutic, but enjoyable for the children and staff so that the weekends would pass more smoothly despite the long shifts.

Brian Stanfield

Mike and Brian first became acquainted as undergraduate social work students at the University of North Carolina–Charlotte. When the Franklin Center hired them both as residential counselors at about the same time, they grew to know and respect each other. As a result of working together, Mike quickly recognized Brian as an "outstanding child care worker."

From Mike's perspective, Brian was an interesting character. "He nurtured this easygoing Goth persona—he usually wore black clothing, had several earrings and a nipple piercing, and had elaborate body art on his back and arms. His musical tastes included Marilyn Manson and The Cure. I liked his style—creative, edgy, out there—but at work he was totally a pro. He was accountable, but not overbearing. He could always relate well with the kids, and they with him." As Brian himself acknowledged to Mike, the Goth style was a reaction to his upbringing. He and his dad had never gotten along very well, and the piercings made his dad crazy. Brian described his childhood home as an "authoritarian environment." That background was definitely not evident in his current style.

Program Success

Inspired by Brian's talent and potential in working with youth, Mike recruited him into the weekend unit soon after he began to supervise it. "Brian excelled at B-mod, he was as good as anyone I've ever seen. Brian was also very motivated and was always trying to keep ahead of me." To complete the core weekend staff, Mike also hired a female counselor, Jenny Ward. Mike described Jenny as "awesome," noting that "she was very creative and was always thinking of fun things for the kids to do."

For a period of eight or nine months after these players came together, weekends at the group home were a time of "pure joy." Good planning with input from the residents and all weekend staff resulted in significant improvements in the behavior and progress of the residents. As Mike explained, "It was my goal to include the children in things, and the children responded by cooperating." The impressive results caught the attention of the other group home staff members and the administration. The weekend shift of the Kennedy Group Home had the fewest holds—staff members physically restraining children to prevent them from hurting themselves or others—and runaway attempts. Before the new weekend program, it was not unusual to have five or six holds per day on the weekends. Now that number sometimes dropped to none.

The Call

On a Wednesday afternoon in mid-July, Brian made a hurried phone call to Mike.

"Mike, I really have to go to Detroit to be with my family. My dad had a heart attack and died. This was all very sudden, we had no idea . . ."

"Oh, I'm sorry, Brian! Don't worry about a thing at work," Mike assured him. "We'll take care of everything here. Just take whatever time you need."

As close as they had grown, Mike had never heard Brian say much about his family. But after hanging up the phone, Mike remembered that Brian had recently mentioned that he and his long-term, live-in girlfriend were having problems. *It doesn't seem that Brian needs any more stress in his personal life right now,* Mike thought.

Brian took the weekend off immediately following his father's death, but returned for the weekend shift one week later.

"It might be too soon," Mike warned. "You may need some more time. Things at work are covered."

"No," Brian insisted, "this is fine. If I'm at home, I'll just dwell on it. I'd rather focus on work."

"The children are sure glad to see you back," Mike commented later that day. "But it still seems to me that you are jumping into things too quickly. Sometimes it gets pretty intense around here."

"Truly, Mike," Brian insisted, "I'm okay. Besides, I'm better off here keeping busy."

As Mike was driving home that night, he couldn't help but think about Brian and all that he was going through. *I'm concerned that Brian's back so soon,* Mike thought, *but I have to admit that he seems to be on top of his game. He seems like himself.*

Falling Apart

The second weekend after Brian's return to work, he showed up a few minutes late for the Friday shift. His first incident of tardiness set a precedent for the next couple of weeks. Then Brian started missing midweek supervision meetings and a required in-service training. He even missed a couple of shifts without calling in to report his absence.

Mike tried talking to Brian several times in a casual manner, but there was no evidence that it was getting through. Finally, one night after work in early September, Mike addressed Brian directly. "Talk to me, Brian, I need to know what's going on and how I can help. I know you've been through a lot, but you've always been such a go-getter."

"There's been a lot going on, but I'm fine. I swear," Brian defended.

"When you first came back, everything was business as usual. I believed you when you said you were okay. Now you're coming in late and you've missed several staff meetings," Mike prodded.

"Sorry about screwing up the schedule a couple of times," Brian said with apparent exasperation. "I won't do it again."

Gently, Mike pushed further. "You wait around for things to happen. That's not like you at all."

"Sometimes," Brian offered, "I just don't know where I'm at."

"You know that I'm here to talk to as a friend," Mike reminded, "and I'll help you in any way that I can."

Brian hesitated as he shifted from one foot to the other, then shared, "To make matters worse, my girlfriend and I broke up last weekend. I knew she was frustrated with a few things, but I didn't see *that* coming either. We've been together for more three years."

"Oh, that's awful, Brian," Mike exclaimed. "I'm so sorry. This on top of losing your dad."

"And right now," Brian explained, "she doesn't even want to talk about it."

"If you can just be here," Mike appealed, "even if you're struggling, I'll help."

Brenda's Intervention

Mike felt a little unsettled as he waited for Brenda to join him in her office. He did not like the way things had been going lately either, and suspected that was what Brenda wanted to talk about. Mike was beginning to fear the spotlight was on him. *Wow,* he thought, *I've been practically offering to help Brian do his job—not that it's helped any. This is so hard for me. Since we started working weekends together, Brian and I have become solid friends. We spend hours talking after work because we're so keyed up after shifts.* As Mike sat there tapping a pen on his knee, he thought further about those conversations and realized that he and Brian talked a lot about their jobs. *I've spent a lot of time reassuring Brian that he does a good job. Given how well he's performed in the past, it's odd that he seems to need that. Up until recently, I've never had any concerns.*

Brenda walked in the room, bringing Mike's thoughts back to focus on the present.

"Thanks for meeting me here. How are you doing today, Mike?" Brenda questioned as she situated herself behind her desk.

"I'm good, thanks," Mike replied, wishing that she would get to the point.

"The last few shift reports you've turned in indicate that the children are quite disruptive these days, more so than usual. There has not been much of a change as far as residents moving in and out. What do you think's going on?"

Reluctant to betray his friend but frustrated at the position he had been put in, Mike offered, "Brian is a very important component to the success of our program at the Kennedy Group Home. The program virtually runs itself when he's on top of his game. Now that he's having some problems since his dad's death, it's reverted to chaos. In the past, Brian always came with notes and a game plan for the weekend. Since his father passed away, that's completely gone. He wants to be led and is much more passive in his job duties."

"I guess I feel partly responsible that this situation has progressed this far," Brenda responded. "Since I took this job nearly a year ago now, it seems I've been putting out fires more than providing supervision. I was hired during a transitional period for the agency, and some of the long-term employees have not responded well to the new emphasis on clinical interventions rather than just the orphanage program it used to be. I hope you realize how impressed I've been with you as a supervisor of the Kennedy Group Home. But I've not provided the support you need to deal with staff issues."

"The situation with Brian has just gotten complicated," Mike admitted. "We've become close friends since working together here. I've been reinforcing to him that he has to get himself together. He seems to have a hard time focusing. It's hard for me to be objective, and in the meantime, Brian continues to spiral downward."

"Yes, but it has to stop somewhere," Brenda said simply.

The Verbal Warning

Mike felt frustrated, even a little angry, about the meeting that he was having with Brian—what a situation his friend had put him in! Brenda had insisted that they begin taking formal disciplinary steps, and this was the first—and hopefully the last. Across the desk, Brian sat looking rather forlorn as he listened.

"Brian, I've given you as much slack as I can. Your unscheduled absences really create a problem for us—you know that. It's been three months now since your dad's death. Your work is not improving. If anything, things seem to be getting worse. This is official and documented in your personnel record—your irresponsible behaviors have to cease or your job may be in jeopardy," Mike warned. "You know the rules. You cannot miss work without proper notification, you have to perform your duties while at work, and you have to attend mandatory meetings during the week."

"I understand what you're doing. You can't imagine how guilty I feel. I'm so sorry for this whole mess—just sorry." Brian kept apologizing.

"Brian, I know you're going through a very rough time, but things are escalating to the point where they're out of my hands. I can only run so much interference with the administration," Mike warned. "They're not just looking at you, they're keeping an eye on the group home altogether. Don't you notice that Brenda is doing spot checks at lot more often?"

"Yeah," Brian admitted, "I noticed that she's in my face every time I turn around." Then, taking a deep breath, Brian said, "Look, there's something I didn't tell you about my dad, and I feel I owe it to you because of all the trouble I've caused around here. My father didn't die of a heart attack—he killed himself."

The Note

Early the next morning, as he arrived at work, Mike found an envelope on his desk. His curiosity quickly turned to exasperation as he unsealed it and read the handwritten note inside. In the note, apparently written the evening before, Brian wrote, "I'm really sorry for letting you down, Mike. I don't want to disappoint you anymore. You've been a great friend and I really appreciate your support lately. This note is to let you know that I won't be able to work tomorrow."

Mike was stunned. *Does he think this meets the requirement for giving advance notice? . . . At 7 a.m., it's basically worthless.* Mike felt resentment welling up. *Not only am I working sixteen hours on this beautiful Saturday, now I'm picking up Brian's slack as well. Brian knows better than this! If he had just taken me up on my offer to schedule some time off immediately after his father died, we would probably all be the better for it, especially the kids. I wish I could go find him, to be sure he's okay, but the cottage can't function with two of us missing. I hope he doesn't do anything drastic. . . .*

The Monday Meeting

The following Monday, Mike paced near the end of the conference table and then took a seat, waiting for Brenda and Brian to join him. *We all knew that this meeting was inevitable,* Mike thought. *Brian's continued to screw up, so here we are. I know he's hurting and all messed up, but we can't turn a blind eye any longer. We have to take some kind of action. I just don't want to make things worse for him.* But Mike wasn't sure what to say or do.

14 | Dying on Time

Rich Schlauch and Terry A. Wolfer

AS THE FOCUSED MEDICAL REVIEW shifted to the final case for the day, Bonnie Delaney, director of social services for Meadow View Hospice, noticed that social worker Miriam Goldstein's face was furrowed into a tight frown. In September 1995, an eight-member committee had convened to review the justification for providing continued treatment services to several patients, including Jean Geddes. Jean had amyotrophic lateral sclerosis, or ALS (a.k.a. Lou Gehrig's disease), and was one of Miriam's patients. Recently, Jean had shown little decline—her symptoms did not seem to be progressing toward the terminal stage—and that, unfortunately, was a Medicare requirement for continuing reimbursement for hospice services. Bonnie noticed Miriam leaning forward in her seat, as if poised for attack. Observing the strained quiet among her peers, Bonnie paused. *How do I proceed without the staff thinking I'm displaying favoritism, not just to Miriam or her patient, but to this particular diagnosis? And how can we justify the patient's hospice eligibility to Medicare?*

Development of this decision case was supported in part by the Project on Dying in America and the University of South Carolina College of Social Work. It was prepared solely to provide material for class discussion and not to suggest either effective or ineffective handling of the situation depicted. Although the case is based on field research regarding an actual situation, names and certain facts may have been disguised to protect confidentiality. The authors wish to thank the case reporter for cooperation in making this account available for the benefit of social work students and practitioners.

Meadow View Hospice

Meadow View Hospice was located near downtown Cincinnati, Ohio. From humble all-volunteer beginnings in 1981, it quickly developed into a small nonprofit organization serving an average of ten to twenty patients daily. Meadow View eventually expanded hospice services across the river into northern Kentucky. By 1995, it had grown significantly larger and served an average daily census of more than 400 patients, placing it among the largest hospice providers in the United States. This growth was attributed in part to the fact that as the only hospice in Cincinnati, it maintained a monopoly on services for the region. But it was also due to the agency's focus on providing quality care. Widely regarded as a "Cadillac of hospices," Meadow View had long had the philosophy: "Do what your patients need—don't be wasteful, but be generous and do all you can to improve their quality of life." Reflecting that focus, some veteran staff members were concerned that the hospice's rapid growth and large size would lessen the quality of care on which it had built its reputation.

Like other hospices, Meadow View served patients diagnosed with a terminal illness—including end-stage cancer, AIDS, ALS, Alzheimer's, and heart, lung, renal, or liver disease—and their families. The hospice sought to ensure that patients received quality care wherever they resided—at home, in long-term care facilities, or occasionally in hospitals for acute needs—by allowing and supporting families, friends, and loved ones to be with and care for the patient. The social workers at Meadow View—core members of the interdisciplinary team, along with nurses, chaplains, nursing assistants, and volunteers—assisted patients and their families in many ways, but especially by helping them work through unresolved emotional issues, fears, conflicts, and feelings. Through expert symptom management, the team enabled patients and families to achieve life closure in a manner satisfactory to them.

Meadow View Hospice received reimbursement for patient services primarily from Medicare. Medicare paid hospices a per diem, or flat rate per day, for each patient. The per diem covered all the services patients received related to their terminal illness (e.g., medications, equipment, visits from hospice team members), but not services unrelated to the terminal illness. Medicare required every patient receiving the hospice benefit to have a terminal diagnosis with a prognosis or life expectancy of six months or less, should the disease run its normal course.

During the mid-1990s, Medicare reimbursement for hospice services involved four distinct benefit periods, time spans for which the patient was approved for reimbursement. Medicare required that patients be reviewed and reapproved or recertified to continue into the next benefit period. The first and second benefit periods lasted ninety days each and the third lasted thirty days. In contrast, the fourth period had an unlimited number of days, but only if the patient remained terminally ill with a life expectancy of less than six months (the admission criterion for hospice). If a patient went into remission or recovered during the first three benefit periods and the doctor determined that the prognosis had changed, the patient could elect to stop hospice services and retain the remaining benefits. Such patients could be reapproved for hospice services at a later time if their illness began progressing. However, this was not the case in the fourth benefit period. If it was determined during the fourth period that a patient had improved or stabilized and the life expectancy was now greater than six months, the benefits were revoked and the patient's lifetime hospice benefits would be exhausted. For these reasons, the hospice interdisciplinary team had to be especially confident that the patient was continuing to decline and that the prognosis remained within the six-month limit before approving the fourth benefit period.

In response to the growth of larger hospice programs like Meadow View and other providers with longer average lengths of stay, Medicare began closely scrutinizing claims made in the fourth benefit period to ensure the cases were appropriate for hospice benefits, and would withhold payment until the review was completed. In addition, Medicare would impose fines and penalties on organizations if they discovered systemic evidence of patients in the fourth benefit period who were unlikely to die within six months.

In response to the new Medicare surveillance, Meadow View Hospice decided to hold its own internal focused medical reviews before clients could enter the fourth benefit period. These included the team serving the patient, the clinical managers who supervised them, and several administrative staff cognizant of the financial implications for the hospice.

On average, approximately 20 percent of the hospice patients being cared for by Meadow View and receiving Medicare were in the fourth benefit period.

If Medicare determined that agency documentation did not support continued hospice services and decided to suspend payment on these patients, the financial repercussions for the hospice as a whole would be devastating. Even though these reviews required considerable time and effort, administrators considered them essential for managing the agency's risk.

Bonnie Delaney

Before taking the position with Meadow View, Bonnie Delaney had done hospice social work and bereavement work for several years. She had started out as a volunteer with a small hospice organization in western Kentucky. She eventually became an employee and was promoted several times before completing her M.S.W., and later became executive director of that agency.

Bonnie had been employed at Meadow View Hospice for approximately four years and was responsible for supervising twenty social workers. She reported directly to the executive director. Her peers included the directors of nursing, pastoral care, volunteers, bereavement, and finance. Early in her career Bonnie had worked with a few ALS patients, and she was especially drawn to them. She had shared with her colleagues at Meadow View on more than a few occasions that if there ever were a specialty team created to work with only these patients, she would happily volunteer to be on it.

Miriam Goldstein

Bonnie had hired Miriam in 1991. From the outset, she perceived Miriam as a "very serious, intense, passionate person and one not always diplomatic in making her needs and wants known." Similarly, many staff thought Miriam was "sharp-edged." One of the few Jewish staff members in the agency, she was also a lesbian and was often idealistic, demanding, and impatient with the other staff. Bonnie thought Miriam's "high standards often conflicted with others' standards." Consequently, she sometimes came across as strident. On a few occasions, co-workers complained about Miriam's "obnoxiousness" to Bonnie. But Bonnie had the distinct impression that Miriam believed her alienation from her co-workers was due to her religion, sexual orientation, and outspoken political positions rather than a result of her behavior.

In terms of her social work skills, Bonnie saw Miriam as "especially bright, intuitive, and deeply committed to her patients." She also recognized Miriam as an articulate advocate for her patients. Because she was such an idealist, team members did not like to argue with her unless they were well prepared and could provide ample evidence for their positions.

Jean Geddes

Miriam was assigned to Jean Geddes, a patient with ALS who was about to enter the fourth benefit period. Jean also had a long history of family issues. When she'd first come into care, Miriam had done a lot of work with her to overcome significant conflict within the family resulting from the stress of trying to care for Jean. She had been bedfast for a while, and family members were essentially exhausted by the time she was admitted to hospice and placed in a nursing facility. With Miriam's assistance, Jean successfully reconciled with her daughter. Miriam had also recently begun to help Jean work through some of her feelings about dying from ALS.

From her colleagues and the team physician, Miriam had learned that ALS is a neurodegenerative disease that attacks nerve cells in the brain and spinal cord, causing gradual weakness and atrophy of the muscles. Patients eventually lose the ability to move their body parts. The brain stem may be affected, causing difficulty chewing, swallowing, and speaking. Throughout the course of the illness, patients remain mentally intact, alert, and aware, which causes even more frustration for them and their families. Physical pain is usually not a major problem, although patients may have pain problems associated with immobility. Patients with ALS are often unable to sleep well. The disease is usually fatal within two to five years after diagnosis, with most patients dying of pneumonia or stopped respiration.

Jean had been diagnosed with ALS in 1991. Initially, she noticed a peculiar weakness in her left leg that did not go away. Because she did not experience any pain, Jean dismissed this symptom. Not until she began having difficulty walking did she decide to seek medical attention. Throughout the course of her illness, Jean did not experience much physical pain. However, losing the ability to communicate with others was almost too much to bear emotionally. She realized that she would rather experience severe physical pain that could possibly be managed with medications and retain her ability to talk than slowly waste away in silence.

Adaptation and Experimentation

Because the disease progressed so slowly and caused increasing disability and frustration, many hospice social workers preferred to avoid working with ALS patients. Bonnie recalled her first such patient telling her that many people treat ALS patients as if they are mentally retarded because of their diminishing inability to communicate and make their needs known. Miriam, on the contrary, was determined to reach her patient. Utilizing a process of adaptation and experimentation, Miriam discovered that she could communicate with Jean by using a clear Lucite board, which contained answers to basic need questions (yes, no, light on / off, etc.). Adapting the board to also include emotional responses and familial issues, Miriam held it up between them and asked Jean questions. Looking at Jean through the board, Miriam would follow her eyes and speak aloud the word or symbol she saw Jean focusing on to verify that she had the correct item. Jean would then blink once for yes or twice for no. This tedious and time-consuming process required deep commitment, but enabled Miriam to connect on an emotional level with and provide therapy to Jean. Although the intervention process itself was very arduous and demanding, Miriam found her work with Jean very rewarding. She wanted to help Jean complete unfinished business before she passed away, a task she considered paramount in her role as a hospice social worker.

The depth that Miriam achieved in exploring Jean's familial and emotional relationships impressed Bonnie. Considering the communication barriers, not many of Miriam's peers were able to reach the kind of depth that she accomplished with this patient. Having established a therapeutic rapport with Jean and fearing that she might be discharged from hospice care, Miriam became very anxious leading up to Jean's internal focused medical review.

Anticipatory Anxiety

One week prior to review of Jean's case, scheduled for September 26, 1994, Bonnie met with Miriam to rehearse the types of questions that would be posed. *Despite Miriam's anxiety and possible frustration,* Bonnie thought, *I am going to have to ask her about Jean's symptoms if there is any hope of keeping her in the program.*

"Miriam, tell me about any changes in Jean's condition that could justify her stay in the program," Bonnie started. "For example, are there any changes in her symptoms? In her level of weakness?"

"None since the first month or two after her admission," Miriam replied flatly.

"How is her respiration? Does she have any evidence of pneumonia? Any infections or bedsores?"

Miriam slowly shook her head. "Her respiration isn't great, but she isn't in a lot of distress yet, and she hasn't had any respiratory infections, amazingly. The nursing home staff has done a great job preventing bedsores—but she shouldn't be punished for that!" Miriam's rigid body language alone indicated that she knew the lack of changes in the patient's symptoms and the lack of necessity for skilled nursing made it difficult to justify hospice care for her.

Nevertheless, Miriam remained adamant. "We can't discharge her. I'm the only one who knows how to reach Jean—we can't just abandon her!" she exclaimed.

The more Bonnie questioned Miriam about Jean's condition, the more anxious Miriam became. Sensing this, Bonnie attempted to reason with her. "Is she terminal and likely to die in the next six months?"

Miriam simply stared at Bonnie and raised her eyebrows, as if the answer to her question was self-evident. "I can't imagine she would live longer than that—but I can't prove it."

Bonnie sighed, shook her head, and responded, "I just don't know, Miriam. You know that it's extremely difficult to determine how long a patient has with this illness." Bonnie wasn't sure Miriam was listening.

"I know how hard you've worked with Jean," Bonnie continued. "In spite of many obstacles, you have overcome the communication difficulties to provide her therapy. However, Jean's stay in the program has to be medically justifiable."

"These internal reviews won't affect Jean, right?" Miriam demanded, tears welling up in her eyes. "ALS is always terminal. She's going to die, and she needs our support until she does!"

With little information to go on, Bonnie began to dread the upcoming internal focused medical review.

Internal Focused Medical Review

The day of the medical review had finally arrived. The meeting included the director of nursing, assistant director of nursing, hospice team coordinator, chaplain, Bonnie, Miriam, and two hospice nurses. Fearing that things could get ugly, Bonnie scheduled Miriam's patient last in this round of reviews. Indeed, the mood was tense during the other patient reviews leading up to Jean's case. Team members were unusually quiet and cautious, apparently out of fear of setting Miriam off. Like Bonnie, they knew that her high standards and deep commitment to patients made it hard to argue with her. Bonnie observed that Miriam's anxiety notably intensified when the team had to recommend discharge for a patient with another debilitating illness whose condition had remained largely unchanged.

Finally, the team came to Miriam's client. "Jean's condition hasn't really changed very much in the last few months," nurse Gina Coggins began. "Although she's bedfast and can't do anything for herself, she's not going downhill quickly either."

"Jean is definitely severely disabled," Donna Martin, the assistant director of nursing, reflected, "but compared to other hospice patients, she doesn't appear to be as near death."

Miriam shifted in her seat, looking visibly uncomfortable. At the same time, she had a determined look in her eyes. Bonnie could sense the tension between Miriam and the team.

"We cannot discharge Jean," Miriam's voice quavered. "You cannot do that. What we are doing with her makes too much of a difference. She has a terminal illness, and she isn't going to get any better," Miriam said more forcefully. "She doesn't have to be on death's doorstep, does she?"

Miriam's work with Jean is probably her most rewarding and most intense. She knows she's making a difference and doesn't want to stop, Bonnie thought. *She's making a good professional judgment in wanting to stay with this case—but how are we going to defend it or appeal it if Medicare doesn't agree with our decision?*

"She just does not present with advanced symptoms such as dyspnea, respiratory insufficiency, pneumonia, or dysphagia that patients have when they are approaching the terminal phase of this disease," Sharon Lanham, the director of nursing, responded.

Finally, Miriam erupted. "We must keep her," she insisted, her eyes flashing, "even if it means we must eat the cost! Everything any of you said about promoting quality of life and providing holistic care is a lie if we discharge this woman!"

15 | Just Thinking About It

Vicki M. Runnion

AFTER SOME PRELIMINARY, casual conversation, hospice social worker Cindy Burnett shifted toward the real reason for her visit with Tiffany Walker, the nineteen-year-old mother of a terminally ill infant. "Tiffany, it wasn't all that long ago that you were so upset that you cut your wrists and were in the hospital yourself. I know bringing Zoe home has taken up a lot of your time and thoughts. But I have to ask, have you thought about that anymore? About hurting yourself? Especially now that Zoe may have to go back in the hospital?" Cindy kept steady eye contact.

"Well, yeah," Tiffany acknowledged, "I kind of always think about it. Like, if I could get enough of her pain medicine saved up when she doesn't really need it, and where I could go so my mom wouldn't find me and call 911 again. But I've always thought about it—all my life, pretty much. But it's not any more than usual right now."

Remembering what Tiffany's mother had told her, Cindy wasn't sure whether or not to believe this, and didn't know what to say next.

Development of this decision case was supported in part by funding from the Project on Death in America and the University of South Carolina College of Social Work. It was prepared solely to provide material for class discussion and not to suggest either effective or ineffective handling of the situation depicted. Although the case is based on field research regarding an actual situation, names and certain facts may have been disguised to protect confidentiality. The author wishes to thank the anonymous case reporter for cooperation in making this account available for the benefit of social work students and instructors.

Columbus, Ohio

Founded in 1812, the city of Columbus had been the Ohio state capital since 1816. Home to Ohio State University and numerous other smaller colleges, with a busy arts and culture calendar and a thriv ing downtown business district, Columbus had gradually grown into the largest city in the state. In 2000, it had a metropolitan population of more than one million.

Riverside Hospice

Riverside Hospice provided a comprehensive program of health care, counseling, and support services designed to meet the needs of terminally ill patients of any age and their families. It had served Columbus and the surrounding communities for nearly twenty years, growing steadily to become one of the largest programs in the state. Together with patients' doctors, the hospice team worked to promote comfort by managing pain and other symptoms while focusing on the emotional, social, and spiritual needs of both patients and their families. The hospice staff helped them learn more about the diseases they were coping with—and what to expect.

Like many other hospices, Riverside had begun to serve pediatric patients very gradually and tentatively, about three years after admitting the first adult patients. But as the organization grew in census, community support, and expertise, early leaders recognized the need for specialized care for terminally ill children and their families, and established the first pediatric hospice program in the state. It took time and extensive community education, but the pediatric census had become fairly stable at around fourteen or fifteen patients and families at any one time.

Cindy Burnett

Cindy Burnett had completed her M.S.W. in June 2001, fifteen months previously, but she had been working in hospice in several different positions for nearly eight years, based on her previous degree from seminary and her volunteer work. Upon completing her social work degree, she joined one of the teams serving adult patients, but about six months later the director of patient care services asked if she would consider also carrying a pediatric caseload. She had agreed with only slight hesitation about becoming involved with children who were going to die, and so far she was satisfied with her decision.

As a thirty-four-year-old single woman, she had wondered if parents would find it difficult to trust what she had to say, since she didn't have children herself, but that had not come up in the year she'd been on the "Kids' Team." By and large, the parents had simply been glad for additional support as they dealt with the unknowns of their child's treatment, decline, and eventual death—or the occasional unexpected recovery.

A Family with Troubles

Zoe Walker was one of the pediatric patients in Cindy's caseload. She was just sixteen months old and diagnosed with a Wilms' tumor. Because the tumor had already spread from one kidney to the other (stage V), the prognosis was very poor. Although the tumors were shrinking a bit, apparently as a result of a first round of chemotherapy, the team knew not to build up too much hope prematurely.

In the two months since Zoe had been admitted to the hospice program, Cindy had spent much of her time trying to sort out her family's history and dynamics. Although Zoe's mother, Tiffany Walker, was listed as primary care-giver, her grandmother, Eugenia Rollins, actually provided most of Zoe's care. Tiffany was only nineteen, a single mom, and Eugenia was a young grand-mother of forty-two, although the lines around her eyes made her look older. Tiffany insisted she didn't know for sure who was Zoe's father. However, Eugenia had confided privately to Cindy that she was fairly positive about the man's identity, but didn't push the issue because she didn't want him to become involved in their lives again.

Tiffany and Zoe lived with Eugenia and her third husband, Bill Rollins, although Tiffany didn't seem too happy about that. Gradually, in bits and pieces, Tiffany had revealed a troubling story.

Cindy's first meeting with Tiffany, at the time of Zoe's referral to hospice, had been held in the inpatient psych unit of the same hospital where Zoe was hospitalized, two floors down, just three days after Zoe's cancer had been confirmed. Tiffany had cut her wrists with razor blades the day she learned of Zoe's diagnosis—and this was not her first hospitalization for suicidal gestures. Cindy had expected to find a distraught young mom, worried literally almost to death by her child's life-threatening illness. But she had been somewhat surprised by Tiffany's fairly calm demeanor, the minimal bandages on her wrists, and the superficial appearance of the previous scars, and had wondered about the seriousness of this attempt.

Over the next several visits, however, Tiffany had disclosed that her mother's second husband had sexually abused her, repeatedly, from the time she was about six years old until they finally divorced when Tiffany was twelve. According to Tiffany, she had told her mom about the abuse when she was nine, but her mother had not believed her until she caught him in the act when Tiffany was eleven years old. It was another year before she finally split up with him.

There had never been any legal action against Tiffany's stepfather for the abuse, but the divorce proceedings were ugly, and Tiffany had gone to live with her father and stepmother in another state until about two years ago when she got pregnant. She told Cindy that she'd had a boyfriend at school when she was living with her dad and had been sexually involved with him, but she said she had also been raped by her stepbrother, so she wasn't sure who the father of the baby was. She said she had not wanted to have an abortion and felt sure her mom would have pushed that if she'd known about the stepbrother, so she didn't say anything about it. "You're the only one who knows about that," she told Cindy. "It's over now, so please don't say anything."

Cindy felt special compassion for Tiffany, and honored that the young woman had trusted her with this story. Cindy herself had been molested, also more than once, by an older cousin when she was young. She had never told anyone and, as a child, had always felt guilty about what had happened. She could only imagine how it would have been to have told her mother and not been believed—allowing the abuse to continue unchecked for another two years.

Two months after their initial visit, Cindy was still observing, and puzzled about, the relationship between Eugenia and Tiffany. It seemed somewhat superficial. There was evident tension between them from time to time, but much more the kind of tension she saw between other parents and younger adolescents—a control and rebellion kind of tension, alternating with times when they seemed more at ease with each other. But Eugenia had never mentioned any problems other than their worries about Zoe, and Cindy had not felt comfortable asking her about what Tiffany had related, since that wasn't the focus of the services she was there to offer. Cindy often felt something was missing between Eugenia and Tiffany, in spite of Eugenia's air of long-suffering indulgence with a difficult teenager. *But I don't know if it's attachment that is missing or an acknowledgment of all they've been through together.* Something just didn't feel right to her.

There's more to this story than I know yet, Cindy found herself thinking on more than one occasion.

Still Suicidal?

It was a gorgeous October Monday morning as Cindy made her way to work—one of those days when she was so thankful to have a job that allowed her to be out and about rather than stuck in an office. It had been a pleasant weekend, and she felt rested as she anticipated getting into her work week.

Greeting co-workers cheerfully, she checked her mailbox and settled in one of the care provider work areas to schedule visits for the day. Around 9:15 she heard Mary, the receptionist, page her: "Cindy, you have a call on 102."

"Hello, this is Cindy."

"Cindy, this is Eugenia Rollins, Zoe's grandmother."

"Hi, Eugenia, what's going on?" Cindy responded.

"We're at Dr. D'Angelo's now," Eugenia began. "Zoe has a high fever, and he told us to bring her on in."

"Would you like for one of us to come down and stay with you while you wait?" Cindy offered.

"No, Bill is with me, and we're okay here. But I need for you to go to the house and see about Tiffany. I'm worried." Eugenia hesitated. "I don't really want you to tell her this, but I was in her room yesterday, and I found a suicide note."

"Oh, no! What did it say?" Cindy asked.

"Just that she didn't feel she could go on with things anymore, and that she was sorry but she was going to put an end to it, and that it would be less trouble for me. There wasn't a date on it, but it was on top of her desk. I was just shocked when I read it—I thought she was doing better since we brought Zoe home, even if I do most of the taking care of her.

"She would be so angry with me if she knew I was in her room, so I wanted to just watch her closely for a few days. But then the baby got sick during the night, and we called the doctor first thing this morning. Tiffany was still in bed when we left—I woke her up and told her where we were going, but she was still pretty sleepy. I don't know how long we'll be here, and they might send us right on over to the hospital for Zoe to be admitted. Can you go check on Tiffany? And if you think she needs to be hospitalized, can you help with that?"

Whoa! Cindy thought. *I don't really like the way this feels. But I guess I should go now and be sure Tiffany is okay, and deal with my icky feelings about it later.*

"Okay, I'll go," Cindy agreed. "If you find out anything about the baby, if she's going to be hospitalized, call back and have the office page me. Once I see what's going on with Tiffany, I'll call you at the doctor's office if you haven't called first."

"Remember, I have a pager," Eugenia said.

"Oh, that's right, it's a text pager, isn't it?" Cindy recalled. "I'll either page you to call me at your house or back here at the office, depending on what I find, or I'll have the office text page you if I'm not going to be in a good place to get a call back, okay?"

"Sure. Thanks a lot," Eugenia responded.

Driving up the street to Eugenia and Bill's house thirty minutes later, Cindy recognized her anxiety by the twisting feeling in her gut. *Gosh, I hope she's all right.*

Taking a deep breath, Cindy rang the doorbell. Everything was quiet. She rang again a few seconds later and listened more closely, and was relieved to hear footsteps approaching the door.

Tiffany's face lit up when she saw Cindy. "What are you doing here?" she asked, backing up so Cindy could come in. The young woman was dressed in her usual ragged jeans and Grateful Dead T-shirt, but her tousled hair suggested that she had not been out of bed for long.

"I heard Zoe is at the doctor's with your mom, and I thought you might be worried," Cindy replied. "I was in the area, so I just decided to stop by and see if you were here."

"Yeah, I was up late watching a movie on TV last night and I was sleeping kinda late this morning. My mom woke me up and said the baby had a fever and she was taking her to the doctor's office. She said she would call after she sees the doctor, if Zoe has to go into the hospital, or else she will be back. I would've gone with her, but she was ready to leave right then."

"Well, since I'm here, can we visit for a bit?" Cindy asked.

"Sure, if you can stay," Tiffany responded with a smile. "Come sit down," and she turned and plopped down on the sofa, tucking her legs up under her. Deciding that the only chair in the room was too far away, Cindy faced her from the other end of the sofa.

"So, how has it been going since you all brought Zoe home from the hospital last week?" Cindy asked. "I know it's a lot of responsibility, watching her so closely, and the medicines she's taking. Are you and your mom working things out okay?"

"Yeah, it's been going okay, I think. We just take turns keeping the baby monitor at night, so every other night we get to sleep all night, unless she's really fussy and wakes everyone up. Sometimes I get a little bugged with Mom for kind of taking over, though, acting like Zoe is her baby instead of mine. She jumps to do everything for her at the least little peep, when I'm right there and would do it. But I'd really get worn out if I had to do it all myself, so I just try to bite my tongue and not complain. It does get on my nerves sometimes, though."

Hmmm, different story than I get from Eugenia, Cindy thought. *She really minimizes Tiffany's role. But I'm not here to sort that out right now.*

"How are you feeling about things overall, Tiffany?" Trying to push a little deeper, Cindy continued. "It was crisis time while Zoe was in the hospital, just finding out what was wrong and getting her started on the chemo, and of course you were pretty upset then, and in the hospital yourself. How are you doing now that you're home with her?"

"I'm just kind of trying to take it one day at a time, pray for her every day, and hope for a miracle. I know her chances aren't too good, but there's a little room for hope, Dr. D'Angelo told us." She paused. "I do think sometimes about what it would be like if she doesn't make it, though—how I would handle it, and what I would do afterward."

"What do you think you'd do?" Cindy probed gently.

"I think I'd like to go back to school, maybe go to nursing school," Tiffany said. "I feel kind of bad saying it, because it sounds positive, like something good would happen if Zoe dies. That's not what I mean, though. I just would want to do something to make this not totally a waste."

"I understand what you mean, I think. I know you want desperately for her to be okay, but she's got a lot stacked against her and you can't help but think about that sometimes."

She doesn't sound suicidal to me, Cindy thought. *And she doesn't seem suicidal. She actually looks almost bright. But she's good at pretending, good at saying what she thinks someone wants to hear. I'm going to have to be more blunt.*

"Tiffany, it hasn't been all that long ago that you were so upset that you cut your wrists and were in the hospital yourself. I know bringing Zoe home has taken up a lot of your time and thoughts. But I have to ask, have you thought about that anymore? About hurting yourself? Especially now that Zoe might be sick again?" Cindy kept steady eye contact. "Well, yeah," Tiffany acknowledged. "I kind of always think about it. Like, if I could get enough of her pain medicine saved up when she doesn't really need it, and where I could go so my mom wouldn't find me and call 911 again. But I've always thought about it—all my life, pretty much. It's not any more than usual right now."

Okay, so now what do I do? I really don't think she's suicidal now; what she's telling me about seems like that same low-level suicidal thinking that a lot of sexual abuse survivors do—that I've done. Shall I bring up the note?

"Wilms' tumor, also called nephroblastoma, is a cancer that originates in the kidney. The disease gets its name from a German doctor, Max Wilms, who wrote one of the first medical articles about it in 1899. . . . Wilms' tumor is the second most common type of all childhood solid tumors, not including brain tumors. It accounts for approximately 6 percent of all childhood cancers. The average age at diagnosis is between two and three years when the disease is unilateral (affecting only one kidney), but it is generally diagnosed at a younger age in children when the disease is bilateral (affecting both kidneys). If caught early, prognosis is very good. If it has spread to the other kidney, however, prognosis is very poor." O'Reilly and Associates. 1999. *Childhood Cancer Center: Wilms' Tumor:* http://www.patientcenters.com/childcancer/news/wilms_tumor.html (accessed August 16, 2005).

16 | A Painful Predicament

Barbara Head

DIALYSIS SOCIAL WORKER Mindy Callahan remained at Elliot Marshall's bedside, talking softly and gently massaging his hands and arms. "I promise you, Elliott, I won't let your death be in vain." Just before leaving, she told him, "I will do everything in my power to make sure patients' wishes aren't ignored in the future." These turned out to be her final words to Elliott. He died quietly that night. His brother and minister made the funeral arrangements.

St. Anthony's Medical Center and Dialysis Clinic

Located in Parkersburg, West Virginia, St. Anthony's Medical Center served a town of 32,000. Farming and factory work were the occupations of most residents in its service area. Thought was generally conservative and religion fundamental in this predominantly Republican county seat.

St. Anthony's was a 100-bed acute care facility owned and operated by the Sisters of Charity. Known as a regional referral center for more than a dozen

Development of this decision case was supported in part by funding from the Project on Death in America and the University of South Carolina College of Social Work. It was prepared solely to provide material for class discussion and not to suggest either effective or ineffective handling of the situation depicted. Although the case is based on field research regarding an actual situation, names and certain facts may have been disguised to protect confidentiality. The author wishes to thank the anonymous case reporter for cooperation in making this account available for the benefit of social work students and instructors.

rural counties in West Virginia and several surrounding states, the medical center prided itself in offering medical specialties and technologies usually found in much larger urban settings. St. Anthony's competed with a similar-sized hospital owned and operated by the city of Parkersburg.

The hospital operated a major dialysis clinic with four satellite centers. Patients usually received treatments as outpatients at one of the satellite centers. If the need for inpatient care arose, they were sent to the acute care facility. Each unit served eight to ten patients at a time in three daily shifts, Monday through Saturday.

The dialysis center employed two master's-level social workers. Together they were responsible for assessment, counseling, education, intervention, and advocacy for more than 260 dialysis patients and their families in western West Virginia. Since 1976, as stipulated in the Code of Federal Regulations, Medicare had mandated that every End Stage Renal Dialysis (ESRD) treatment facility have a master's-level social worker to provide such psychosocial services. The vast majority of dialysis patients were covered by Medicare under the ESRD program, either because of their age or because of their disability. The two social workers counseled dialysis candidates in the hospitals and at home to explain the procedure and lifestyle of a dialysis patient and to determine reimbursement resources. One or the other made almost daily rounds at the satellite centers to check on patients and assess ongoing needs. During hospitalizations the dialysis social workers would visit the patients and assist in developing discharge plans.

The social workers participated on an interdisciplinary team consisting of the nurses, aides, social workers, physicians, and any other therapists working with the patient. The team at St. Anthony's met every other week to discuss cases and develop or update the plan for each patient's care. Team meetings were important opportunities for communication regarding the patients, but informal updates occurred almost daily depending on the changing needs of each one.

Mindy Callahan, Dialysis Social Worker

Mindy had received her M.S.W. from West Virginia University. Her past employment included social work with inpatient psychiatric patients and outpatient mental health therapy with individuals, families, and groups. With more than fifteen years of social work experience, she was well suited to address the diverse needs of dialysis patients. She was an active member of the Council of Nephrology Social Workers and the National Association of Social Workers, and she served as co-chairperson of the hospital's ethics committee. As such, she was responsible for the initial review of cases sent to the committee and developed the agenda for each meeting.

In addition to the routine responsibilities of the dialysis social worker, Mindy provided staff education related to psychosocial issues and participated as a member of the multidisciplinary nephrology care planning team. Her fellow team members respected her opinions and admired the energy and compassion she brought to her job. Patients immediately connected with this perky, petite blond whose vivacious personality and commitment to their well-being made her so easy to like.

Dr. Sharma, Nephrologist

Dr. Sharma, a native of Calcutta, India, received his medical education in India and had just completed a fellowship in nephrology at a medical center in Oregon. He had been heavily recruited to join the only private nephrology practice in the area. St. Anthony's Dialysis Clinic contracted with this practice to provide medical management for its patients. Now two physicians would share the demanding responsibilities for the dialysis center. The two nephrologists had privileges at the hospital and would follow clinic patients during any inpatient stays.

Dr. Sharma spoke softly with a heavy accent that complicated communication with the dialysis staff, especially those who did not often encounter people from other countries. He was a man of few words and very little self-disclosure. Clinically, he was quite astute and competent, but team members were never quite sure where he stood on issues such as futile care, patient self-determination, and palliation of symptoms.

Elliott Marshall

As Mindy learned while completing Elliott's psychosocial assessment, he was one of five children born to an alcoholic coal miner and the wife he had married when they were only teenagers. Frequently sent to the tavern to fill his father's coal bucket with beer, Elliott soon learned that sipping on the beer during his trek back home made the inevitable beatings easier to bear. He came to enjoy drinking and carousing with other youths as an alternative to the depressing surroundings of home. At the age of eleven, he was a passenger of a drunk teenage driver; they were in a wreck that broke Elliott's back and left him with excruciating chronic pain. When Elliott was ready to leave the hospital, he was informed that his parents would not be picking him up. He never knew exactly why, but he assumed his ongoing care was just too much for a family already in crisis due to his father's alcoholism. No other relative could be located as the time for his discharge approached, so Elliott lived in a series of foster homes. After his abandonment, Elliott never felt pain without also feeling anger and despair. He would become impatient and demanding, alienating the professionals charged with his medical care and pain relief.

At the age of sixteen, Elliott was hospitalized a second time for back surgery. Often belligerent and antagonizing toward staff, he got into a scuffle with a housekeeping employee, an American Indian, whom he harassed while the employee attempted to clean the room. During the confrontation, the employee's mop got tangled in Elliott's catheter and tore it from his body. Screaming in pain and striking out at people trying to help, Elliott was sent to the psychiatric unit of that hospital because he refused to accept any effort to console him. He confided in Mindy that while he was there a staff member of the unit physically abused him.

Released from the hospital, Elliott decided he did not want to live in foster care. He ran far enough away that no one would recognize him. Lying about his age, he applied for a position in a factory, asking only for a place to sleep in payment for his labor. With evident pride, he told Mindy how he worked his way up in the factory and was able to have a place of his own. He married in his early twenties. After beginning to abuse his wife, Elliott saw himself repeating his father's behavior and felt frightened by his own potential for violence.

"My behavior was really scaring me. I didn't want to torture others the way my family tortured me," he told Mindy with tears in his eyes. "The only choice I thought I had was to divorce and live alone. I get along better with people if they keep their distance." Eventually, Elliott had reconnected with one foster mother who was especially kind and understanding, and sought out one of his biological brothers and developed a meaningful relationship. He had even asked this brother, Leroy, to be his durable power of attorney.

Elliott's Later Life

While employed, Elliott progressed to a supervisory position in a plant that manufactured chairs. He became very active in a local Baptist church. "I met the Lord, and my life changed for the better," he told Mindy. "Some folks think I'm crazy, but Jesus means everything to me and I'm not afraid to tell anybody." He often shared his fundamental, conservative beliefs, especially when they discussed life and death issues.

Unfortunately, Elliott's career was cut short by the progression of his renal failure. At the age of fifty-eight, he was forced to go on dialysis. He tried to continue working but did not have the strength and endurance to undergo dialysis and maintain his position at the plant.

Elliott received hemodialysis three days a week, for a minimum of five hours each time. The treatment involved being hooked up to a dialysis machine. His blood was shunted via a surgically inserted catheter through a machine that would filter out impurities. The procedure itself was not particularly painful except for the venipuncture required to connect him to the machine, but the dialysis often left him weak and nauseated and the withdrawal of fluid and changes in his electrolytes sometimes gave him a headache. But he never missed clinic appointments unless he was hospitalized. During his treatments, Elliott could watch television or read, but he usually chose to make conversation with the nurses, aides, social workers, and other patients. Between treatments, he tried his best to comply with the strict diet, including limited salt, protein, and potassium, and fluid restrictions recommended for optimal functioning. If he planned to be away from the area for longer than two days, he had to make arrangements to be treated at a facility where he was visiting. Elliott knew that his life depended on this procedure.

As if renal failure weren't enough of a disability, Elliott had severe diabetes and the attending complications of hypertension, atherosclerotic cardiovascular disease, peripheral vascular disease (which had resulted in the amputation of his right toes), and peripheral neuropathy. He walked with an unsteady shuffle and talked in a gruff, somewhat hoarse voice. Osteoarthritis and degenerative disk disease of the lumbar spine added to the pain of his neuropathy, creating a chronic pain syndrome.

Mindy developed a professional relationship with Elliott over a period of two years. Despite his reserve, she came to appreciate his determination and honesty.

The staff and patients at the dialysis unit became his family. Upon entering the clinic, he always took time to greet the other patients. An avid fisherman, he often shared his catch with those on limited incomes who might appreciate a fresh fish dinner. He knew all the staff well and didn't hesitate to converse and joke with them. Everyone was happier when Elliot was at the clinic. In honor of a nurse named Grace, he dubbed it the "Grace Unit," claiming that it was his "saving Grace," giving him life he would otherwise not have known. Even with dialysis, the body eventually deteriorates, and Elliott began a slow decline. He started having difficulty walking and became wheelchair dependent. Unable to maneuver the wheelchair in his apartment alone, he reluctantly accepted the nursing home placement Mindy arranged for him at the county's best facility. The dialysis staff suffered with him through his physical deterioration. He developed a decubitus ulcer (bedsore) the size of a grapefruit at the end of his spine. Mindy occasionally assisted in dressing the sore because it took several staff members to hold him up while the wound was packed. It tortured her to see her client suffer and have to deal with such indignity.

Elliott's Final Wishes

As with all the patients in her caseload, Mindy had entered into discussions with Elliott about his condition, the consequences of dialysis, and his desires related to how he would live out the rest of his life. He had signed an advance directive instructing that he be allowed to die naturally when his disease became terminal. Elliott did not want artificial nutrition or hydration or to be placed on a ventilator, but he initially stopped short of deciding to discontinue dialysis when he became imminently terminal. He named his brother, Leroy, to be his health care surrogate and gave him durable power of attorney, but the brothers had not had any serious conversations about Elliott's desires should Leroy become his decision maker.

Mindy saw Elliott as a determined soul, a survivor with many scars from fighting illness and disability, but his renal failure and other comorbidities eventually began to win out. Elliott's decline continued to the point that his extremities became dusky. His dialysis treatments had to be shortened due to his inability to maintain a stable blood pressure. He was hospitalized at St. Anthony's. Mindy visited him again to discuss his wishes about whether or not to continue dialysis. Because his religion had taught him that suicide was sin, initially Elliott could not even fathom discontinuing dialysis, which seemed akin to suicide. But as he and Mindy talked, he came to view it as withdrawing a treatment and allowing natural death rather than an intentional act of suicide.

After one of their discussions, Elliott told Mindy, "I don't want no more dialysis. Just let me go on."

"Do you want a Do Not Resuscitate order?" Mindy probed.

"Don't do nothing to me," he reiterated, "just let me go on."

That same evening, Elliott intentionally pulled the feeding tube from his abdomen. When asked why, he responded, "If I'm going to go on and die, why put a bunch of food in me? I don't want this feeding tube any longer. Please don't put it back in. You're only wasting time and money."

Mindy agreed to communicate this decision to the other members of the health care team, Elliott's minister, and Leroy. Before leaving the hospital that night, Mindy made these calls and left an explanatory note on Elliott's chart stating, "Patient desires comfort measures only. He wants no further dialysis and no artificial hydration or nutrition. Please refer to patient's living will on this chart." She talked with the nurses on the floor about his decision. Many of them had cared for Elliott numerous times and respected his wishes, knowing how he was now suffering.

As much as she hated to lose this special client, she was relieved that he had made a choice that would put an end to his suffering. Once dialysis was discontinued, Elliott would be moved to a designated "compassionate care" bed in the hospital with the focus of keeping him comfortable until death. She and Elliott had discussed how a person dies after discontinuing dialysis. Generally the toxins build up in the body, leading to a comalike state that is not uncomfortable. Dialysis patients generally live from several days to several weeks after treatment stops.

A Disappointing Turn of Events

When Mindy returned to the hospital the next day, she was shocked to find an empty bed in Elliott's room. Mindy asked Suzanne Henderson, the charge nurse on duty, "Where's Elliott?"

"He's gone down for his dialysis treatment," Suzanne replied.

"But he wanted to quit dialysis," Mindy insisted.

"Dr. Sharma visited Elliott early this morning to discuss his decision. He convinced Elliott that discontinuing treatment was indeed an act of suicide, and he promised to provide adequate pain medication if only Elliott would continue dialysis," Suzanne explained. "I know you wrote last evening that he wanted no further treatment, but the doctor told us to send him on for his treatment today."

Mindy was speechless. *How could this have happened? Elliott was so sure of his decision last night. His advance directive was on the hospital record, and I know I was clear about his decision in the progress notes.*

Mindy searched through his medical record to see what Dr. Sharma had written in the physician's progress notes. It said: "Patient has reconsidered his earlier wishes and will continue dialysis. Dialysis to be provided three times weekly per previous orders. Begin Total Parenteral Nutrition (TPN) after insertion of a central line."

Mindy hoped to have further discussion with Elliott, but when he returned to his bed, he was heavily sedated and wearing an oxygen mask. The TPN, aggressive nutritional support via direct intravenous infusion, had been started, as evidenced by the big bag of white fluid hanging beside the bed. *He looks so pitiful and helpless—just like he must have looked when he was sixteen, hurting and alone. I can't believe this happened to him. Even when he was sick, he was so full of life, but now all he can do is moan and gasp for each breath.*

Mindy spent hours at his bedside, but Elliott was not able to respond to her verbally. *I wish I could talk to him again about all of this. Does he know I did my best to convey his wishes? What did Dr. Sharma say to him that changed his mind? Or did Elliott feel he had no choice in the matter?*

To Mindy, it seemed that Dr. Sharma avoided her. Privately, the nurses and technicians expressed support for her concerns, but none dared broach the topic with the doctor.

According to the chart, Dr. Sharma had ordered a gastrointestinal endoscopy to evaluate Elliott for swallowing difficulty and/or pain. The chart read "procedure aborted when pt's heart rate accelerated and he demonstrated a change in mentation accompanied by weakness of right upper and lower extremities." Finally, Dr. Sharma decided to stop aggressive treatment, sent Elliott back to his room, and wrote an order for hospice care.

The next morning, Mindy was horrified when she entered Elliott's room. His eyes were pulled to the right and he was unable to make eye contact. His face was contorted and he groaned continually. Elliott's upper torso jerked intermittently. His breathing was labored and he was perspiring profusely. Torn between staying at his side and wanting to intervene, she turned and ran for the nurses' station.

"Get Elliott something for pain," Mindy demanded indignantly as she approached. "Don't you realize how badly he's hurting?"

"I knew there was a change in him and thought it might be pain," the nurse replied defensively. "But all that Dr. Sharma ordered was one hydrocodone with acetaminophen tablet by mouth, and Mr. Marshall can't swallow for twenty-four hours after his test. . . . Dr. Sharma doesn't like for us to bother him during the night, so I just let it be."

"That's ridiculous!" Mindy didn't even try to hide her anger at the situation. "You need to call Dr. Sharma immediately, and tell him this is not acceptable." Mindy returned to Elliott's bedside to attempt to comfort him.

Minutes later, the nurse reported that she had reached Dr. Sharma, who was making rounds at the clinic, and he had begrudgingly ordered morphine for Elliott. After the first intravenous dose of the drug, the patient's pain began to subside.

Mindy remained at his side, talking softly to Elliott and gently massaging his hands and arms. "I promise you, Elliott, I won't let your death be in vain." Later in the day, Mindy left, but only after promising, "I will do everything in my power to make sure patients' wishes aren't ignored in the future." Those turned out to be her final words to Elliott. He died quietly that night. His brother and minister made the funeral arrangements.

Pondering Her Predicament

After allowing some time for her own mourning, Mindy seriously pondered how to honor the promise she had made to Elliott. Dr. Sharma had never acknowledged that there was anything problematic about Elliott's treatment and death. What were her options if the responsible physician did not recognize a violation of a patient's right to choose? As co-chair of the ethics committee, she had the responsibility of ensuring ethical practice related to patient's expressed wishes, and this loomed large in her thoughts.

This man suffered enough through a difficult life, and I did my best to assure a dignified, pain-free death. This is just not right, and it shouldn't ever happen again.

Mindy became preoccupied with this failure to realize a patient's last wishes. She knew she couldn't let the issue die with Elliott. But what recourse did she have?

Mindy's colleague, Brenda Harmon, who co-chaired the ethics committee with her, called to schedule an appointment to plan for the next regularly scheduled meeting. Mindy had received several requests to review cases at the meeting, but perhaps the most important one was Elliott's. Mindy wondered whether she should place a case so close to her heart on the agenda. Could she remain impartial during such a discussion? Was this the best way to assure that others would not suffer as Elliott had when his wishes were ignored?

17 | 'Til Death Do Us Part?

Barbara Head

STANDING WITH MR. ANDERSON, geriatric social worker Linda Nickels wasn't sure how to respond. Mrs. Anderson had just left Fredonia Hospital on a stretcher. The ambulance would take her to Mount Meadows Nursing Facility, where hospice would follow her. Linda was covering for Michelle Humphrey, who had taken Friday off to enjoy a long weekend, and she hadn't anticipated any problems with this discharge.

"I would never have agreed to that surgery," Mr. Anderson said, tears flowing down his ruddy cheeks, "if I'd known it would come to this. This is no way to spend the last days of our life together—and after sixty-five years of marriage. We've never been apart for more than a day. I can't bear to go home without her."

The tears of this heartbroken elderly man were gut-wrenching for Linda. Obviously, this hospitalization hadn't been routine and the Andersons were not headed to a happy ending. In order to help him, Linda knew she had to explore the source of his sadness.

Development of this decision case was supported in part by funding from the Project on Death in America and the University of South Carolina College of Social Work. It was prepared solely to provide material for class discussion and not to suggest either effective or ineffective handling of the situation depicted. Although the case is based on field research regarding an actual situation, names and certain facts may have been disguised to protect confidentiality. The author wishes to thank the anonymous case reporter for cooperation in making this account available for the benefit of social work students and instructors.

Fredonia Hospital

Fredonia Hospital was renowned as a progressive teaching and research institution associated with one of the best medical schools in the nation. Located in central Missouri, the regional facility served the metropolitan area and 10 surrounding counties. The hospital had 600 beds and numerous specialty units, including the geriatrics wing where Linda did most of her work, a women's pavilion, and an extensive oncology department.

Fredonia provided the setting for the training of residents and fellows, and many of the staff physicians were also faculty of the medical school at the University of Missouri at Columbia. A public institution committed to serving the indigent as well as those who were well-insured, the hospital attracted patients who wanted state-of-the-art, research-based care.

The Department of Social Services

Fredonia Hospital had a large, well-respected Department of Social Services. All social workers in the department had master's degrees and most had substantial experience prior to their employment at Fredonia.

The role of the hospital social workers included providing counseling, procuring resources, referral, facilitating patient and family education and support groups, and planning discharges. Their caseloads ranged from twenty to twenty-five cases at any one time. The workers were assigned to various departments of the hospital (i.e., geriatrics, oncology, pediatrics), but all were expected to cover any department when a colleague was off.

Planning for discharge was one of the most essential and challenging responsibilities. It began at the time of admission and included an assessment of caregiving conditions and family and community resources, and a description of the home environment. As specific needs became evident, plans for discharge would be adjusted accordingly to assure that the patients' needs could be met. With elderly patients, increased care needs often required placement outside the home, at least temporarily. Matching needs with available resources and securing a placement satisfactory to the patient and family were often challenging. Timing was of the essence, as the plan must be finalized to coincide with the patient's discharge date. With very short hospital stays being mandated by insurers and third-party payers, the social workers were under pressure to quickly assess the patient's and family's needs and condition and almost immediately secure a suitable situation for posthospital care.

Linda Nickels, Social Worker

Linda began her career with a bachelor's degree in education. After two years of teaching junior high school English, she decided she was more suited to social work and returned to school to get an advanced degree. She had never regretted this decision.

Linda joined the staff at Fredonia Hospital as a master's-level social worker in the Department of Geriatrics. She had completed her master's at South State, the large state university with which the hospital was associated. Prior to accepting this position, she had been a social worker at an extended care facility for patients needing ongoing skilled medical care, many of whom were elderly.

Linda had a knack for working with geriatric patients. She was compassionate and patient and enjoyed spending time learning about her patients and their experiences. Her respect and appreciation for the elderly quickly endeared her to patients and their families. Both her patients and her colleagues appreciated her animated communication style and "down home" sense of humor.

The Andersons

The Andersons married young—he was twenty and she only eighteen. Mr. Anderson farmed with his father until he was able to purchase his own land. The couple had three children—two girls and a boy—and eight grandchildren. Their lives centered around family, farming, and church.

Although they were now in their mid-eighties, Mr. Anderson still helped his son farm the acreage he owned. Mrs. Anderson kept busy with cooking, canning, gardening, and helping care for her grandchildren since both of her daughters were employed full-time. Mr. Anderson had moderate visual impairment due to macular degeneration and his wife had adult onset diabetes; otherwise they had been in excellent health for their ages.

They had not been so fortunate with their financial situation. As farming became more and more mechanized, it became harder and harder for the

Andersons to make a living, let alone set aside much for retirement. They had sold some of their acreage to their son and some to a neighbor when Mr. Anderson turned sixty-five, but the proceeds were long gone. They were both embarrassed and grateful to have medical assistance from the state as well as their Medicare.

About eight months prior to this hospitalization, Mrs. Anderson had started having abdominal pain and bloating. Thinking the problem was just constipation or indigestion, she didn't visit her family physician until the discomfort became severe enough to limit her activities. The CAT scan of her abdomen revealed that she had advanced ovarian cancer. She was referred to Dr. Anthony Browning, an oncology surgeon.

Dr. Anthony Browning

Dr. Browning was a respected faculty member and researcher at the South State University medical school. A specialist in gynecological oncology surgery, he had secured numerous substantial research grants for the university. He usually had several fellows or residents making rounds with him to observe and learn this specialty from a renowned expert. A rather small man, he was always well-groomed and distinguished-looking. He was polite, but reserved. Like many other surgeons, he was meticulous and demanded perfection from himself and his colleagues. Dr. Browning was driven to adhere closely to his research protocols, recruit adequate numbers of participants for his studies, and meet his research objectives, as these were essential criteria for maintaining ongoing funding from major sources.

Mrs. Anderson's Condition and Care

By the time it was diagnosed, Mrs. Anderson's ovarian cancer had metastasized throughout her abdomen, affecting her reproductive organs and the adjacent tissues. The prognosis was poor. She and her husband were overwhelmed by this sudden, devastating diagnosis. Although they were advanced in years, their good health had precluded any discussion of separation due to illness or death. The Andersons were totally dependent on each other, and neither could fathom the end to their relationship as they knew it.

Based on his reputation, Mrs. Anderson placed her hope in the able hands of Dr. Browning. His recommendation was that she have a pelvic exenteration.

This surgery would include a radical hysterectomy (removing both ovaries and the uterus), pelvic lymph node dissection, rectal resection (redirecting bowel contents through a surgically created opening [ostomy] on the abdomen into a bag), and removal of the bladder and urethras. The patient would need to adjust to both a colostomy and a urostomy (surgically created opening on the abdomen through which urine empties via the ureters from the kidney into an attached bag) after the surgery. Other consequences included extreme changes in digestion and elimination as well as total loss of sexual function, disturbance of body image, and, sometimes, loss of self-esteem.

As with all surgeries, Mrs. Anderson had to sign an informed consent. This form was intended to verify that the patient understood the surgery and potential outcomes, had any questions answered, and agreed to the procedure. At Fredonia, it was the physician's responsibility to ensure that the patient understood the surgery, the expected results, and the possible complications prior to the procedure. Most often, the nurse caring for the patient before surgery actually got the form signed after making certain that the physician had clearly explained the procedure. Since Mrs. Anderson was apparently competent and capable of deciding for herself, discussion with and a decision by her alone would be seen as adequate. There was no formal requirement that family members be involved in the informed consent process.

Mrs. Anderson had signed the informed consent, but had she fully grasped the impact of this surgical intervention on her life as she knew it?

"If I'd known it would come to this . . ."

Michelle Humphrey, the social worker on the women's surgery floor, had located a nursing home bed for Mrs. Anderson earlier in the week. She was fortunate to find one available in the only nursing home close to the small town where the Andersons lived. It was Fredonia Hospital's policy that a social worker be present for discharges to nursing facilities. The social worker had to verify that all the necessary forms went with the patient and that the ambulance personnel were adequately informed about the placement, the patient's condition, and other relevant factors.

In covering for Michelle on the Anderson case, Linda had expected that this discharge would be routine. She had gotten to the floor early to make sure all the paperwork was complete and the ambulance was on its way. After discovering that Mr. and Mrs. Anderson lived in the same rural farming community where she had taught school for two years after completing her undergraduate education, Linda had had a nice chat with the couple. Mrs. Anderson had no complaints and expressed her appreciation for the excellent care she had received in the hospital.

After Mrs. Anderson left for the nursing facility, Linda remained with Mr. Anderson, trying to calm him down so that she could better understand his tears. Finally he was able to tell Linda about his frustration related to Melba's condition.

According to Mr. Anderson, he had not understood the care that would be required after the surgery. He was not familiar with medical terminology and had not comprehended the frequent, meticulous procedures required when a patient had newly created bodily openings that constantly drained into bags. Additionally, Mrs. Anderson had a wound that needed regular sterile dressing changes.

Mr. Anderson wanted so much to take his wife home. He had thought that the surgery would buy them time together, but the reality was that it required her to be placed in a skilled nursing facility where registered nurses could care for her wounds, and where conditions were more sanitary than those at the farm house. Mr. Anderson's visual impairment made it impossible for him to tend to her alone, so, with his children all needing to maintain their employment, returning home was not a realistic option.

Mr. Anderson told Linda that he had left the decision regarding surgery to Melba. Dr. Browning always made his rounds early in the morning, before Mr. Anderson's children could get him to the hospital, so he had had no in-person discussion with the physician about his wife's surgery or other possible options. Mrs. Anderson had told him what she remembered the doctor saying, but she had led her husband to believe she'd be returning home after a few days of recovery in the hospital.

"I wish I'd asked more questions, but I'm not much on words and I don't talk like those nurses and doctors. I just thought they knew what was best for Melba. But I don't think it's best for us to be apart like this, and I don't think she'll ever get used to having all those bags to deal with. Those hospice people say she only has six months or less anyway. At least she could have spent her last days in our home and I could have been there and slept beside her."

Linda drew some comfort from knowing that the local hospice would be involved in Melba's nursing home care. Because Mrs. Anderson had both

Medicare and Medicaid, she could receive visits from the hospice team members (nurse, social worker, chaplain, nursing assistant, and perhaps a volunteer), who would direct her plan of care and provide support just as if she were at home.

Linda talked further with Mr. Anderson about his plans for visiting and being with Mrs. Anderson at the nursing facility. One of his children planned to drop him off every day on her way to work and pick him up on her way home. "But it's not like lying beside her at night and being there whenever she needs a listening ear," said Mr. Anderson sadly. "Our home ain't much, but it's a castle to us."

About ten minutes after Mrs. Anderson had left, the Andersons' daughter, Thelma Mattingly, hurried into the room.

"C'mon, Dad. We've got to get on to the nursing home so they won't just dump Mom off in that room all alone. Sorry I'm running late, but I had to finish filing some records at work before I could get away."

As Thelma helped Mr. Anderson get his coat and hat on, Linda quickly introduced herself. But there wasn't time to further discuss Melba's placement or the reactions of other family members.

"Thanks for listening to an old man like me," Mr. Anderson said as he shook Linda's hand. "It's hard for a farmer to understand all this medical talk and newfangled operations. I only wish you'd talked to me and Melba before all this happened. Things might have ended differently if we had only understood."

The Aftermath

After Mr. Anderson left with his daughter, Linda sat alone for a few minutes trying to collect her senses. Seeing this elderly man with leathery skin and callused hands weep openly and bare his soul to her left her feeling both melancholy and angry. She couldn't believe that the hospital staff had apparently ignored appropriate principles of proper informed consent.

Linda opened the medical record to enter her discharge note. While seated at the nursing station, she reviewed the record, hoping to get a better picture of what had occurred. The consent form was completed, signed by Mrs. Anderson and witnessed by one of the nurses who usually worked the evening shift. The nursing note said only: "Surgical consent form signed. Patient voiced understanding of the procedure as explained by Dr. Browning and said she had no questions."

When Linda's co-worker, Michelle, returned to work on Monday, Linda reported on Mrs. Anderson's discharge and her husband's regrets. Michelle was unaware of the emotions surrounding the surgery and discharge. She said the Andersons seemed agreeable to the placement when she spoke with them together on Thursday.

For some reason, Linda could not let go of this case without taking action to prevent further incidents in which patients and families were not truly informed about their care. Questions kept running through her mind: Did Mrs. Anderson really understand the consequences of the surgery when she signed the informed consent? Did Dr. Browning fully explain the care she would require? Did communication issues or memory problems affect the Andersons' comprehension? Why didn't someone talk with her husband about the surgery and its results? Was informed consent taken for granted at this research-oriented facility?

As an advocate for her elderly patients, Linda could not let the issues raised by this experience be forgotten. She knew she had to report the incident to others who would help her ensure that the informed consent process included all affected people and provided understandable information on which the patient could make an informed decision.

Who will listen to and help me? How can I do this in a professional manner? Are research and its related protocols more important here than the patient's informed choice? The questions kept coming, and Linda couldn't rest until they were answered.

The issue took on a new urgency when Michelle told her that it was routine for Dr. Browning to perform aggressive surgeries on elderly patients even when the treatment for their disease was futile. "No one dares question his right to recruit patients for his teaching and research. The man brings too much cash into the university with his research grants," Michelle had declared rather flippantly. "And did you know that he just recently received more money to study aggressive surgical interventions for gynecological cancer?"

Linda needed no further incentive for action, but she kept questioning herself as to what the next step should be.

18 | I Want to Talk to Your Supervisor!

Vicki M. Runnion

HOSPICE SOCIAL WORKER Marie Vincent was just walking into the office when the receptionist said, "You've got a call here, Marie—it's that same woman, and she's really hot."

Marie picked up the phone rtly. Immediately, without introduction, Suzanne began, "What is this you told my mother about APS [Adult Protective Services] and going home? She was adjusting to being at Eastminster and you got her all stirred up. She isn't competent to make these decisions, and certainly not to go home. I want to talk to your supervisor, and I don't want you to visit her anymore."

Knowing there might well be unpleasant consequences to what she needed to say, Marie tried hard to keep her voice under control. "Well, I do need to call APS and let them sort through this. Actually, your mother's competence doesn't have to be proved, incompetence has to be proved, and you'd have to be the one to initiate that, since you are the one who sees her in that light."

Development of this decision case was supported in part by funding from the University of South Carolina College of Social Work. It was prepared solely to provide material for class discussion and not to suggest either effective or ineffective handling of the situation depicted. Although the case is based on field research regarding an actual situation, names and certain facts may have been disguised to protect confidentiality. The author wishes to thank the anonymous case reporter for cooperation in making this account available for the benefit of social work students and instructors.

"I want to talk to your supervisor, I want her name," Suzanne practically shouted.

"Her name is Becky Sammons," Marie replied. "You're welcome to call her."

Her ear ringing, Marie put down the phone. In her stomach she felt the slight gnawing she had come to recognize as a response to uncertainty and misunderstanding. *I'd better go warn Becky that she's likely to get a call,* Marie thought. *That is, if Suzanne hasn't already gotten to her.* As she walked to Becky's office, Marie vacillated between feeling angry at Suzanne and feeling perplexed about her inability to connect with this daughter whose mother desperately wanted to go home once more before she died.

Nashville, Tennessee

Nashville boasted a wealth of health care resources for a city of its size—just over half a million in the 2000 census. Its status as the capital of Tennessee and also as the home to Vanderbilt University, along with its strategic geographic location, attracted a wide range of resources to the area.

Hospice of Central Tennessee

Hospice of Central Tennessee (HCT) served six counties surrounding Nashville and Davidson County. Founded in 1983 as a not-for-profit organization, it had grown to the point that it was in the top category of census and budget size in the statistics kept by the National Hospice and Palliative Care Organization. It had a solid track record of meeting needs in the various communities in its service area and was well regarded, and well supported, by those communities. Thus far, there was no competition, but the administrative staff were well aware that this could change, and they paid particular attention to the actions of two for-profit chains of hospices that were moving into adjacent states.

But HCT had had its share of hard times too—upheavals in administration, steep increases in regulation, staff layoffs during a protracted slump in the census, some mid-level managers with personal issues that made them problematic as supervisors of direct-care staff—and some employees who had been there during many of these difficulties found it hard to recover their sense of confidence, trust, and being valued and supported. The mood around the office could swing pretty wildly from one day to the next, depending on whom one encountered. But overall, the organization's response to the challenges it faced was to reexamine everything about its functioning and try to foster creativity and an openness to change among its staff.

The health care staff were assigned to one of ten teams serving patients in their own homes, four teams serving patients in long-term care facilities, a specialized pediatric team, or one of six teams that staffed the two inpatient units around the clock. Each of the home care teams comprised two nurses, a chaplain, a social worker, and a nursing assistant, but given each team's unique blend of temperaments, experience, and particular strengths, they differed significantly.

Marie Vincent

Marie Vincent had been a hospice social worker for seventeen years, and she still loved her work—not just liked it, *loved* it. Loved meeting people at a deep level, hearing their stories, their pain, and the ways they were making sense of their lives as they were nearing the end. She had weathered many of the storms and "sea changes" in the organization—changes that were difficult for some of her colleagues to adapt to, and that often caused grumbling and sometimes deeper distress. But she had found a way to move through them without losing her balance or her passion for her work. She often said it was the work itself that helped her maintain perspective—focusing on the families she served. And then she might also smile and say that the time she spent each week with her three long-and-eagerly awaited grandchildren probably had something to do with it as well.

Sixty-two years old, Marie lived alone next door to her son and his family, which included two of the three grandchildren. One of the features of home that delighted her was the protected pathway between the two houses, so that the grandchildren could easily walk over to visit their "GrandMarie." She enjoyed babysitting frequently, one night almost every week, but had chosen to keep her weekends free for visiting with friends, longer treks than her daily walk, working on projects with the little neighborhood Unitarian church she had joined, reading, and just puttering.

Marie was known among the social workers at HCT to be especially intuitive, and empathic even with some clients who were hard to like. On her team, she was usually the one who offered an interpretation that helped the others come to understand clients' difficult, demanding, even seemingly unreasonable behavior and thus lessen their frustration or irritation.

Hospice Care for Doris Blackwell

The hospice team—nurse Annie Eldridge, chaplain Betsy Overton, and social worker Marie Vincent—first met Doris Blackwell in March 2002. Doris was seventy-three years old and living alone in an established older neighborhood in Nashville, on Warner Parkway, near the park. She had chronic obstructive pulmonary disease (COPD), partly the result of lifelong heavy smoking. She had an oxygen concentrator in her living room, with plenty of tubing to reach into the bedroom and kitchen. In spite of the constant air hunger she felt, she wasn't interested in quitting smoking at this point, so she alternated between smoking and using the oxygen. Doris acknowledged that lately she'd been sleeping in the recliner in her living room, because she felt like she was suffocating when she lay down in her bed. So, in effect, she now used only a small circle of rooms—living room, kitchen, and bathroom—in order to minimize exertion as much as possible, a restriction common to many of the team's patients with COPD.

Doris was not able to do much at all toward maintaining her home, due to her shortness of breath. She told the team that she had a housekeeper who came twice a week, a reliable handyman, and a lawn-care service. Her daughter bought prepared meals for her at Kagan's Market, a small but full-service neighborhood grocery, and all she had to do was heat them in the microwave. Even though she was tiny, weighing less than 100 pounds, Doris said her appetite was fairly good, and that she ate something at every mealtime. The nurse, Annie, asked if she could check in the fridge to see what sorts of things she was getting, and confirmed to the others that there were meals for another couple of days.

Doris reported that her daughter, Suzanne Winters, and Suzanne's husband, Ed, and two daughters, Sarah and Jessica, ages thirteen and ten, lived across town. The team recognized the address as one of the newer, very upscale housing developments. Doris said Suzanne stopped by every two or three days. She also reported that a neighbor, Martha, helped her out anytime she needed it. Martha was a widow herself, a little younger than Doris.

She still had a car, so she would take Doris to the store or run errands for her and then stay and visit, or do minor chores. Doris paid her nominally for her help; the arrangement was beneficial for both of them.

Doris seemed fairly reserved in talking about her daughter, answering the team's questions but offering little else, but it did seem that Suzanne was involved and helpful, and Doris had some other supports in place. The team went through several variations of the questions they usually asked about her goals, her wishes for this time, but Doris's responses were all some version of, "I can't think of anything, honey." She seemed safe and contented.

They were quiet as they left Doris's home and got back into Marie's car, but as she pulled away from the curb, Betsy said, "Well, that may have been the least informative first visit I've ever had. She seems satisfied with how things are, and the basics are covered for now, so I guess it's okay, but I surely don't have a good sense of who she is at any depth."

"I know," Annie agreed. "I feel like we just barely scratched the surface with her. I hope we have time to get to know her a little better before there's a crisis."

As they walked back into the office for a meeting, Marie said, "You know, I remember this woman. It's been bugging me the whole time—while we were there, and on the way back—but now I remember. I used to live on Warner Park Court years ago, when my kids were young, and she had a daughter a couple or three years older than my Kendra. I didn't actually know her, but I would see her out walking. She was always immaculately coiffed. I noticed her because she always kept her eyes focused straight ahead and she never smiled, at me or anyone else that I saw. She really was not a relational neighbor at all. So the way she was with us today was pretty consistent with how she was back then—courteous, but not offering much more than that. I wonder how her daughter turned out. Oh well, I guess we'll find out soon enough—I'll call her and see if she can be there for one of our next visits."

When Marie called Suzanne, she sounded very much like her mother—courteous, but not volunteering much information. She indicated that she was very busy, but that she visited her mother every few days and was sure she would run into one of the team when they happened to be there at the same time. Marie pushed a little, to inquire about her availability to provide more care if and when Doris's condition deteriorated, and Suzanne told her that there was a trust fund established by her father to provide care for her mother. She said she would call Marie or the nurse if she had any concerns. As she hung up, Marie thought, *Okay, I'll go at it from the other direction—ask Doris if she will let me know when she's expecting Suzanne to visit, and make sure to drop in at the same time.*

Things progressed smoothly for the next several weeks. HCT began to send a nursing assistant to help Doris with taking a shower. She agreed to have a Lifeline installed so that she could call for help if she were in a crisis, and—a little surprising to Marie—agreed for a keybox to be put on the front door so that they could have access to the house in case she wasn't able to come to the door.

Visits were always pleasant, but Marie expressed some frustration to Annie and Betsy at one of their regular team meetings: "The conversation is always just about a quarter-inch deep—it never goes beyond the superficial!" Betsy acknowledged that her visits went pretty much the same way.

Then one morning, just as the team was wrapping up a meeting, Marie was paged to take a phone call. Gail, the receptionist, said, "I'm sorry to bother you, I know you're in your meeting, but this lady sounds really upset."

It was Suzanne, and she was indeed upset. "Mother has taken to calling me at any hour of the day or night, for the least little thing. She called at two this morning to tell me she was cold!"

Marie could hear the stress in Suzanne's voice as she went on. "She's really confused a lot of the time. She's not only sick physically, she's mentally ill too. I don't know how much more of this I can take—it upsets me and interrupts my sleep, but the calls wake my husband and sometimes my daughters too. I think we are going to have to start looking into nursing home placement for her."

Trying to get a sense of whether the patient's mental status had deteriorated significantly since her last visit two days before, Marie asked, "Has your mother ever been diagnosed with any mental illness before now?"

"No," Suzanne almost snapped back, "but she should have been!"

When Marie tried to explore her response, Suzanne calmed down and returned to talking about needing to explore nursing home placement. Marie assured her that she would visit Doris that day, to see how she was, and asked Suzanne to let her know some times that they could have a family meeting to discuss plans for whatever increased level of care her mother might need. They set a meeting for Thursday morning, two days later, and Marie left voice mail messages for her team members so that they could plan their schedules accordingly.

When she visited that afternoon, Doris seemed about the same as on previous visits, although perhaps even a little thinner. Marie asked whether she had times when she felt anxious, maybe at night, and called her daughter. "She's a little worried about you, Doris, wondering if perhaps you need someone here with you, or maybe to begin to think about moving to a facility where someone will be there to care for you anytime you need it. We're planning to meet here Thursday morning to talk about some options with you."

"Oh no, honey, I inherited a lot of money from my parents, and my husband set up a trust fund for me before he died, so that there would be plenty of money to pay for someone to stay here with me so I don't ever have to go to a nursing home. My daughter is the trustee for the account. But I don't think I need someone here all the time yet."

"Well, maybe not quite yet. We'll talk about that with Suzanne Thursday morning, okay?"

Thursday morning, Marie was just heading out of the office to meet Annie and Suzanne at Doris's house when her cell phone rang. It was Suzanne. "I'm so sorry, Marie, but I'm not going to be able to get by Mother's this morning. I had completely forgotten that I have an appointment to get my nails done. We'll have to do it another time."

Taken by surprise, Marie agreed, and Suzanne ended the call. She went back inside to ask the receptionist to page Annie and let her know the meeting was off. Then she called Doris to let her know that since Suzanne couldn't come and since team members were visiting other days that week, they wouldn't have the meeting that day.

"That's okay, dearie," Doris replied, "I didn't really think it was necessary anyway. But you girls just come visit anytime you can."

Feeling a tinge of frustration over the last-minute change in plans, Marie made another call to set up a visit with another family, and headed out.

Early the next week, there was another lengthy call from Suzanne. Another family meeting was scheduled, and then canceled the morning of the meeting. "I'm so sorry, Marie, but I'd completely forgotten that I'm starting a new exercise class at the gym this afternoon."

The same thing happened the following week, only it was a hair appointment that time.

In their team meeting the morning after the third last-moment cancellation, after venting for a bit, Betsy remarked, "You know, Marie, obviously this is becoming a pattern. And I'm wondering if this isn't maybe how Suzanne is coping—setting up the meeting, thinking she is going to start the process of getting her mother placed somewhere, relieves some tension or anxiety, and then she feels better and doesn't need the visit after all. Her feeling of being at the end of her rope goes away once she dumps it on you."

"I agree," Annie chimed in, "but I did notice a little more forgetfulness in Doris yesterday and Monday, so I think we do need to try to set a meeting that Suzanne can actually come to, and talk about plans for when more care is needed. Maybe we can find out more about the trust fund and how that can be used."

"Okay, I'll try again," Marie promised. "This time I'll ask her to go get her calendar and be sure there isn't a conflict."

Finally it happened—a meeting scheduled, and no last-minute cancellation. And this time, they all found Doris to be quite confused. At one point she was telling a nearly incoherent story about Billy Joe and how he made the best mud pies ever. Marie looked to Suzanne for clarification, and Suzanne said Billy Joe was a childhood neighbor she hadn't seen in thirty years or more, since second grade—not even a close friend. After listening for a little while longer, Annie and Marie went out into the kitchen to confer.

"She hasn't started any new meds, and it looks like she has been taking her usual ones—I just set up her pill box Tuesday, and yesterday's and today's pills are gone," Annie noted.

"Annie, could she possibly have had a stroke?" Marie wondered aloud.

"I guess that's a possibility. But I'm going to see if we can get her into the IPU [inpatient unit] for evaluation, maybe do some labs," Annie responded.

When Annie called the IPU to ask about a bed, none was available, but a patient was scheduled to go home the next day, and the unit manager said Doris could have that one. They went back into the living room to make plans with Suzanne and Doris. Suzanne agreed to the admission, and she and Marie made a couple of calls to people on Marie's list of private-duty caregivers and were able to find someone to stay with Doris until she could be admitted to the IPU.

The morning following Doris's admission to the IPU, Annie left a voice mail for her teammates: "Hey y'all, I just talked to Dr. Morris down at the IPU, and he said Doris's problem was that she wasn't using her oxygen. Her oxygen level was way low—82 percent. But she started to improve immediately once she'd been back on the oxygen for a few hours. They said they will be ready to discharge her later today."

Later that morning, when Marie called to check on Doris, Jaime Ellison, the IPU social worker, told Marie that Doris was eager to go home. "She says she feels fine and that she doesn't even know how she got here, but she wants to go home."

But Jaime said that when she had called Suzanne to say she could come pick up her mother, Suzanne's response was, "No way. We are going to California on vacation in just a few days, and I can't have her alone at home while I'm that far away."

After concluding her conversation with Jaime, Marie called Suzanne to talk with her about plans for Doris.

"Suzanne, your mother and the sitter who stayed with her right before she went into the IPU got along very well, and that sitter will do twenty-four-hour care. What about having her stay with your mom while you are in California, and then you can reassess how she is doing when you get back?"

"No, Marie, I'm just not willing to take that chance. What if the sitter gets sick, or something else happens so that she can't stay? I just can't count on that. We'll be too far away. I have been making some calls, and there is an assisted living room at Eastminster Terrace. She can go there while we are away, and then we'll see how she is when I get back. Can you let her know that?"

Marie shook her head as she listened, and then responded, "Suzanne, she is very clear-minded now, and she wants to go home. I think she should hear about your concerns from you."

"All right," Suzanne sighed deeply, "I'll go up to the unit right now to tell her. I want to get this settled today so I can get ready for my trip."

Knowing it was quite possible there would be a scene when Suzanne announced her plans to Doris, Marie decided to go and see whether she could help.

She could hear Doris as soon as she walked onto the unit an hour later. "No, Suzanne, I am not going to any nursing home! Ed left money for me so that I wouldn't have to do that! I want to go home! You are keeping me here against my will, and I want to go home! Right now! They said I could leave, and that's what I want to do."

Jaime came out of another patient's room and caught Marie before she entered Doris's room. "Doris already tried to call a cab to take her home this morning, but she wasn't able to manage all the extra digits necessary to get an outside line. She's pretty upset—as you can undoubtedly hear. Good luck!"

Marieentered Doris's room quietly, not wanting to disrupt their conversation until she knew what was needed. Doris became more and more agitated, and angry, roundly cursing out all the staff, including the medical director. "You all are Nazis, keeping me here against my will. I have my rights, and I want to go home!"

Dr. Morris did a quick mini-mental status exam, which Doris passed. "She really is competent to make this decision," he told Suzanne.

"Well, get another opinion. You aren't a psychiatrist, are you?"

So Dr. Morris called for a psychiatry consult, and a staff doctor was able to come right over from the psychiatry unit. He also found Doris competent to make her own decisions. Talking with Suzanne in the hall after the exam, he said, "She's really frail, and I agree that twenty-four-hour care is most appropriate for her, but I think a judge would determine that she legally could make her own decisions."

Suzanne went back into Doris's room to try to persuade her. "Please, Mother, Ed and the girls and I are going to California next week on vacation. You know how excited the girls have been about it. I just can't think of being that far away from here knowing that you are home without any family in town to call on if something was wrong. I'd be worried sick the whole time, and none of us would be able to enjoy the trip. Please just go to Eastminster while we are gone. As soon as we get back, you can go home, I promise."

"Well, let me go home tonight and stay there," Doris began to relent, "and I'll go to Eastminster tomorrow."

"No, Mother," Suzanne insisted, "we have to take that room today if we're going to take it at all, and arranging for the sitter to stay another night at home with you is just too complicated. I've got a lot to do to get ready to go. It won't be for long, but I need for you to go on to Eastminster while we're gone, and you can go home when we get back from our trip. Please."

Very, very reluctantly, Doris agreed.

Eastminster Terrace was well known as a lovely facility and the staff were kind and attentive, but assisted living wasn't designed to provide medical supervision. The third morning after Doris arrived, the housekeeper came into her room and found her bottle of Oxycontin pills spilled on the bedside table. Doris was confused and seemed weaker, so they sent her to the hospital and called HCT to report the transfer. More lab work was done, and the hospital

ER called both Annie and the director of nursing (DON) at Eastminster to report that she had not overdosed on any medication. Her oxygen level had been very low when she first came in, but since they had had her on oxygen, she had improved significantly. So the DON called Suzanne in California and reported the situation. Suzanne agreed that she could call the sitter who had stayed with Doris previously and ask that person to stay with her twenty-four hours a day at Eastminster until Suzanne returned.

Doris was eagerly awaiting Suzanne's return so that she could go home. She made the same plea to everyone who visited: "Will you take me home? Can I pay you to take me home?"

Several days after Suzanne's return, she agreed to meet Marie at Eastminster to talk with Doris. Doris could hardly wait. But when Suzanne arrived, she had a long list of reasons why her mother couldn't go home. "I'll still have to be involved in scheduling people to be there with you, and it will just be too complicated." To every one of her objections, Doris had a response. Finally Suzanne reached the end of her list. "No, Mother. I cannot care for you at home, and there is no one we can trust or pay enough to take care of you around the clock, and you can't be alone anymore. It's just too hard."

Seeing her mother's disappointment, Suzanne turned to Marie. "*You* manage it, Marie. *You* arrange it all, take care of it all, and then she can go home."

Swallowing her irritation, Marie responded, "That really isn't how it works, Suzanne. The thing is, your mother—" then, turning to Doris, "The thing is, Doris, that the doctor felt you were competent to make your own decisions, and you, Suzanne, are in charge of the trust fund, so you are in charge of paying for the things that would make it possible for your mother to do what she wants to do. Somehow the two of you need to reach an understanding."

Doris turned and reached for the telephone.

"Wait, Mother, "Suzanne interrupted. "You can go home. But not today. The air conditioning has been off for a couple of weeks and it's very hot out, so we will have to go by the house and turn it on, and get things ready for you. You can go tomorrow or the next day at the latest, okay?"

Doris settled back into her chair with a small smile. "That will be wonderful."

Marie left the meeting not entirely convinced that Suzanne had given in so quickly and would work toward getting her mother home promptly, but trying to give her the benefit of the doubt.

The next morning, however, she was not surprised to hear from Suzanne. "My husband and I had a long talk last night, and we talked to some other friends of ours, and we all agree that it's just not a good idea for Mother to go home, and we just can't do it."

"Are you going to tell your mother this?" Marie asked.

"Yes, I'll go there tonight and tell her," Suzanne replied. But she didn't.

Two days later, Suzanne visited and told Doris, "This woman who has been staying with you and was going to be with you at home is just not acceptable, Mother. Some of your medicines are missing. You're going to have to move over to the nursing home part of the building, where someone can take better care of you." And she began to push her mother's wheelchair through the halls to the nursing home wing.

Doris was livid. As soon as Suzanne left, she tried to get up and leave as well. She got as far as the parking lot before staff caught up with her, and brought her back and restrained her. Another psych evaluation was ordered, and the next day, Marie read in Doris's chart at Eastminster Terrace that the new doctor found Doris to be very depressed and frail, but still competent to make her own decisions.

Dreading the conversation, Marie called Suzanne with news of the newest evaluation. "Suzanne, the doctor has said Doris is competent to make her own decisions, and she desperately wants to go home. Would you be willing to let her try it with another sitter? Just to see if it can work?"

"Marie, that would cost over $100,000 a year; I don't think very many people could afford $100,000 a year—could you?"

Marie replied, "Well, this isn't really about me, it's about the trust, and your mother. What if you don't think about how much it would cost for a year? Your mother said she wished she could just go home for a day, that she left her home not knowing she was leaving it, much less that she wouldn't go back. What about a month? Would there be enough money to let her go home for a month and see how she functions with a sitter?"

"Well, you may be able to think in terms of a month, Marie, but I am a long-term thinker, and I think in terms of a year, and that would be too expensive. I know she would not be satisfied with just a month there, and a year would be too expensive."

Gently, Marie raised the issue of Doris's hospice prognosis. "Suzanne, you know your mother is very ill, or she wouldn't be a hospice patient. We think it's very unlikely that your mother will live as long as a year, according to what her physician has said. It's really more likely to be a matter of just a few months."

"No, that just wouldn't work at all. I'd have to call all those people, and they'd get sick or have car trouble or something. And are *you* going to come in the middle of the night to take care of her when the schedule falls apart? Because if you aren't, then it just can't work."

Completely out of ideas for any further persuasion at the moment, Marie ended the call as quickly as she could.

Turning to Betsy, who sat at the desk next to hers, Marie quietly exploded. "Oooh, that woman! She has all the warmth of a fish. She has *not once, ever,* expressed any regard for how her mother feels or what she wants. She's so . . . so damned busy with her tanning appointments and her exercise classes that she can't be the least bit inconvenienced so that her mother can spend her last days where she wants so much to be!"

Betsy hesitated for a moment, and then said, "Marie, I struggle to connect with her too. But I keep asking myself, how did their relationship get to be like this?—and since I don't know the answer to that, I try not to judge it."

"You're right, of course you're right," Marie responded, "and remembering to ask that usually helps me get some perspective, with other families. But it hasn't helped so far with this one . . . and, Betsy, I don't like it that I can't find any empathy in me for Suzanne because I don't feel any in her for her mother. The very sound of her voice, that saccharine sing-song way she speaks to Doris, hits me like fingernails screeching on a blackboard."

"Maybe you should ask for another social worker to be assigned," Betsy suggested.

Marie paused. "Well, that would feel like admitting total failure, and I feel like I'd be letting you and Annie down, not to mention Doris, having to bring another social worker onto the team. But I'll think about it."

The following week, Eastminster scheduled a care planning meeting. It was routine, but Gerri Evans, the social services director, pleaded with Marie for the hospice team to attend. "We're really struggling here, and we need your participation," she said. "We've never had someone who was actually lucid and oriented and also cursing at our staff and angry all the time—sometimes some patients with dementia are like that, but this is really different."

"We'll be there," Marie promised. "At ten o'clock, right?"

"Right," Gerri said, "and thanks!"

Marie was surprised to walk in to the conference room at Eastminster and find Suzanne there. Doris herself was not present, though it was customary for patients who were able to participate in a discussion to be included. But the tiny conference room was very nearly full, with Helen Lillard, the Eastminster DON; Karen Godfrey, the activities director; and Gerri Evans, the social services director; plus the three hospice staff members and Suzanne.

As Marie and her colleagues sat down, Helen started the discussion. "Mrs. Blackwell is really unhappy about being here. We all need to think of ways we can help her adjust to being here, to be more contented," she said, and Suzanne was nodding.

"I think we need to be truthful with her, and we need to attend to her grief. She has really strong feelings about this, and we need to get with those feelings," Marie countered.

Just then, Doris was wheeled into the room. As Marie watched the others respond, it was like seeing a swarm of bees hovering around Doris.

"Oh, Doris, we want so much for you to be happy here," said Karen Godfrey. Marie thought she might gag at the saccharine tone of Karen's voice. Karen went on to ask Doris about several suggestions, from participation in the Bible study group to getting two ice creams with her evening meal. Marie looked at Betsy and Annie, wondering whether they heard the same level of condescension and patronizing that she did.

Meanwhile, Doris just kept saying, "No, that won't help. I want to go home." Finally she asked the aide if she could return to her room, saying that she needed to take a pain pill and lie down.

After Doris left, Suzanne looked around the room and announced, "You just have to help her adjust. That has to be the focus."

Marie responded, "I believe that she needs to hear the truth, not to be deceived. If she can't go home, she needs to know that so she can deal with it."

"Oh no, there would be the biggest blow-up," Suzanne insisted. "If you think she has acted out thus far, you can't imagine how it would be if she is told that it's final."

"I think the blow-ups now are at least in part due to the fact that she isn't being told the truth." Marie tried to keep her voice even. "So she is constantly hoping and crashing, hoping and crashing."

"Well, I'm not going to be here to clean up the mess," Suzanne retorted.

"I agree," Helen said. "I think it's better not to close off that hope. So, for now, we won't tell her."

Talking with Doris

Marie dreaded her next visit with Doris, not sure how she could get through it and not be truthful if Doris asked her directly about what was going to happen. She walked in and found Doris clearly waiting for her.

She'd barely gotten a greeting out when Doris asked, "Is there anything I can do, legally, to get out of here? Suzanne isn't going to take me home, I've realized."

Marie hesitated, and then responded, "I'm not positive, Doris. You can call Adult Protective Services and ask them to investigate, to sort things out and see if it would be possible, in their opinion, for you to return home. I don't know if it will do any good or not."

And Doris said, "Would you do that? Would you please call them?"

Marie said that she would.

The next morning, Marie was just walking into the office when the receptionist said, "You've got a call here, Marie—it's that same woman, and she's really hot."

Marie picked up the phone reluctantly. Immediately, Suzanne said, "What is this you told my mother about APS and getting out of here? She was adjusting to being at Eastminster, and you got her all stirred up. She was doing better, and you got her all stirred up. She isn't competent to make these decisions, and certainly not to go home. I want to talk to your supervisor, and I don't want you to visit her anymore."

Knowing there might well be unpleasant consequences to what she was going to say, Marie tried hard to keep her voice under control. "Well, I do need to call APS and let them sort through this. Actually, your mother's competence doesn't have to be proved, incompetence has to be proved, and you'd have to be the one to have to initiate that, since you are the one who sees her in that light."

"I want to talk to your supervisor, I want her name," Suzanne practically shouted.

"Her name is Becky Sammons," Marie replied. "You're welcome to call her."

19 | Drowning Sorrows (A)

Vicki M. Runnion

Telephone Assessment

"Howard," hospice social worker Karla Thomas asked, "do you remember that you agreed not to be drinking before my next visit?"

"Yeah, I remember," Howard Harriman acknowledged.

"Your voice sounds like you have been—am I right?"

"Yeah." Silence.

Karla paused, wondering whether to stick with what she had told Howard at her last visit, and about the risk to his safety as well as her own.

Dandridge, Tennessee

In 2001, Dandridge was a small town with a population just under 10,000. Located in Jefferson County, about 35 miles east of Knoxville, Tennessee, and a similar distance from Sevierville and tourist mecca Pigeon Forge, it was situated along Douglas Lake, one of the Tennessee Valley Authority series of lakes.

Development of this decision case was supported in part by the University of South Carolina College of Social Work and the Project on Death in America. It was prepared solely to provide material for class discussion and not to suggest either effective or ineffective handling of the situation depicted. Although the case is based on field research regarding an actual situation, names and certain facts may have been disguised to protect confidentiality. As indicated by the (A), the instructor's manual provides a continuation of the case. The authors wish to thank the case reporter for cooperation in making this account available for the benefit of social work students and practitioners.

It was the second oldest town in Tennessee, with a once-notorious stagecoach stop. That slight historical significance, along with the natural beauty of the area, drew visitors and more than a few retirees not interested in becoming sunbirds.

The newcomers gradually learned about their long-established neighbors: a few well-to-do old families, whose homes were set apart by their long driveways and the whitewashed wood fences that contained their Tennessee walking horses, and the many more middle-class and poor mountain people whose ancestors were among the first settlers to move west across the Blue Ridge and Smoky Mountains.

This mix of origins made for an equally distinctive mix of socioeconomic status, political persuasions, priorities, and lifestyles. People mostly practiced a live-and-let-live philosophy of not meddling in their neighbors' business, but occasionally there were conflicts between what some called "the haves and the have-nots," often regarding issues such as zoning and community planning.

Hospice of the Smokies

Hospice of the Smokies (HS) had been established as a not-for-profit organization in Knoxville in 1981, first serving only the increasingly urban Knox County. But over the years, it had extended from one neighboring county to another, primarily because of its firm commitment (along with that of two other large hospices in the state association) to work toward assuring that every Tennessean had access to hospice care. But the more financially oriented staff and board members also acknowledged that it helped their bottom line to spread administrative costs over as large a patient census as possible. By 2001, Hospice of the Smokies served fourteen east Tennessee counties and had four regional satellite offices, in Newport, Gatlinburg, Greenville, and Dandridge. Each of these offices had a manager and kept its own medical records for the patients to whom it was currently providing services, but most of the administration was centralized in the Knoxville office.

Karla Thomas

Karla Thomas was in her late forties, and had worked at Hospice of the Smokies for most of her professional career. She had gone back to college in her early thirties, choosing social work because it would allow her to move quickly through both undergraduate and graduate programs, and she felt she didn't have time to waste. She'd already done enough of that, partying her way through one year of college right after high school, then leaving school to get married and raise a family. She worked part-time and, as her children grew up, full-time as a bookkeeper in a law practice. And she worked to recover from what she had come to acknowledge was her alcoholism.

In her social work studies, two of Karla's three field placements were with Hospice of the Smokies—first with the bereavement department in her B.S.W. program, and then with the social work department in her second M.S.W. placement. When she graduated in 1987, HS was just expanding into two new counties and establishing the first of its satellite offices in Dandridge, and offered Karla a position as a social worker. She worked for a little over two years in that job, then began to pick up some responsibilities as a bereavement counselor. She enjoyed bereavement work, although she didn't like trying to prioritize the needs of patients who were dying against those of family members who were bereaved. So when a bereavement counselor position opened up in her office, she jumped at the chance. She'd been offered several possible promotions since then, each time HS grew again, but she was contented and believed she was effective in what she was doing, and she chose to stay put.

Shannon Worley

Shannon Worley came to Hospice of the Smokies in 1996 after several years' experience in mental health. She had earned a B.S.W. in 1990 and immediately entered an M.S.W. program. After earning the master's degree, Shannon had worked four years at the Smoky Mountain Community Mental Health Center. At Hospice of the Smokies, she first worked four years as a social worker in the Newport office, then applied for a supervisory position based in the Dandridge office. She had been a little hesitant about that at first, not wanting to compete with Karla Thomas, who had been so supportive and helpful when she first started, but Karla had assured her that she was not interested in the position and urged her to apply.

Shannon's responsibilities included supervision of all the counseling staff for the Dandridge office—three social workers besides Karla and two chaplains. The chaplains and other social workers had all been hired more recently than she, but had varying levels of experience. She'd had difficulty with only one, a woman who had been through a nasty divorce and whose work had deteriorated seriously during that time and not recovered. Shannon had had the difficult experience of coaching and then terminating her. "I hope I don't have to do that again anytime soon!" she told her own supervisor, Cheryl Wetherly, the vice president for counseling services. But Shannon felt she had learned a lot in the process.

At first she felt uncomfortable supervising Karla, who was both about fifteen years older than she and had almost ten years more experience at hospice. But Karla was reliable and conscientious about her work and straightforward in her communication, and gradually they settled into a comfortable relationship. Karla didn't seem to need much in the way of supervision, either clinically or administratively. Now and then she would stick her head in Shannon's office and ask a quick question to confirm her own thoughts about how to proceed with one issue or another, and Shannon often found herself doing the same thing with Karla.

Referral to Bereavement

At a team meeting in mid-April, Natalie Morris, one of the hospice nurses, reported, "Sarah Harriman died April seventh at the hospice care center. She was seventy-two years old. Her ex-husband, Howard, seventy-nine, was her primary caregiver, and he will be the primary bereaved person needing follow-up. Sarah was our patient twice. She was admitted in February 2000, for lung cancer with bone metastasis. Rhonda was her nurse then. Evidently she seemed to have stabilized, because she was discharged in early October. Then we readmitted her at the end of December, and I got her since Rhonda wasn't here anymore. Rhonda's notes indicated that both of them were big drinkers, and that Sarah was always pushing for more and more pain medication. And she said the caregiving was less than ideal. But Howard had evidently stopped drinking around the time we readmitted her—I never saw or smelled or sensed any effects of alcohol anytime I was there, and I think that's true for the rest of the team. Anyway, he took really good care of her, and I didn't have any problems with her wanting too much medicine. She got extremely short of air about a week before she died, and we admitted her to the care center on the fourth, and she died there, like I said, on the seventh.

With Howard's history of alcohol abuse, I'm concerned about how he will do, and I hope you can follow up with him pretty soon, Karla. Oh, I nearly forgot, they have a son, James, but they have not had any contact with him in many years. But James has a son, Jimmy, who has a baby girl. They visited about weekly while Sarah was alive, and I think they will be a good support to Howard. He really lights up when he talks about that baby."

"Sure, I'll give him a call this week and see if I can go out," Karla agreed. She was able to set up a visit for the following Monday.

First Visit

Karla missed the driveway the first time she drove along the one-lane road to Mr. Harriman's house. *I'd have hated to have to come out here on call late at night,* she thought. *I don't know how I'd find it in the dark, if I missed it in broad daylight. And there aren't any neighbors to ask, for sure.* Turning around, she drove a quarter mile back and finally saw the narrow gravel drive, lined with trees.

Howard was waiting out on the porch of the old white farmhouse when Karla drove up. As she walked past him through the front door, Karla caught a whiff of bourbon. *Uh-oh,* she thought. *He's drinking again. That didn't take long.*

Sitting on the sofa, Karla was bit surprised when Howard scooted the armchair closer to her and sat down. "Tell me about Sarah, Mr. Harriman. I know you were divorced, but you'd been together a long time, even after that, right?"

"How did you know that?" he asked, seeming a little disgruntled.

"Her nurse, Natalie, told me."

"I guess Sarah told her about everything," he said, shaking his head. He went on to talk about how they had met, and to describe his wife. "She just loved to do . . . well, everything, seemed like. She was pretty strong-minded. She loved to travel, and she was in this club that traveled together, and they would pay for her to go someplace they were interested in as sort of an advance scout or something, and report back to them how it was, the accommodations and the food. And by damn, she was going to do it, whether I liked it or not. I'd just as soon stay right here—I can probably count on my fingers the nights I spent away from here, and I didn't really like it when she was gone, but she went right ahead and went by herself. She's been all kinds of places—Europe, out west. Sometimes I'd go with her, but mostly I stayed home. I think she divorced me over that Europe trip—I didn't want her to go, and she didn't want me telling her what to do. But we always lived together, mostly got on pretty good except for that."

"Tell me about the rest of your family, Howard. You have a son and grandson, right?"

"We had a son. He's still living, but I don't see or hear from him—we had a parting of the ways while he was in high school and just never have gotten it worked out. But he has a son, Jimmy, who lives over in Sevierville, and he comes by about every week. He's married, got a baby girl that I think the world of."

"Oh? How old is she?"

"She just turned one a few weeks ago—while Sarah was in that care center. She's a smart little thing, just jabbers away, sounds like nonsense to me, but I think she's real clear about what she means. She's just started to walking, but she's a little crab when she's crawling—fast! Hard to keep up with her."

Karla listened without interrupting for a long while, but Howard seemed to stay mostly on the surface, so she began to probe a little. "Was drinking always part of your relationship with Sarah? Was there ever a time when it wasn't?" Learning that Howard had once stopped for a period of two years, some fifteen years earlier, she asked, "How was that time?"

"Frankly, ma'am, it was one of the worst times in my life. It was right around the time we divorced, and I was just trying to see what I could do to hold on to her." Karla thought he was going to continue in that vein and was rather surprised at Howard's next words. "I hope this is helping you some, 'cause it's not doing me a lick of good."

Karla encouraged Howard to talk about how he was feeling now, since Sarah's death, and what he was thinking about how his life would be.

He thought for a moment and started to answer, but his voice cracked and tears came to his eyes. He waited another moment to compose himself, and then shook his head. "It's just so damn lonely. I just don't know if I can take it." And then he reached out to her, placing his hand on her thigh.

Startled, she said, "Howard, you know why I'm here. I'm here to talk with you about your loss, about your grief. I understand your being lonely, but we have to be clear about what we're doing here."

"Are you afraid of me?" he asked. "'Cause I would never hurt you."

"I believe you, Howard, I don't think you'd try to hurt me, but you touching my leg like that makes me uncomfortable, and I just needed to be clear with you about why I'm here."

"Okay, I understand."

"Howard, I know you're hurting a lot, and I need to ask you, do you ever think about hurting yourself?"

"Yeah, sometimes I do, that I could just put a stop to it if things get too bad."

"Do you know how you would do it?" she pushed.

He replied in a matter-of-fact way that sent alarms up her spine: "I'd shoot myself."

He insisted that he wasn't thinking about doing it anytime soon, and he was open to her return but declined information about the mental health center. "No, I've not been there, and I'm not going to go now." And he gave the same response when she asked if he would consider trying some AA meetings.

"Howard, I'd like to be supportive, like to help you if possible, and I think that it *is* possible. But if you continue to drink, I don't think grief counseling will do you much good, because your head isn't clear. You can't really take things in if you're drinking, and you can't do much about any changes. Do you think it's possible you could be sober if I come back another time?"

"Yeah, I think I could. I'll give it a try, I really will," he replied, nodding. So Karla made an appointment to come back in two weeks, on a Wednesday, and then stood up to go. Some instinct made her wary as she walked past him to the door, and she sidestepped just in time to avoid a hug. Shaking her head, she put out her hand and offered to shake his.

He held her hand just a second or two longer than seemed right to her, and then said, "Thank you for coming," just as she pulled her hand back and stepped outside.

Back at the Office

When Karla got back to the office, she looked for Shannon. Knocking lightly on her office door, she looked in and found her on the phone.

"I'll catch you later," Shannon mouthed to her.

Karla went on to her own desk and did some charting. Just as she had returned the charts to medical records and was gathering her belongings to go home, Shannon came to her door. "I'm sorry—the day just got away from me. Can we talk tomorrow?" she asked.

"Okay," Karla agreed.

As it turned out, it was a week later, the next Monday, before they had a chance to talk. Karla told her about Howard. "This whole thing makes me nervous, Shannon. I'm not comfortable going out there by myself anymore. He lives way out in the country, with lots of trees around and no neighbors— it's pretty isolated. And he's drinking, and he's lonely. He was inappropriate with me. And I think he's a high suicide risk."

"Well, see if he will agree to see you in the office," Shannon suggested. "I'd say to ask Nick to go with you, but he's at the doctor's right now and it looks like he's going to be off for back surgery."

"He did tell me he doesn't drive when he's drinking, so maybe that will be an added reason not to drink before the next appointment," Karla responded. "Well, I'll give it try."

One Week Later

Karla tried to call Howard the day before their scheduled appointment, but he didn't answer the phone, so she left a message on the answering machine. "Hi, Howard, this is Karla from hospice. I was calling to confirm our appointment tomorrow. I was wondering if it would be possible for you to come in and meet with me in our office, right downtown in Dandridge. If you could call me back, I'd appreciate it."

By the end of the day, when there'd been no call back, she looked for Shannon to plan her next steps, but the receptionist told her that Shannon had gone to Knoxville for a meeting and wouldn't be back in the office until the following week.

Karla came to work the next morning with an uneasy feeling. She completed some notes from the day before, and then sat and thought. *I'm going to call him before I head out there. If he's drinking, I'm not going to go. It won't do any good anyway, and I just don't feel safe.*

She dialed Howard's number. After about five rings, just as she was starting to hang up the phone, he answered. She could tell right away that he had been drinking. *Damn it, I knew he would be drinking!* she thought.

"Howard, this is Karla from hospice. I was just calling to check with you before I came out there this morning, since you didn't call back yesterday. How are you doing?"

Silence.

"Howard, do you remember that you agreed not to be drinking before my next visit?"

"Yeah, I remember," Howard acknowledged.

"Your voice sounds like you have been—am I right?"

"Yeah."

Karla paused, wondering whether to stick with what she had told him at her last visit, and about the risk to his safety as well as her own.

20 | Seizing Hope (A)

Gecole Harley and Terry A. Wolfer

AS HE NAVIGATED rush-hour traffic, case manager Tim Reilly reflected on thirty-four-year-old Gilbert Shealy's worsening situation. Gilbert lived in a group home for people with developmental disabilities. He suffered from repeated seizures and had near constant low-grade seizure activity in his brain. His various seizure medications offered limited control and, as it turned out, carried their own extreme side effects. Elizabeth Parsec, the administrator at Gilbert's group home, had just proposed a risky and expensive solution. But first, Tim and Elizabeth had to decide whether and how to help Gilbert make a decision about it.

"This is serious, Tim," Elizabeth's words rang in his ear, "and I want to be sure. . . . Well, I don't know if we would ever be sure, even with a person of average IQ, but I want to be fairly certain, in my own heart and mind, that Gilbert is doing what he wants."

Development of this decision case was supported in part by funding from the Project on Death in America and the University of South Carolina College of Social Work. It was prepared solely to provide material for class discussion and not to suggest either effective or ineffective handling of the situation depicted. Although the case is based on field research regarding an actual situation, names and certain facts may have been disguised to protect confidentiality. As indicated by the (A), the instructor's manual provides a continuation of the case. The authors wish to thank the anonymous case reporter for cooperation in making this account available for the benefit of social work students and instructors.

Sacramento, California

Sacramento, the capital of California, sat in the upper middle part of the state. Although the city had a population of nearly 400,000, it was still surrounded by fertile farmland in a valley bounded by mountains to the east and west. Like most of California, Sacramento was ethnically and racially diverse. In 1996, the population was 48 percent white, 17 percent Asian, 15 percent black, 22 percent Latino, and 1.3 percent American Indian. Sacramento boasted some of the most affordable housing in California. About 1 percent of the population lived in institutionalized group quarters.

Alta California Regional Center

The Alta California Regional Center (ACRC), located in Sacramento, was one of twenty-one locally managed regional centers serving individuals with developmental disabilities and their families statewide. All were nonprofit private corporations that provided local resources to help clients find and access the many services available.

If California were pictured as an arm with a slight bend, ACRC's sprawling catchment area would sit in the crease. The area consisted of Alpine, Colusa, El Dorado, Nevada, Placer, Sacramento, Sierra, Sutter, Yolo, and Yuba counties.

The mission of the ACRC was to provide or coordinate services for individuals with developmental disabilities and their families. These services included information and referral, assessment and diagnosis, counseling, service coordination, purchase of the services required to meet the individual's life goals, and monitoring of those services through the regional center. There was no charge to the individuals or their families.

Tim Reilly

Tim Reilly was one of 200 service coordinators who worked at ACRC. Each had a caseload of about 80 people, organized around age and geographic location. Tim worked in the adult and aging unit, so all the people he served were at least 25 years of age. Although this position was Tim's first job as an M.S.W., he had worked with people with developmental disabilities for about

7 of his 14 years in human services. In fact, he knew many of the people on his caseload through prior work experience. Except for state hospitals, California offered residential services to individuals with mental retardation only in private group homes. To place them, the state hired case managers like Tim to help individuals and families locate appropriate services and monitor their satisfaction. Tim would ascertain what services the client required, negotiate contracts with various private providers, and ensure that the client received quality services.

One reason Tim chose to work for ACRC was the agency's strong commitment to self-determination. Most of its brochures included a prominent caption: "People with developmental disabilities have the right to make their own decisions." Tim's experience was that ACRC did not just write the words—self-determination was indeed a coveted value. Tim boasted to social workers from other agencies that he participated in case management staff meetings where a client with profound mental retardation would be wheeled into the room and stare at the ceiling as staff members asked the client for an opinion and carefully watched for signs of some preference. While some people might question the relevance of that deliberate attempt to facilitate communication, Tim thought, *I am proud to work for an agency that takes self-determination so seriously, even when it's inconvenient or appears to be unnoticed.*

Tim's curly hair had a natural orange hue and the hair on his head matched the well-groomed, close-cut beard that accentuated a chiseled chin. When Tim engaged in conversation his eyes twinkled, yet he also seemed unflappable and meditative. Each word was carefully measured, each thought concisely constructed.

139 Nickerson Place, a Holding of Pacific Care Home Services

When California experienced the fervor for deinstitutionalizing people with developmental disabilities that swept the country in the 1990s, entrepreneurs began a cottage industry by buying single-family houses and converting them into group homes. One of these, Pacific Care Home Services (PCHS), was created to answer the need for community-based group homes. This private for-profit company specialized in providing residential placement for people with developmental disabilities who needed twenty-four-hour nursing care. Since its creation six years earlier, PCHS had grown dramatically to a total of twenty-four homes, including six in ACRC's catchment area. Although the company met government standards, it did not have a stellar reputation. But few group homes did. Most met government standards and operated as best they could in an imperfect world with high performance requirements and minimal financial resources. Though not a model operation, PCHS was considered a good placement among the alternatives.

Among PCHS's very first acquisitions, 139 Nickerson Place was one of three homes the company purchased on a single property, with one house facing the street and two located behind it. Each had three bedrooms and housed six residents. The professional staff consisted of an administrator, a registered nurse, a consulting physician, and a licensed vocational nurse for each shift. They floated among the three homes. In addition, there were caregiving employees assigned to each home who provided direct nonmedical care such as bathing, feeding, and personal care. They worked eight-hour shifts. There were always two caregiving employees on duty at each of the three homes at any given time.

139 Nickerson Place was in a beautiful location. The street was lined with trees and the well-planned neighborhood had fresh rows of prefabricated homes with perfectly manicured lawns. Some neighborhoods had resisted attempts to establish group homes in their "backyard," but to Pacific Care's surprise, the neighbors had not complained once clients moved into Nickerson Place. The group home occupants were quiet and hardly went outside. Most were physically incapacitated and only ventured beyond the front=yard fence for weekly physical therapy and occasional doctor's appointments.

Elizabeth Parsec

Elizabeth Parsec had been the administrator for the three homes at 139 Nickerson Place for seven months. With a B.A. in criminal justice, she had worked for six years as a practitioner and then program manager in the Florida juvenile justice system. She moved from Florida to California to accept the administrator position shortly after she divorced at age thirty. Although people sometimes questioned the quality of PCHS's services, Tim had never heard anyone question Elizabeth's professionalism. Like most administrators of small nonprofit organizations, Elizabeth wore many hats. She was integrally involved in programming and overseeing client care in addition to her administrative responsibilities. She quickly developed a reputation among the regional center coordinators who worked with her as a strong consumer advocate and intelligent administrator. In fact, Elizabeth's strong clinical skills landed her contract work from a local psychologist who asked her to do assessments for him after her normal work hours for PCHS.

Gilbert Shealy

Gilbert Shealy was thirty-four years old and had been one of the first residents to move into 139 Nickerson Place, six years earlier. Gilbert's mother had cared for him all his life. The two lived on their own with little support from other family members or friends. After Gilbert reached the age of majority, he was legally independent but continued to live with his mother, who still provided supervision. After she died in 1991, Gilbert moved into 139 Nickerson Place under arrangements by ACRC, which contracted with PCHS to place individuals like him in group homes. Each placement involved a separate contract, although all the contracts included the same standard language. Gilbert was financially dependent on state resources for his room and board and medical treatment, but otherwise remained legally independent.

Gilbert's IQ was low and he was diagnosed with moderate mental retardation, but no one argued that Gilbert was incompetent or needed to be a ward of the court. For that reason, he did not have a guardian ad litem or other similar advocate appointed to make decisions for him. The legal standard for competence was quite low and Gilbert was generally considered capable of making his own decisions. To engage in more complex decision making, he just required more time, more structure, and simpler explanations.

Medically, Gilbert was diagnosed with tonic-clonic seizures, a type of generalized seizure previously referred to as grand mal seizures. In addition, he occasionally suffered from status epilepticus, "a potentially life-threatening condition in which a person either has an abnormally prolonged seizure or does not fully regain consciousness between seizures" (National Institute of Neurological Disorders and Stroke 2007). In Gilbert's case, some seizures lasted more than twenty minutes. But the specific seizures were only part of his physical challenges. Gilbert's brain was in a near-constant state of low-level seizure activity, and he suffered from full-body tremors as a result of the

excessive stimulation. Over the years, doctors had prescribed a variety of medications to control the seizure activity—including phenytoin, carbamazepine,
valproic acid, Topamax, and, most recently, valproate sodium—but with little
success. To prevent head injury, since childhood Gilbert had worn a protective
helmet that framed his olive-complexioned face. The doctors insisted that he
wear the helmet for protection from serious and violent grand mal seizures
that occasionally and unexpectedly sent him crashing to the floor.

As is typical of people with medically intractable epilepsy, Gilbert had a
conspicuous, awkward gait that made people watching wish he would just sit
down. But when he did, he sat hunched with his hands gathered at his chest,
shaking fiercely. He looked a little peculiar, even to Tim, who felt genuine
affection for him. Gilbert seemed to be aware of people's reaction; he was a
highly sensitive person whose feelings were hurt easily. Gilbert understood
that he was different from other people and found it easier to retreat into his
own world than to be confronted with his rarities in the outside world. Most
of the time he sat quietly at the dinning room table or lay on his bed within
the confines of his room.

But even at 139 Nickerson Place, Tim noticed that Gilbert had no close
peer relationships. Communication was a challenge for most of the residents.
Some with profound mental retardation were unable to have a meaningful
exchange with Gilbert. Other residents, like Gilbert's roommate, possessed
average IQs, but had to rely on computer-assisted communication because of
severe physical limitations resulting from cerebral palsy.

These communication challenges did not apply to the staff, however, so it
was not surprising to Tim that Gilbert endeared himself to them. Compared
to many other residents at 139 Nickerson Place, Gilbert was low maintenance
and fairly well versed in the activities of daily living. He could brush his teeth
and bathe with minimal assistance. He could also dress himself, although
staff had to make sure he did not put his shoes on the wrong feet.

Tim also noticed that Gilbert would use his personality to engage staff
members, as best he was able. Tim described Gilbert to others as incredibly
cooperative, nonconfrontational, and friendly. The powerful medications he
took had a sedative effect, producing a relatively flat affect. The combination of constant seizure activity and powerful medications caused lengthy
language-processing delays. Sometimes, while seemingly staring off in space,
Gilbert would take ten seconds to respond in conversation. Nevertheless,

within the confines of the group home, he enjoyed talking to staff in his distinctive slow monotone about his "job" at a "sheltered workshop" run by the Association for Retarded Citizens. It was especially apparent that Gilbert enjoyed his relationships with Tim and Elizabeth. It seemed to Tim that Gilbert adored Elizabeth. Sometimes they felt uneasy because Gilbert listened carefully to everything they said. Sometimes they felt the full weight of their responsibility not to influence him inappropriately.

Creative Problem Solving

As they started to worry about Gilbert, Elizabeth and Tim formed a friendship that sometimes allowed work-related discussions to spill into dinnertime conversations. With their busy schedules and Tim's long commute to his personal residence, dinner meetings near the group home were often the only solution to time constraints. The group home was between Tim's office and his home, so it was convenient for him to stop for dinner, miss the brunt of rush-hour traffic, and then continue home.

One evening at a dinner meeting, Elizabeth said to Tim, "I wanted to check something out with you." They were seated in a booth at a neighborhood restaurant, having dinner after one of the monthly care planning meetings. The crowd had dissipated, so all that remained was the whirring of the dishwasher and the clanking of dishes.

"I think this is a good idea, but I want to make sure you approve," she said, sounding a bit hesitant.

"Sure," Tim said, "let's hear it."

Elizabeth paused before she began. "Gilbert has a long history of putting objects in his rectum when he's alone in his room or late at night after his roommate is asleep. Unfortunately he steals what he can, toothbrushes, pencils, and the like. I know from his chart that the previous administrators have tried a number of behavior management plans to stop this, but none of them seemed to work. I have two thoughts."

Elizabeth dropped her eyes momentarily to stare at an empty coffee mug. Then she looked up at Tim. He nodded so she continued, "If we can't stop his behavior, we need to think in terms of harm reduction and find a way to reduce the possibility he will injure himself . . . not to mention the hygiene issues for the house. And more importantly, do we have the right to stop the behavior? It seems to me that as long as he is not hurting himself or others, how he finds sexual gratification is none of our business. Am I being too far out here?"

Tim thought for a moment. "I don't think you are being too far out at all. And I agree with you, it's not our place to judge him or tell him what to do, but we have his and his housemates' safety to think about. What do you suggest?"

"Well," Elizabeth paused, "How about if I take him down to that adult novelties shop on Clark Street and buy him a sex toy?"

Tim laughed. "Am I supposed to write this into his behavior plan?"

"I think this might be a case for discretion."

"I think you're right," Tim said. "But are you sure you're the appropriate person to go? I mean, since you are female, do you think Gilbert might feel awkward?"

"Well frankly, Tim, I don't have confidence that the few male staff members we have would handle the situation appropriately, and Gilbert is so child-like in some ways." She paused for a moment. "I just don't think it would occur to him to be embarrassed or uncomfortable with me. He trusts me."

"Yeah," Tim concurred, "I'd be willing to take him, but I don't really have the kind of relationship with Gilbert that you do. And it sounds like you've already had some good conversations about it."

"Besides," Elizabeth added, "I am the senior person here. I should be the one to take ultimate responsibility."

"I tend to agree," Tim said. "Go. You have my support."

Good News and Bad

With the purchase of a sex toy, Gilbert's life at the group home seemed to settle into a quiet pattern, but not for long. A few weeks later, Tim received a call from Elizabeth as he was preparing to leave the office at the end of the day.

"Hi Tim, it's Elizabeth. Hey, would you mind stopping by here on your way home? I have something I want to talk to you about regarding one of the residents."

"Sure," Tim replied. He often visited residents in the afternoon because of his long drive home from the office. Stopping on the way provided a welcome break.

On the way to the house Tim thought, *Elizabeth seemed uncharacteristically unsure and tentative. I wonder what could be going on over there.*

"Gilbert went for a lab test follow-up with his personal physician, Dr. Parker, today," Elizabeth said breathlessly when Tim arrived at the home.

"Good," Tim said, waiting for the other shoe to drop.

"Well, you know he takes valproate sodium. Dr. Parker has tried all the other alternatives and Gilbert just has not responded. The medicine he takes is necessary, but it's toxic."

"Yeah . . ."

"Well the bad news is that Dr. Parker said Gilbert will only live another eighteen months if he keeps taking those meds. They're killing him, and he's only thirty-four. He really isn't much older than we are."

"I see," Tim responded softly, trying to sort through all of the information. *Toxic? Killing him!?* "What do you mean? How?"

"Well," Elizabeth explained, "it can cause both kidney and liver damage, especially at the high dosage he needs. I think the frequent medication changes, in an effort to find something that works, have been hard on his health too."

"I know nothing seems to work for long," Jay agreed.

"The good news is that I found a medical option that we might at least explore that could make things better for Gilbert. I've done some checking on the Internet and I have kind of a radical idea for a medical referral. I asked you to stop by because I want to talk to you about it. You might want to sit down for this." Elizabeth looked straight into Tim's face. Her expression was grave.

"Okay, I'm listening," Tim said, moving his chair so close to the table so that he could feel the edge pressing into his ribs.

As Tim waited, he thought, *I've always supported Elizabeth's recommendations before. I wonder why she seems so anxious.*

"It's called functional hemispherectomy. It's been used to help people with seizure disorders like Gilbert's, according to information I found on a couple of reliable Web sites. What happens is that a surgeon cuts the connections from one hemisphere to the rest of the brain so that seizures arising in that hemisphere have nowhere to go. Basically, it means that a brain surgeon would cut Gilbert's brain in half to prevent the stimulation from causing seizures. If it were successful, Gilbert would not have to take the medications anymore. He would live longer. The success rate is 75 to 85 percent."

Elizabeth paused for a second, but Tim could tell there was more. "The thing is, Tim, that besides being dangerous it is also really, really expensive."

She was right, Tim thought, *I'm glad I'm sitting down for this one.*

"Do you know what the risks are?" Tim asked.

"All I know is what I found on the Internet," Elizabeth said. "Of course, the surgery could be unsuccessful and Gilbert could continue having seizures. After the surgery he will almost certainly have some muscular weakness, but that should be temporary." She looked at Tim. He was still listening, so she continued. "Also, he could hemorrhage while in surgery. He risks infections. It is possible that he could lose his ability to sense pain. He may lose his peripheral vision. It's also possible that the surgery could do damage to the functioning part of his brain. And although fatalities are rare, it could happen."

Tim held his breath for a moment. "Gosh, that is really serious," he said quietly. "Did you run this by Dr. Parker? What does he think?"

"I haven't, because I didn't learn about the procedure until after Dr. Parker told me, in his usual forthright manner, that Gilbert was going to die without help."

There was a pause, and then Tim said, "So what we really want is a referral for a medical doctor to investigate whether this procedure is an appropriate option for Gilbert?"

"Right. Obviously I don't know. I'm not a doctor. But I feel that Gilbert should have a right to explore all of his options."

"And then there's the cost, right? You said it was expensive."

"Yep," she said, "very, although I don't have an exact figure."

"Well," Tim said, resting against the back of his chair, "If Gilbert is a potential candidate for surgery, we can certainly help him advocate for the referral. Obviously, it would be a battle and we might not win, but we could try."

Tim's mind wandered for a minute as he reviewed agency protocol. *Okay, he thought, as a case manager, I have a menu of medical services that I have free rein to approve, but functional hemispherectomies are certainly not on the list. So I go directly to the medical director. Of course, I could discuss it with Rick [supervisor] first, but I know what he'll say. He'll tell me my chances are limited but I should ask anyway. I could also consult with the team but, like Rick, they can only help me process. They can't authorize anything. The medical director makes the decisions. She's the clear choice.*

Tim became conscious of his surroundings again. He thought Elizabeth might be waiting for him to refocus, but she wasn't. She was thinking too.

"What does Gilbert think?" Tim asked, prompting Elizabeth to return to the conversation.

Elizabeth reclined a little in her chair, then said, "Well, I'm not sure. I haven't asked him yet." Elizabeth drank slowly from a glass of ice water before she continued. "I was hoping you would come and help. You know how Gilbert is. He is so compliant. He just sort of does what we ask, and even if we don't ask, he will say yes if he even slightly senses what we want." Elizabeth lifted herself from the reclined position and leaned toward Tim. "But this is serious, Tim, and I want to be sure. . . . Well, I don't know if we would ever be sure, even with a person of average IQ, but I want to be fairly certain, in my own heart and mind, that Gilbert is doing what he wants."

"Well, does Gilbert know what it means to die?" Tim asked. His face was solemn; his eyes lost some of their brilliance.

"I have no idea. The subject just does not come up in our daily activities."

"His mother died," Tim volunteered, "but that was at least five years ago, before I started working with him. I don't know how well he understood that. But it might give us a place to start."

"You know," Elizabeth sat up a little straighter, "now that I'm thinking about it, I have talked to Gilbert once or twice about heaven. Sometimes he talks about his mom and how she is in heaven. That would be where to start."

"Okay. Hmmm. What do you think about talking with him on a couple of different occasions about his concept of dying? We can check to see how clear he is about the finality of death and see if he is consistent over time." Tim looked at Elizabeth and she was nodding, so he continued, "Then we can try to see if he can understand anything about the potential risks of doing and of not doing the surgery."

"Ohhh, this is crazy!" Elizabeth exclaimed. "If he stays on the current meds, he will die soon. If the surgery goes wrong, he could die sooner."

"Yeah, well, let's hope it works," Jay responded, feeling the gravity of the options. "We can't just give up on him!"

"I noticed you scheduled some visits on Monday. Can you stay a little longer and talk to Gilbert then?"

"No problem. I'll give some thought to how we should lead into it, and what to say."

Reference

National Institute of Neurological Disorders and Stroke. 2007. *Seizures and Epilepsy: Hope Through Research.* http://www.ninds.nih.gov/disorders/epilepsy/detail_epilepsy.htm#How%20can%20Epilepsy%20be%20Treated? (accessed November 22, 2007).

21 | Gifts (A)

Gecole Harley and Vicki M. Runnion

SOCIAL WORKER and group leader Phyllis Watts reflected on yet another monthly meeting of Mothers and Others, a support group for people whose loved ones were dying of AIDS. There were fabulous meetings, for example, when the group came together to organize a week's worth of casseroles for a family whose loved one was in the final stages of dying, when someone in the group was processing what it meant to be a devout Christian and have a gay son, or when the group collectively offered counsel far exceeding any individual therapist's best effort.

But lately the group seemed stuck on the same old issues: their grief and frustration with other people's religious intolerance toward gay men. Yes, some of them realized the importance of moving through grief and getting on with life. Yes, some made efforts to reach out to other communities affected by AIDS.

But here we are, Phyllis reflected, *in 1993, affluent white people talking about past experiences of a disease in a rapidly evolving medical and social ser-*

Development of this decision case was supported in part by the University of South Carolina College of Social Work and the Project on Death in America. It was prepared solely to provide material for class discussion and not to suggest either effective or ineffective handling of the situation depicted. Although the case is based on field research regarding an actual situation, names and certain facts may have been disguised to protect confidentiality. As indicated by the (A), the instructor's manual provides a continuation of the case. The authors wish to thank the case reporter for cooperation in making this account available for the benefit of social work students and practitioners.

vice environment. She had to ask herself, *When does the point come to let go, Phyllis? When?*

Cincinnati, Ohio

Located in the hilly southwest corner of Ohio, Cincinnati was the seat of Hamilton County. The third largest city in the state, after Columbus and Cleveland, it was the transportation, industrial, commercial, and cultural center for a region extending over southern Ohio, northern Kentucky, and southeastern Indiana. The city's strategic location on the westward-flowing Ohio River had made it a focal point for migration in the nineteenth century, and it was often referred to as "the Gateway to the West."

In 1990, Cincinnati had a population of more than 350,000. The population was split almost evenly between whites (53 percent) and people of color, including blacks (43 percent) and other ethnic groups (4 percent). In 1990, the category of "unmarried partner" was added to the "household" section of the U.S. Census. Although it could include partnerships that were not gay or lesbian, the category offered an opportunity, albeit imperfect, to estimate the number of gay and lesbian partnerships (Gates n.d.).

AIDS: A Dawning Crisis

Like many other large metropolitan communities, Cincinnati found itself facing a mounting health crisis in the mid-1980s as the number of HIV-positive people grew. At the very start of the AIDS epidemic, before there was money available for services, everything was done by grassroots volunteers. Volunteers scoured news sources for information and developed channels for passing that information along to others. They scraped together money to pay for what little medication there was. They prepared meals for exhausted caregivers. And volunteers took turns sitting with friends, and with strangers, as they sweated or chilled or vomited or talked deliriously, and as their breathing slowed and then finally stopped. At that time, nursing homes refused AIDS patients.

A bit later, things began to change—bringing both good news and bad news. Good news came because the epidemic was finally being taken seriously, and research funding became available. The bad news stemmed from increasing public worry and willingness to blame gays and intravenous drug users. In short, it became easier for people to take out their anger and fear on those two already stigmatized groups. (Not until the death of Ryan White, a hemophiliac, in 1989, did Congress pass any legislation to provide funds to improve the quality and availability of care for people living with HIV.)

June Sorenson

June Sorenson, a professional social worker, was personally affected by AIDS, back in 1984. June was a petite woman with flyaway, straw-colored hair that had nearly turned gray. Strangers who caught a glimpse of her, often with her brow furrowed and eyes downcast, thought she was cold. Then the little lady with the knitted brow would burst into a raucous laugh that would leave no doubt about her ability to see humor in the world.

June's laugh lost a little of its luster when her son, James, became one of the first people in Cincinnati to contract AIDS. While James fought a losing battle against an unknown disease, his father suffered from denial; he just could not accept that his son was gay.

June sought help. She found it through a gay man in the local community who gave her the phone number of a mothers' support group in New York City. At the time, Mothers and Others was one of few AIDS support groups in the United States. After talking to the group in New York, June started a Mothers and Others group in Cincinnati. They met in the community room in the basement of Holy Cross Episcopal Church. Holy Cross was an established presence in an old downtown neighborhood. Although it was not in the heart of the inner city, it sat in the first ring outside and had an urban edge, but not a full-fledged urban feel.

Depending on a person's perspective, Holy Cross was either renowned or reviled as one of the first churches in Cincinnati to accept gays and lesbians into the congregation and to champion issues surrounding sexual orientation. The church welcomed Mothers and Others and permanently reserved the community room for their meetings. The room had a couple of large rectangular collapsible folding tables and steel-gray folding chairs lining the perimeter of each. The cinder block walls would have seemed oppressively drab except that colorful children's artwork, depicting scenes from the Bible, decorated them and made the room cheerful.

Phyllis Watts

Phyllis Watts, a social worker, was a professional acquaintance of June before James got sick. She soon became June's personal friend after the crisis of his illness arose.

Phyllis was a sturdy middle-aged woman whose bright red glasses, full mane of white hair, and purposeful stride alerted strangers to the fact that she was a woman on a mission. But Phyllis was not hard. You could feel the warmth as she advanced down the sidewalk in her no-nonsense shoes, smiling to herself. She was tireless—or so she appeared.

Phyllis had grown up on the West Coast and often said she came from a "progressive religious family." Her father was a communist labor organizer, her mother was an immigration activist, and both advocated for gay and lesbian rights. "Their spirit kind of crept into me," she would say with a chuckle.

Phyllis remained a devout Christian into adulthood and served as a lay reader at her church. Still, she had her own special version of religious expression and most folks in town knew it. "I am not afraid to take on church-based or religiously based homophobia," she said. "I will speak out." In quiet moments while reflecting on Mothers and Others she realized, *I think that has always been part of my legitimacy with the community, my willingness to say things . . . to speak out.*

Phyllis graduated from UCLA with a degree in history and political science and supplemented her B.A. with a master's in counseling psychology. That credential allowed her to work in public welfare and child welfare positions all along the West Coast. When Phyllis and her husband relocated to Cincinnati, she worked as a hospital social worker at a teaching hospital before returning to school to earn her M.S.W. Upon graduation, Phyllis became a faculty member at a local medical school, teaching a range of courses, including some focused on gay and lesbian issues, while raising her three children. During her tenure there, she had the rare opportunity to spend a significant amount of time with Dr. Elisabeth Kübler-Ross when she came to the hospital as a consultant. When the AIDS epidemic arose, Phyllis found a perfect marriage between her interest in death and dying and her interest in gay and lesbian issues. She immediately became a vital part of the early AIDS community.

The Invitation

Phyllis, like most volunteers in the AIDS community, was familiar with Mothers and Others. The group had been serving the Cincinnati area for about eight years when Phyllis received a call in late summer 1992 from her friend June.

June sounded casual. "Hey, remember we were talking about Mothers and Others after the Community Trust board meeting last month? Well, just wondering if you would come to the next meeting."

"Now, June, you know full well how much you are respected by everyone in the AIDS community, including me. You're a saint! How am I going to say no?"

Phyllis heard June chuckle into the phone and then whisper, "Thank you."

"But can you tell me why? What's up?"

June paused, and Phyllis wondered why. It seemed out of character for her to be so hesitant, especially when asking for something specific.

"I would just like for everybody to get to know you better; you're a resource for these people. It's a wonderful group," she said and then added, "about thirty to forty people come every month."

Phyllis's First Visit to Mothers and Others

"Well, it's seven o'clock," June said. "I guess it's time to start." The chatter in the room died down. "The rules are the same. You can talk or not talk. Some people want to talk. Some people don't. You can wait and hear what other people have to say, if you want. We go around the table giving each person an opportunity to share. Please feel free to stop the person who is talking to add a comment. We want this to be a discussion group, not a lecture."

June made a motion as if to sit back in her chair, then straightened and looked to her left, where Phyllis relaxed quietly in a chair. "Oh," June said, "I forgot to introduce my friend and fellow social worker, Phyllis."

Phyllis smiled, nodded, and said, "Pleased to be here," in response to a chorus of welcomes.

The group quieted again and looked toward June. She then settled into her chair in earnest and said, "Who would like to start today?"

"You know, we have a potluck supper at my church every Wednesday," a steady baritone voice boomed from the far end of the table. Phyllis recognized a man who had introduced himself earlier as Edwin. "Claudia and I found that the church community really helped us get through the hard times when Kevin was sick." His voice faltered for a minute. He wife pulled some Kleenex out of her purse and mopped a few tears from her face.

Her husband's face suddenly hardened. "But you know, this man . . . this . . . this so-called Christia n at our table last week, had the gall to say that AIDS is God's way of punishing sinners." The man's face flushed with anger. The previously silent group began to stir.

Phyllis could not follow any one story in the confusion that followed, but it was clear that nearly every person at the table had had a similar experience. The group then fell into what seemed to be a familiar routine: group outrage. Group grief. Group unity, in the face of a common enemy.

Phyllis noticed that the group mainly talked about people who had already died. She also noticed that these were people who had been with June from the beginning and that they treated her with both reverence and familiarity. It appeared to be more of a bereavement group, although Mothers and Others described its mission as supporting people and families living with or affected by AIDS. Phyllis was impressed by the exchange among them. It was not a few people talking; everyone became actively engaged in the discussion.

At the end of the evening, June turned toward Phyllis and said, "Phyllis, would you like to say a few words?"

"Sure," Phyllis responded. Then, turning to the group, "I hear that you are tired of experiencing hostility toward gays from some religious folks." She paused and then added, "And I hear that you are grieving. Even though your loved ones are gone, you are still very sad. I am sorry for your losses and I thank you for welcoming me into your community this evening and sharing so honestly. I wish you all well."

After the meeting ended, Phyllis grabbed her sweater from the back of the chair and prepared to leave.

"Would you come again next month?" June asked matter-of-factly. "The group likes you so much."

Well, that's odd, Phyllis thought. But it was a time of volunteerism, and you just kind of did whatever people wanted, at least in Phyllis's mind, so she agreed.

Finding a Different Place

Next month came quickly. Although Phyllis had only been to Holy Cross once before, she was happy to see the place. She had felt inclined to advocate for AIDS-related causes almost from the moment she heard about the disease. She already spent many of her volunteer hours working with people affected by HIV, so attending this group just seemed like a natural extension of her pursuits.

As Phyllis walked into the building, she realized that she felt comfortable there. *Folks seem pleased to see me, most especially June,* she thought as she walked into the room, greeted several members who welcomed her back, and found a seat. She loved the way Edwin, the man who had raged about the insensitive comment at the church potluck, greeted everyone by name as they walked through the door. His wife, Claudia, noted who was missing. "Abigail hasn't arrived yet. I wonder if she's caught that nasty flu?" *They're almost like family,* Phyllis thought as she settled into her chair.

June raised her voice, "Well, it's seven o'clock. I guess it's time to start." The group began as usual, going around the table, person by person, until every voice was heard.

After the meeting ended and the last group member's car pulled out of the parking lot, June asked Phyllis if she would mind joining her for a walk in the park across the street.

"I cannot do this group even one more month," June said abruptly. "I have grieved for my son for eight years, and it's over. I can't do it anymore." Phyllis looked to June's face for evidence of tears, but there were none. She just looked resolute.

June gestured toward the parking lot, now empty but for their two cars. "They like you, and I want you to take the group."

"WHAT?!" Normally, Phyllis could look cool, even as panic welled up inside, but for a moment she reacted, unchecked. A few moments passed before she responded in a steady voice. "It seems like most of the people there are grieving."

"Oh, Phyllis, I have been trying to get them to move on, and that's part of my reason for leaving. They are stuck where they are and if I stay here, so am I." She glanced over to the parking lot. "We all just need to be in a different place."

Group Transition from Peer Leadership to External Leadership

Phyllis accepted the challenge. She confirmed that her liability insurance would remain in effect, and arranged to see another social worker for supervision for the first few months. June sent the group members a farewell letter.

As Phyllis walked down the church stairs leading to the basement conference room, she heard the muffled voices echoing down the hall. "Hi," she said as she found an open chair along the circumference of the long table.

"Welcome back," someone said as the others took their seats.

Phyllis felt like a substitute teacher walking into a classroom. She was an outsider, and although the group supported her assuming June's role, she sensed tension. Phyllis decided it was best to allow the group to take the lead.

"Well, it's seven o'clock. I guess it is time to start." Phyllis deliberately started with the welcome that June had used. Although she knew she would have to find her own ways of doing things eventually, she wanted to ease everyone into the transition. "Who would like to begin?"

"So June really isn't going to come back here and be with us at all?"

"No, Edwin, she isn't. How do you feel about that?"

"Well we thought she might change her mind. I mean, she started this thing and then we all grew it and it is a part of us, and then she just disappears? We know who you are," he said, squirming as he suddenly became a little more self-conscious. "You have supported the AIDS community and we all respect you, but June was a part of us. Now she's just going to pretend like we don't exist?"

"Well, I don't think she's pretending that we don't exist," said Gretchen, a lady whose delicate silver hair was pulled neatly into a taut bun. "John, Ethel, and I just had lunch with her today." Gretchen glanced over to John and Ethel, who nodded in unison.

Phyllis noticed that some members of the group sat quietly. Others were leaning and whispering. Some looked sour. Others listened, sometimes to more than one conversation. *Gosh,* Phyllis thought, *seems like there are some major dynamics going on. What's that all about?* She then said it aloud, "Gosh, there seem to be some major dynamics going on here. What's that all about?"

Silence fell on the room. Phyllis casually folded her arms, rested them on the table, and waited, looking at no one in particular.

"We are THE group for AIDS in this community, the only one, and have been for a long time. We," Edwin looked into the space above the table as if he'd find the right words there, "we are Mothers and Others. We all are, including June, and I just don't understand why she left us."

Phyllis heard a few people whisper, "Yes." "That's right, Edwin." "Yes." "That's how I feel too."

Phyllis didn't move. She remained focused on Edwin. So did Gretchen, who looked back at him and said softly, "June holds a special place in her heart for this group and she encourages us to continue. She just feels the need for a little distance." Gretchen looked sincerely at Edwin as if she wanted him to know that she could feel his pain. "I will miss her too."

"But you just saw her. I haven't seen her since the last meeting," Edwin said, more to himself than to the rest of the group. "She is a part of us. She wasn't just our leader."

Leader: the word resonated for Phyllis. Although group members were aware of June's profession as a social worker, she had been a founding member and the peer leader of Mothers and Others. Phyllis quickly scanned the room to make a visual appraisal of how people were doing. Some, mainly those who had mentioned seeing June since her resignation from the group, seemed at ease. Others were whispering and/or gesturing. Still others just sat stoically, listening carefully.

Phyllis brought up June's departure over the course of the first few meetings, and to a greater or lesser extent the group was able to process her absence. Despite her extensive experience with group leadership, Phyllis often found herself wondering, *Should I have intervened sooner?* The group had a life of its own, which on the surface was a leader's dream—it could function without directives—but Phyllis worried about the undercurrent of tension that she sensed but could not define. And she did not feel the group would help, or perhaps could help, give definition to that tension. Even the members who accepted the transition always made clear that Phyllis was the external leader—the other. She found herself alternately feeling the urge to grab hold of the conversation and then backing away.

Phyllis also understood why June had said the group was stuck. They were.

On the way to one of the meetings about six months into her tenure, Phyllis thought about a phone call she had received earlier in the week. They had hardly gotten beyond, "Hello, my name is," when the woman blurted, "My husband is HIV positive, but no one knows, not even our thirteen-year-old daughter. My husband and I are ministers of a very large, very conservative church in town. I don't think people will understand."

"Well, we understand," Phyllis had told her.

But when the woman came to the Mothers and Others monthly meeting, the membership really didn't understand. Not really. The group, stuck in a rut, obsessively focused on their pet issues of religious intolerance toward the gay community. They did not hear the pain in the heterosexual woman's voice, nor did they seem to notice when she tried to casually peek at her wristwatch for the third time that night.

Phyllis could feel her own frustration welling up, but she did not want to seize the power as facilitator. *Mothers and Others belongs to them. I am just the leader, the professional facilitator, whatever that means. I want to help the group be productive, but I do not want to be directive, and I'm having trouble determining the essence of the group. Without knowing the essence, I cannot help it be healthy and focused.*

Phyllis then noticed the woman glance at her watch again. *So, there sits this woman with this need to learn to live with someone with HIV and AIDS and to talk about her issues with her child, and the group is focused on their grief and not supporting her experience in the place where they have all been.*

Phyllis had seen the group reach out to the woman in their own way. Edwin and Claudia greeted her warmly when she arrived, the group listened intently as she shared her family's challenges, and several people even politely interrupted and asked questions as she talked, which certainly demonstrated their interest. But after the woman completed her story, the group fell into its habit of retelling stories and renewing the familiar battle against certain organized religions' insensitivity toward gay men. And then the bomb fell.

One of the old-timers mentioned that he had been counseling a member couple's son, now deceased, for two years before he came out to his parents.

Phyllis seemed to be the only person in the group who reacted to the breach of confidentiality. Everyone else just focused on the couple's bewilderment. "You mean, *you* knew about Chad before *we* did?" The newcomer's issues were forgotten and Phyllis's efforts to stop the flow of confidential information were in vain. The group careened forward, gaining momentum but seeming to lose direction.

Phyllis was stunned. She had noticed that the group lacked boundaries. Subgroups formed. Unspoken liaisons existed. Confidentiality was a foreign concept. *The group may be beyond my control, even with the best facilitation,* Phyllis thought as she drove home that night. *What on earth should I do?*

Reference

Gates, G. N.d. *Census 2000.* GLBTQ, Inc. http://www.glbtq.com/social-sciences/census_2000,2.html (retrieved November 30, 2005).

22 | Patty's Girls

Heather Bennett, Karen A. Gray, and Terry A. Wolfer

IT WAS JANUARY 5, 2004, the first day back at Chicora Elementary School after Christmas break, and Patty Morris felt excited about resuming her M.S.W. internship there. During the break, she had often wondered about the Dawkins girls, Dominique and Shante. Patty felt she and Dominique had made excellent progress in their last sessions, just before the holidays. Patty had new ideas for treatment and couldn't wait to see the girls.

Patty arrived at Chicora and headed toward her office. As she passed the principal's office, his secretary called out, "Mr. Green wants to talk to you."

Patty assumed he wanted to say hello and welcome back and ask about her Christmas. But when she stepped into the office, there was no light conversation.

"Patty," Mr. Green went right to the point, "I have something I need to tell you about. The Dawkins girls' mother was killed in a car accident over the break."

Development of this decision case was supported in part by the University of South Carolina College of Social Work and the Project on Death in America. It was prepared solely to provide material for class discussion and not to suggest either effective or ineffective handling of the situation depicted. Although the case is based on field research regarding an actual situation, names and certain facts may have been disguised to protect confidentiality. The authors wish to thank the case reporter for cooperation in making this account available for the benefit of social work students and practitioners.

Stunned, Patty went numb. Her eyes welled up with tears, and she felt that stabbing in her heart with which she was so familiar. At first, all she could say was, "Oh, no! What?! When?"

North Charleston, South Carolina

Chicora Elementary was located in North Charleston, a low-income suburb of Charleston, South Carolina. The immediate neighborhood was about 87 percent African American, and more than half of the families with children lived below the poverty level. Although the number of crimes dropped over the past few years, the rates were still higher in this neighborhood than in surrounding areas. Scattered efforts were under way to revitalize the neighborhood.

Chicora Elementary School and the School-Based Mental Health Program

Chicora Elementary School was one of four public schools that served the North Charleston community. Most of the faculty and staff were white, while almost all of the students were African American. Approximately 97 percent of its students received free or reduced lunches. Many students, including the Dawkins girls, lived in a subsidized housing development near the school.

As part of an innovative school-based mental health program, Charleston County Community Mental Health Services (CCCMHS) placed mental health counselors on site at Chicora and other schools. Like their traditional counterparts at CCCMHS, these counselors provided mental health services for children and their families, but they worked from offices on the school premises. Working parents often preferred the flexibility and convenience of having their children receive mental health services at school. As a result, counselors found it was often easier to arrange counseling sessions with children, though sometimes harder to involve parents or caretakers. Unlike school social workers, who had multiple responsibilities (e.g., attendance, crisis intervention, case management), counselors in the school-based program spent most of their time providing direct mental health services and for some students, did so over extended periods of time. Like other CCCMHS counselors, most members of the school-based professional staff were social workers.

Patty Morris

Patty Morris, a young white woman, was an advanced standing student in the M.S.W. program at the University of South Carolina in Columbia and maintained residence just outside the Charleston city limits. She commuted to Columbia twice a week for classes and did her fieldwork in North Charleston. Her field placement was at Chicora Elementary.

As an undergraduate, Patty began with a major in education and received training as a teacher. But during a semester of student teaching, she realized that education was not her calling. Instead, she wanted to work with children in and out of the classroom in a more holistic manner. A career in social work seemed to provide the opportunity to do just that. Furthermore, ample life experience had sensitized her to the profound needs of children.

In particular, Patty had a great deal of personal experience with death and loss. It began when she was just a year old—her seventeen-year-old sister died in a car accident. She was four years old when her maternal grandmother died, and eight when her maternal grandfather died. When she was in fifth grade, her favorite uncle died of cancer. During that year, Patty experienced separation anxiety about leaving her mother for school; she cried every day. Later, during high school, several classmates died or were seriously injured in car wrecks, including her best friend and her friend's brother. Several of these accidents happened in January, so every January Patty got a little nervous.

During her sophomore year in college her father's best friend, who was also a longtime family friend, died of a heart attack. Patty had been close to this man all her life and was very upset by his unexpected death. Over the next two years, two more people she knew well died or were permanently injured in car accidents. She lost the aunt she was named after, due to complications associated with emphysema. In addition, an acquaintance committed suicide while Patty was in college, and even though she didn't know him very well, she wondered whether there was something she could have done.

One year before Patty's field placement, her sister's boyfriend of three years was killed in a plane crash. The young man had become a pilot after becoming close to Patty's father, who was an airline pilot. Patty's sister blamed herself, saying, "If we'd never met or dated, he'd still be alive." Patty's elderly neighbor, to whom she was close, also died that year.

Patty's mother once told her, "It's in the valleys we grow."

"Pretty soon," Patty had replied, "I'm going to be taller than the mountains."

Although Patty knew these experiences had profoundly shaped who she was, she hadn't connected them with her work or identity as a social worker. She was keenly aware that it made people uncomfortable to hear about the multitude of losses she had experienced, and she tended to keep that part of her history to herself. It had never occurred to her to tell Sarah about them.

Sarah Davis

Sarah Davis, white and in her mid-thirties, supervised Patty's field placement in the school-based mental health program offered by CCCMHS. An experienced social worker, she had worked with the agency in several capacities for six years. She was responsible for Oak Park, another elementary school, as well as Chicora. She supervised two M.S.W. interns, one at each school. She had a rather unorthodox sense of style. In Patty's opinion, Sarah dressed too casually. She sometimes wore sweatpants and a cotton T-shirt and her clothes looked well worn, as if she'd had them for years. But Patty observed that Sarah had great relationships with parents, students, and educators at Chicora, and recognized and appreciated her expertise. She was not a micromanager and provided supervision on an as-needed basis. She trusted her social work interns and gave them freedom to perform. However, if there were problems, she would help them discuss the case and resolve the issue.

The Dawkins Family

Patty learned about the Dawkins family when she was assigned to their case during her first weeks of field placement. Each year the Dawkins girls were assigned to a new social work intern.

Mabel Dawkins, their mother, was plagued by strained relationships with men. In one instance she had been beaten almost to death in front her daughters by one of her male friends. For six years before her sudden death, Ms. Dawkins had had a boyfriend who lived in their home and, from Sarah's perspective, served as a rather questionable father figure to her daughters. Nevertheless, the girls called him Daddy.

There were three Dawkins girls. Sarah told Patty that the oldest, Jocelyn, was in middle school, and was the spitting image of her mother. Jocelyn's two half-sisters, Dominique and Shante, still attended Chicora. Dominique, a fourth-grader, was very slender with long legs and beautiful eyes. Shante, a third-grader, looked a lot like Dominique. It was obvious, just looking at them, that they were sisters, but their smiles and their shared aptitude for jump rope made the resemblance even stronger.

Patty felt so sad even thinking about their mother, Mabel Dawkins. *She was so full of life—voluptuous and with a captivating smile. That slight gap between her two front teeth made her lisp when she spoke—that just made her seem so sweet and vulnerable. Mabel Dawkins never met a stranger and was as honest as they come. Her girls were her life!*

Patty and the Girls

Patty Morris had been assigned to work with the two youngest Dawkins girls, just as several other interns had done before her. Dominique and Shante had each been referred by their first-grade teachers to the school-based mental health program for poor grades, withdrawn behavior, depression, and problems with anger management. The girls' cases carried over each year because teachers echoed the same concerns. Initially, Patty was concerned about working alone with the girls because she feared that her inexperience would hinder her effectiveness as a therapist.

After a few weeks, however, Patty became more comfortable with her duties as an intern, and the Dawkins girls began to show signs of improvement. Over the course of her work with the girls, Patty developed a close bond with Mabel Dawkins as well. Often, meetings scheduled to discuss the girls turned into private counseling sessions for Ms. Dawkins instead. Although Patty realized that the meetings were getting off track, she believed that they were ultimately benefiting the girls as well. She believed that patterns in families often repeat themselves, so the more work Mabel did to correct her own patterns, the less likely the girls would be to follow them.

Patty used art therapy and play therapy as her main techniques with the girls. Shante had always been engaged in the sessions, but Patty found it difficult to engage Dominique. Patty and Sarah suspected that Dominique might be depressed, and Mabel agreed to let a psychiatrist examine her. That appointment was scheduled for January 3.

As Christmas break approached, Patty had a breakthrough with Dominique. One morning, Patty met with Mabel, who told her details about things Dominique had done and said that week. Armed with this information, Patty decided to use an indirect approach with the child.

In their session, Patty began by telling Dominique a "story." "I just want to tell you about this little girl I know. She's a nice girl, about your age, who lives with her mother and her sisters. She really loves her mother and her sisters. Most of the time she's good, but she doesn't always do her homework and sometimes she won't talk to her mother and she goes to her room and closes the door and won't let anyone come inside."

Dominique brightened. "I do that too! I do the same thing!"

It was the first time Dominique had opened up. As the session continued, she opened up even more. Patty felt elated that Dominique was sharing some of her inner thoughts about school and about her home and family. Dominique reflected that excitement, and truly came alive. Patty thought it was obvious how empowering it was for the young girl to finally talk about her feelings. For the first time, she felt hopeful that Dominique might improve.

"The girls aren't coming back . . ."

On January 5, 2004, Patty arrived at Chicora and was on the way to her office when she passed the principal's office. His secretary called out, "Mr. Green wants to talk to you."

"Patty," Mr. Green went right to the point, "I have something I need to talk to you about. The Dawkins girls' mother was killed in a car accident over the break."

Stunned, Patty went numb. Her eyes welled up with tears, and she felt that stabbing in her heart with which she was so familiar. At first, all she could say was, "Oh, no! What?! When?"

"Just before Christmas," Mr. Green reported.

With tears suddenly trailing down her face, Patty asked, "Where are the girls? Are they okay?"

"Yes, they're with their grandmother. I saw them at the funeral and they seemed to be okay."

"Does anyone at mental health know this happened?"

"No."

I can't believe no one called us! Patty thought. But then, swinging into action, she said, "I need to talk to their teachers and see how they're doing."

"They're not coming back to this school."

"They're not? Why not?"

"Their grandmother wants them to attend Dunston Elementary because that's closer to her home."

"Do you have her phone number?"

Mr. Green gave Patty the number. She quickly left his office but then collapsed on the bench outside. *Why?* she thought to herself. *How could this have happened?* Patty felt a jumbled wave of emotions: grief for the girls, anger that she hadn't been contacted, and anxiety as an intern with little experience. *When we last met, Dominique was so specific about seeing me again. I'm so worried about her. I'm sure she missed the appointment with the psychiatrist, now the one with me.* Then she told herself, *Get with it, Patty! You're a professional. Keep it together.* Sarah was out of town until the next week and Patty wasn't sure what to do, so she decided to begin by speaking with the girls' teachers. She calmed herself down, gathered her thoughts, and went to their classrooms.

The girls' teachers had all gone to the funeral. They all reported that none of the three girls cried and that they seemed happy to see their teachers. None had had contact with the girls since. With this news, Patty began crying again. *Those girls need to come back to this school! Everything in their lives has changed. They need some consistency.*

Next, Patty decided to call Mrs. Dawkins. From the phone in her office, Patty dialed the grandmother's phone number, still unsure exactly what she was going to say. It was obvious from the grandmother's tone of voice when she answered that she was still very grief-stricken.

"Ms. Dawkins?"

"Yes, how can I help you?"

"My name is Patty Morris, and I have been working with Dominique and Shante as their counselor. I just heard about Mabel . . . I mean Ms. Dawkins . . . I am so sorry for your loss."

"Thank you," Ms. Dawkins paused. "I'm hangin' on for them. I am trying to be strong for the girls . . ."

"Ms. Dawkins, I wanted to mention that I have spoken with the principal here at Chicora, and he will make arrangements so that they can stay at this school."

"No, I don't want them to go to Chicora. I don't want them going back to that side of town at all. I don't want them to go to school or stores or anything over there. Everything will remind them of their mama, and that's too hard on them."

Patty disagreed but decided not to say so. Instead, she continued with the conversation. "How are the girls?"

"They're happy. They're well. My minister has spoken to them and brought them a lot of comfort. Shante said she was happy her mama isn't hurtin' anymore. Their older sister is very angry that her mother was the only one in the car who died. I tell her it's okay to have all those feelings. I feel the same. I keep telling them we're going to stick together, we're going to get through this.

"I am tryin' to get legal custody. I don't want them to have contact with Mabel's boyfriend. He showed up the night they found out about the wreck. He reeked of alcohol and made a really big scene because he wanted to be the one to tell them. We went through the same ol', same ol'. I told him, 'No, sir, you're not going to see the girls like this.' Since then he's been harassing us on the phone. He won't give us any of Mabel's personal things. But he is not going to see these girls, not if I can stop it."

"How is Dominique?"

"Well, she doesn't say much. She sits and looks off in space. She seems okay, though." This concerned Patty, especially because she suspected Dominique had been depressed even before this terrible loss.

"Ms. Dawkins, I was wondering if it would be all right if I came by to see the girls . . . just to check on them?" *I just don't want them to think I've abandoned them or that I don't care about the work we were doing together,* she thought.

"I think they'd love to see you. Just give me a little bit of time to think about it, though. I think the girls would like to see you, but they're doing okay."

Patty gave Mrs. Dawkins her personal cell number. "Please, tell the girls I called and I'm thinking about them."

She's not going to call me back, Patty despaired after hanging up the phone. *I wonder if the girls want to see me as badly as I want to see them. I'll have to trust their grandmother to relay my regards.*

Patty didn't know what else to do, so she left Sarah a written note saying it was urgent that they speak as soon as Sarah returned. Then she decided to leave a phone message too. She did not say what they needed to speak about; Sarah had known Mabel too, and Patty thought it best to tell her in person. Patty felt very concerned about the girls, and anxious to help in some way. She wanted so badly to do what was best for them, particularly Dominique. She waited with great anticipation for Sarah to return to the office and to hear what she advised.

The Next Week

Sarah returned to work on Monday, and by late Monday morning, Patty still hadn't heard from her. So she stopped by Sarah's office.

"Hi, Sarah, did you get my messages?

"Yes, it's been really hectic, first day back and all. Can it wait until after lunch?"

"No, I'd rather not." Patty had been very anxious to tell Sarah about the Dawkins tragedy, and knew that Sarah would want to know what had happened.

"Okay then."

"I have some very bad news. Mabel Dawkins was killed in a car accident over Christmas break."

"What?!" Sarah was stunned. "Why didn't anyone call me?! I can't believe the guidance counselor didn't call me. Have you talked to him?"

"No, I didn't know what to do. You weren't here and there's no one else to talk to." Patty went on to relate briefly what had happened and how she'd learned the news.

Sarah sat in silence for a minute before responding further. She had known the Dawkins family for a number of years and been close to the girls and their mother. Patty's news was obviously painful for her to hear. "I really need to get something to eat. Let's talk more after lunch."

Patty recognized Sarah's need to digest what had happened by herself for a while. She agreed to be back in Sarah's office at 3:00 p.m.

When Patty and Sarah met at 3:00, Sarah asked Patty if she'd spoken to Mrs. Dawkins yet. Patty relayed the conversation in detail.

"You need to call Lesley Streeter at Dunston right now," Sarah told Patty. "She's the school-based counselor over there. We need to set up a time to see the girls."

"But Mrs. Dawkins asked us to wait, to let her think about it." Patty felt relieved to get some direction, but concerned about where this was going.

"No, you can't wait," Sarah insisted. "You need to call Lesley today and meet with the girls ASAP."

"But we don't have consent," Patty objected.

"Yes, we do. Sure we do. We have Mabel's consent."

"But she's dead. Does that still count?"

"Look, Patty, we have consent. Mabel would want us to meet with them. You know she would. You know that Mabel's relationship with her mother was strained. Think about the children, think about what's best for them. Patty, those children need to see you. You need to go to their new school ASAP—preferably tomorrow—and see them. It's the right thing to do and it's what Mabel would have wanted."

Patty wanted badly to see the girls, but was still concerned that she was violating client self-determination, after Mrs. Dawkins's request. *Then again,* after listening to Sarah, *who was the client? The grandmother? Not really.* "But I'm not sure it *is* the right thing to do . . ."

"It is, Patty. I'm sorry, but I don't have any more time to talk about this now. I've got a bunch of catch-up work to do after being gone so long—you know how it is. A few fires here and there. You'll be fine. Check back with me in the morning to let me know what progress you've made."

What should I do? As Patty exited Sarah's office, thoughts flooded her head. *Should I respect Mrs. Dawson's wishes or listen to Sarah? What would Mabel really have wanted? Those girls need me . . . they need to see me . . . they probably* want *to see me . . . I am the only thing they have left that's the same. What should I do?*

23 | I Don't Want Them Mad at Me (A)

Vicki M. Runnion

"DONALD, LET ME BE SURE I understand, okay?" hospice social worker Emily Prentice asked. "You want your brother Thomas, Thomas Jones, to be guardian for your girls after you're gone, is that right?"

"Yeah," Donald said weakly.

"But you told Betty Jane, the social worker who visited on Saturday, that you don't want to tell the girls` about it?"

"No," he said, his eyes closing.

Taking a deep breath, Emily pushed on. "Donald, I think it's really important for them to know what you want for them, and why. You're their dad, and they need to know what you think would be best for them."

Tears slipped out the corners of his eyes. "I don't want them mad at me," he said.

Emily was silent for a few moments, trying to figure out what to say or do. In those few seconds, Donald drifted back to sleep.

Development of this decision case was supported in part by the University of South Carolina College of Social Work and the Project on Death in America. It was prepared solely to provide material for class discussion and not to suggest either effective or ineffective handling of the situation depicted. Although the case is based on field research regarding an actual situation, names and certain facts may have been disguised to protect confidentiality. As indicated by the (A), the instructor's manual provides a continuation of the case. The author wishes to thank the case reporter for cooperation in making this account available for the benefit of social work students and practitioners.

Elizabethton, Tennessee

Elizabethton was a bedroom community just northeast of Johnson City, Tennessee. It still had a small-town feel—traffic was much easier to negotiate, for one thing—but its proximity to Johnson City allowed for ready access to some of the features of a larger city, many of them associated with East Tennessee State University.

Beyond Elizabethton, there was "out in the country": some farmland in the foothills, and then the Blue Ridge Mountains. The community was relatively stable—there had never been a great deal of industry, but that meant it had not experienced the economic upheaval associated with the closure of plants suffered by some other areas in the region. All the same, the population was fairly diverse in terms of economic well-being and educational level, if not racial and ethnic or religious diversity.

Hospice of the Tri-Counties Area

Hospice of the Tri-Counties Area (HTCA) celebrated its fifteenth year of service to the community in October 2002. Initially developed as an offshoot of the larger Hospice of the Blue Ridge, it had become independent a couple of years later. There had been some lean times during HTCA's history, but it had earned a solid reputation in the community. A not-for-profit organization, it received support from United Way and various community businesses as well as several fund-raising events throughout the year, in addition to reimbursement by Medicare, Medicaid, and commercial insurance companies.

In 2001, a national for-profit chain of hospices, Transitions, moved into HTCA's service area and began to compete aggressively for clients. HTCA initially saw a slight dip in census, and staff members were concerned about job security for the first time in more than a decade. But the executive director, Helen Mower, who had been a board member for many years, including some of the troubled ones, prior to becoming director, had extensive business experience and a passionate belief in HTCA. She challenged the staff to reexamine everything they were doing, to be sure they were providing top-notch care with an increased focus on customer service, and assured them that they could survive and even thrive.

One of the changes—the Open Door Policy—was intended to make it easier for physicians and potential clients to decide on hospice care and then easier to choose HTCA to provide it. The board of directors had approved Helen's recommendation that they risk getting some patients earlier in their disease process than had been customary and thereby incur more expenses for them, in the hope that they would also increase their census and average length of service, which would result in increased income. The gamble had paid off, and the census had doubled over a fifteen-month period—resulting in a need to increase staff, rather than the decrease that they had feared—and continued to grow.

Emily Prentice, M.S.W.

One of the new social workers hired as a result of the increased census was Emily Prentice. Emily was beginning a second career. Thirty-four years old—although with her long dark-blond hair and slightly funky wardrobe, she looked younger—she had taught middle school in a couple of different special education programs for students with emotional and behavioral problems. Emily had become increasingly aware of and involved in the lives of her students outside of school, and had been fascinated by the complex interplay between things happening in her classroom and things happening in students' homes. She decided to get a master's degree in social work rather than the master's in education she had been planning to pursue.

As she approached graduation, Emily decided to explore working in some other social service settings rather than returning immediately to a school. She had been intrigued by a classmate's account of hospice care for her grandmother and, when she saw the posting of a social work position with HTCA, decided to apply. As a new graduate, she was a little surprised to get even as far as an interview, and quite pleased when offered the job.

Five months later, Emily had become fairly comfortable with the organization's procedures—most days were no longer so overwhelming. But she knew she was still very much on a steep learning curve when it came to the larger realm of the community social service system. She still gave the phrase suggested by her new supervisor—"I don't know, but I'll find out"—a regular workout. Hardly a week went by that she didn't have to research some new resource or benefit for one client or another.

Emily found that her work regularly drew on not just her academic preparation but also her life experience. She had dealt with juvenile rheumatoid arthritis since she was about ten—including several surgeries to fuse various joints in an effort to reduce pain, the need for periodic major adjustments to the complex combination of medications she took to keep symptoms at a tolerable level, and occasional flares of inflammation that forced her to slow down drastically for a couple of weeks or more, and sometimes even necessitated hospitalization for intensive intravenous therapies. As a result, she had a keen awareness of what it was like to live with debilitating chronic pain and fatigue and in-depth familiarity with the carousel-like experience of navigating the health care system.

In December, immediately after four intensive weeks of orientation, Emily had approached her supervisor about working thirty-two rather than forty hours per week, to give herself a day off in the middle of the week for rest. Then, as she began to set her own schedule, Emily found she was less tired, and decided to go back to the forty-hour week for a little longer. But by early April, she had to admit to herself that her pain was increasing, and as a result her energy was fast becoming depleted.

Donald Jones and His Daughters

Donald Jones was forty-two years old and dying of acute myeloid leukemia. He had been diagnosed not long after his wife had died of complications of diabetes, about five years earlier, and had been disabled for three years. He had two daughters—Elizabeth, who had just turned sixteen, and Sarah, age twelve.

When Emily and nurse Sallie Earles first met him, on April 21, Donald was sitting in a rocking chair with one broken rocker and chain-smoking. The family lived in a duplex apartment that had apparently not been seriously cleaned or straightened in a long time, and it seemed evident to Emily that financial resources were pretty limited. The kitchen sink and small counter were overflowing with dirty dishes, the kitchen floor was sticky and missing tiles, the carpet in the living room and dining area was stained and matted, three of the four chairs that went with the kitchen table were broken. The only furniture in the living room was a sofa, there were no sheets on the bed that Donald was using, and the bathroom sink and tub were crusted with soap scum and dirt. The refrigerator was empty except for a partly full aluminum tray of spaghetti and one can of beer. The telephone had been disconnected for the past three weeks, and utilities were scheduled to be disconnected at the end of the week if the bill was not paid by then.

Donald's speech was slow and somewhat slurred, and one side of his face seemed swollen. It apparently took considerable effort for him to talk, and it was difficult for Emily and Sallie to understand him. *I wonder if he might have had a stroke or something,* Emily thought. *I'll have to ask Sallie what she thinks when I get a chance.*

He had been receiving platelets on a twice-weekly basis, transported via Wheels (the community transportation service offered by the American Red Cross for ambulatory patients who could not drive themselves to medical appointments) to the doctor's office. "Do you go again tomorrow, Donald?" Sallie asked. "If so, I will arrange the transportation for you. Maybe it'll be a little less tiring if you just go and come directly, rather than sharing the trip with several other people."

At one point, Donald needed to go to the bathroom. When he got up, he was very weak and unsteady on his feet, and Emily and Sallie looked at each other with some alarm.

"I don't know how his daughters will be able to manage him here for much longer," Sallie said softly to Emily while he was out of the room.

When he came back, Sallie said, "Donald, we can get a wheelchair for you—would you want that?"

"Yeah," Donald replied, "could you get me one of those motorized kind, and get a ramp so I can get outside a little?"

"Well, we can't provide that kind of chair ourselves, but sometimes someone donates one and we sell them in our thrift shop," Emily told him. "I'll see if we have any available. But would you like a regular wheelchair if we don't?"

Donald shook his head no.

One of Donald's medicine bottles was empty, and while trying to make arrangements to get that refilled, it quickly became apparent to Sallie that Donald didn't fully understand what medicines he was taking for what purposes and was relying on his daughters to dispense them whenever he needed something. Sallie was relieved to realize that Elizabeth had a basic understanding of what each medicine was for and how often she could give it. "Elizabeth, I will bring a pill box out next time I come and help you set up a schedule for the medicines. That way, if we need to change some of his medicines, you won't have to try to remember so many details."

While attempting to complete a psychosocial assessment, Emily learned that Elizabeth was missing school most days to take care of her father, but that Sarah attended consistently. It also emerged that Donald had a son, Bobby, age nineteen, who was currently in jail on a drug possession charge.

"And I have a brother, but he don't come over much," Donald added.

"What's his name?" Emily asked.

"Thomas," Donald responded.

"What's his address and phone number?" Emily continued.

"I don't know, he lives in Kingsport," Donald replied.

Knowing that her eyes might give away her surprise that he didn't know how to reach his brother, Emily kept her head down.

Donald continued, "And I got a sister-in-law, Christina. The widow of my brother who died. She lives a few blocks from here." He didn't know her address either, but provided a phone number. Gradually, Emily learned that Elizabeth and Sarah stayed with Christina fairly often, and that Donald would want Christina to have custody of the girls if anything happened to him. By this point, Emily was less surprised to learn that no formal arrangements had been made for guardianship of the girls.

While Sallie continued trying to assess his immediate physical needs, Elizabeth asked Emily to come back to her room so they could talk. Both of them sat on the edge of her bed. Emily was grateful to sit down. "I know my dad is dying," Elizabeth started out, "and I just want to stay home to take care of him and be with him."

Emily began to tell Elizabeth about hospice services, and that she could help find people who could care for Donald during the day, but Elizabeth interrupted her.

"I've already missed enough school that I can't pass this year—I'll have to restart my junior year this fall." She wanted Emily to help her officially drop out for the remainder of the present year, so that she wouldn't be considered truant anymore.

"I'll go by your school and see what I can do," Emily promised.

Emily started to stand up, but Elizabeth stopped her. "Can I ask you one more thing?"

"Sure," Emily responded, and settled back on the bed again.

"Please don't call CPS [Child Protective Services] on us," Elizabeth pleaded. "They took us away after our mother died, and it was awful. Me and Sarah want to stay together, and Christina—our aunt Christina—will take care of us."

"I can't make a promise about that forever," Emily responded, "but for right now, I don't see a need to make any report, and I promise we will try to help your family enough that it won't become necessary, okay?"

"Okay, thanks," Elizabeth said, and got up to go back to her dad.

The intake visit was lengthy because it took so long to get information out of Donald, and because the needs seemed overwhelming. Sallie and Emily had been there for nearly two hours when Emily was paged to go attend another patient's death.

"Will you be at the office later?" she asked as she got ready to leave. "Can we see if Ron can meet with us to do some planning?"

"Yeah, I'll be there about three or three-fifteen," Sallie replied. "Want me to call Ron and see if he can meet us?"

"Yeah, that would be great—see you then," Emily said as she left. *I think I covered most of what I needed for a first visit,* she thought as she drove. *I'm glad to have this time to rest a bit—this pain is really wearing me down.*

Next Steps

When they met later, along with chaplain Ron Amick, they made a list of things to be done and divided up the tasks. Ron agreed to see whether he could help with funeral arrangements. Sallie said she would focus on getting some more information about Donald's condition and treatment plans, and on getting his medications and transportation for treatments straightened out. Emily had a lengthy list, including getting some financial resources to take care of the utility bill, getting phone service restored so they could communicate more easily with the family, checking on the motorized chair and ramp, and talking with a guidance counselor at each girl's school to see what the situation was for each of them. She also planned to talk further with Donald about his wishes for the girls and to see whether she could help facilitate arrangements for guardianship, so that by the time of his death things would be clear and unnecessary confusion and turmoil could be avoided.

"You know, one of the things I love about hospice is that we get to iden-tify the needs that are affecting the patients and families and address them, without rules dictating every little thing we can or can't do—like you help-ing someone drop out of school and me looking for money to get a funeral paid for!" said Ron. "Situations like this really energize me, make me feel like what I do really makes a difference in tangible ways, as well as the intangible stuff."

After they finished, Emily tiredly gathered up her papers and shoved them into her briefcase. "I'm heading home, y'all. I'm wiped out."

A Turn for the Worse

Two days later, on a Friday morning, the team received a voice mail from on-call staff, saying that Donald had been admitted to the hospital overnight because his platelet count had been dangerously low based on lab work from the day before. Emily had already put several processes in motion, toward getting some resources for the family and getting a cell phone. Thinking, *We may not even have the few weeks we thought we would to get all this done,* she headed over to the hospital.

Donald was even more lethargic than he had been at home, but he was still awake and oriented and could nod his responses to Emily's first ques-tions, so she decided to go ahead and talk with him about the guardianship issue. She carefully divided up her sentences into single ideas, and asked him repeatedly, "Do you understand what I'm saying?" Donald seemed to be tracking fairly well, so she continued, "You said that you want Christina to have guardianship when something happens to you, is that right?"

He nodded.

"Do you want me to see if I can find an attorney who will help you get all the paperwork in order, so that everything will be ready?"

Again, he nodded.

"Okay, I will start making some calls, and I'll let you know what I find out."

As she turned to leave the room, Donald spoke up, one of the few times Emily had heard him initiate conversation. "Could you take me out to smoke?" he asked. Emily felt her mouth drop open, but closed it again as she turned back to Donald. "They won't take me if they get busy," he explained.

"Donald, I'm sorry, I don't have time right now—I have other visits that I'm already running late for. But I'll go see if one of the aides here can take you soon. Will that be okay?" Donald nodded slowly, but Emily saw the disappointment in his eyes. She was relieved to see one of the male aides headed toward his room as she stepped out into the hall.

"I'm going to take him down to smoke, if you're through with your visit. We don't want him deciding to go home just so he can smoke," the aide said, smiling.

"Yes, he was just asking for someone to take him out. He'll be glad to see you." As she rode down in the elevator, she thought about what had happened. *Well, we both lucked out that time. He will get what he wanted, and I don't have to sit there in all that pollution for him to get it. I* HATE *cigarette smoke! But is it too selfish of me not to want to sit with him while he smokes, when he has so little time left? I just hate smelling it in my hair and my clothes the rest of the day, not to mention feeling it in my lungs! Is it part of my job, to do stuff like that?*

That afternoon, Emily felt extremely fortunate when, on her fifth call, she found an attorney, Jane Rickert, who agreed to help Donald, pro bono, with preparing the paperwork to designate Christina as guardian. She went back by the hospital later that afternoon to let Donald know, but he was sleeping deeply, so she didn't disturb him.

Undecided

The following Monday morning, Emily listened to her seventy-two voice mail messages, reminding herself to focus on them instead of on how weary she felt and the constant ache in her shoulder, wrist, and fingers. She was dismayed to hear a message from Betty Jane Conner, the social worker who had been on call over the weekend.

"This message is for the team of Donald Jones, and especially for Emily," Betty Jane began. "I went to the hospital on Saturday to check on all our patients there. When I went in, Donald was sitting up in a chair. At first I thought he was asleep, but then he opened his eyes and spoke, so I went in and asked if I could sit down and talk with him. Oh, y'all, this was so sad. He told me that I might want to sit in the chair on the other side of the room, because the nurse had told him he stunk. How could anyone say something like that to that poor man? Well, I told him that he was fine, I didn't smell a thing and not to worry, and I sat on the edge of his bed.

"I asked how he was doing, and he said he was really worried about his girls—and then all of a sudden, he was just sobbing. Just sobbing! It was kinda hard to understand him, you know, but he said, 'I need to tell . . . I need help . . . my girls want to go live with Christina when I die, and I've been saying they could, but I want them to live with my brother and his wife, but I'm afraid they will be mad at me. Please don't say anything to them—I don't want to die knowing they are mad at me.' I just sat with him and held his hand, and I promised him I would tell Emily and she would help him work it out, and I told him to try not to worry. Emily, I don't know what you're going to do with this, but if I can help you in any way, I will. Just let me know. This is such a sad case! Oh yeah, and he wanted to know if you've found a wheelchair for him, Emily."

Hearing Betty Jane's message, Emily's first thought was, *Oh no. I'm supposed to go by the lawyer's this afternoon to pick up the paperwork saying that Christina is to be the guardian. Well, maybe it won't be too much trouble for her to redo it and put in Thomas's name—I just hope.* Even though she had other visits scheduled, she decided to go by the hospital first, to be sure about what Donald wanted.

When she got to his room, Donald was in bed, looking very groggy, but he had company, a young woman in sweatpants, T-shirt, and flip-flops, who looked like she might be in her late twenties or early thirties. Emily looked to Donald, realizing he probably couldn't explain, but then the woman spoke up.

"I'm Christina," she said. "I haven't met you, but the girls are staying with me right now, and they'll be with me if something happens to Donald."

Emily gathered her wits about her enough to think of getting Christina's address and confirming her phone number, and gave Christina one of her business cards.

"Well, I gotta go," Christina said. "Take care, Donald, and I'll see you later."

Emily watched her go, then turned to Donald. His eyes were closed, and she stood quietly for a few minutes, trying to decide what to do next.

She walked out to the nurses' desk and waited for Ginny, the one she knew best, to finish talking with someone on the phone. "Ginny, what can you tell me about how Donald is doing? I really need to talk with him about his daughters—he has changed who he wants to have custody of them since I saw him last week."

"He's not doing good at all, Em," Ginny said. "His platelets aren't staying up anywhere near normal, even with transfusions every day. He can't go on too much longer like this. I think he can understand you, but he can't focus for more than a few seconds at a time. If you can ask him yes or no questions, I think he can answer them—but it's hard to be sure. I wasn't working this weekend, but I know from Terri that his brother came to visit Friday night. Maybe that's why he changed his mind."

"Okay, thanks, Ginny. I'll go see if he can wake up enough to talk with me."

Feeling really uncertain and uneasy, but aware that the time left for finding out what Donald wanted was quickly slipping by, Emily went back to his room.

"Donald," she began, "can you wake up enough to talk to me for a few minutes? I need to ask you some questions."

He opened his eyes with some effort and blinked, finally focusing on Emily. "Okay," he said.

"Donald, last week when we talked, you said you wanted Christina to have custody of the girls when something happens to you, do you remember? And you said you would like for me to try to find a lawyer to get some paperwork together for you?"

"Yeah," Donald said.

Emily paused a moment, but Donald didn't say anything more.

"Then one of our other social workers, Betty Jane, came to see you on Saturday—do you remember that?"

Donald seemed to try to remember, but didn't say anything.

So Emily went on, "And she said you told her that you want your brother to have the girls."

"Yeah," Donald agreed.

Emily waited.

Donald's eyes drifted shut again.

"Donald, please try to stay awake and talk to me—this is important, okay?"

He opened his eyes again.

"I did find a lawyer, and she has done some paperwork for you, but it says you want Christina to be guardian for your daughters. I need to know if you want me to ask her to change it to your brother."

"Yeah," Donald said.

"Let me be sure I understand, okay? You want your brother Thomas, Thomas Jones, to be guardian for your girls after you're gone, is that right?"

"Yeah," Donald said.

"Did you talk to him about that when he was here over the weekend?" she asked, wishing he could say more about changing his mind, but knowing she was already pushing him to his limits.

"Yeah," Donald said.

"But you told Betty Jane on Saturday that you don't want to tell the girls about it?"

"No," he said, his eyes closing.

Taking a deep breath, she pushed on. "Donald, I think it's really important for them to know what you want for them, and why. You're their dad, and they need to know what you think would be best for them."

Tears slipped out the corners of his eyes. "I don't want them mad at me," he said. "I want Thomas to have them, but I can't tell them. I don't want my last time with them to be when they are yelling at me and all upset."

Emily was silent for a few moments, trying to figure out what to say or do. In those few seconds, Donald drifted back to sleep.

Emily stood there for a few moments, then went out to the nurses' station to document her visit in the chart, although she wasn't sure what to write.

"Oh, Emily, I forgot to tell you earlier," Ginny hurried back over to her. "Terri also told me that she had said something to Donald's brother when he was here about their sister-in-law really helping out with the girls, and she said he looked at her kind of blankly, and then said that they don't have a sister-in-law. They only have one other brother, who lives in Indiana, and he isn't married."

"What?" Emily was bewildered. "Well, then who in the world is Christina?"

Contributing Authors

Heather Bennett, M.S.W., is a research associate, Office of Program Evaluation, College of Education, University of South Carolina, Columbia.

Sarah Cearley, Ph.D., L.C.S.W., is Director of Client Services at Arkansas Lawyers Assistance Program in Little Rock, Arkansas.

Laura Cox, M.S.W., L.M.S.W., is a counselor at the Savannah Vet Center, Savannah, Georgia.

Karen A. Gray, Ph.D., M.S.W., is an assistant professor at the College of Social Work, University of South Carolina, Columbia.

Gecole Harley, J.D., M.S.W., is the Ombuds, University of California, Irvine School of Medicine and Medical Center.

Barbara Head, Ph.D., R.N., A.C.S.W., is Research Director of the Interdisciplinary Program for Palliative Care and Chronic Illness at the University of Louisville, Kentucky.

Mary Hylton, Ph.D., M.S.W., is an assistant professor at the School of Social Work, University of Nevada, Reno.

Miriam McNown Johnson, Ph.D., M.S.W., is an associate professor and Associate Dean for Academic Affairs at the College of Social Work, University of South Carolina, Columbia.

Rachel C. Parker, L.M.S.W., is a school social worker at Lexington/Richland School District Five in Chapin, South Carolina.

Vicki M. Runnion, M.S.W., C.S.W., is a social worker at Hospice of Louisville, Kentucky. Since 1980, she has been involved in hospice and end-of-life care in a variety of roles, including volunteer, social worker, bereavement counselor, supervisor, and executive director. She has taught social work courses at the University of Louisville, Columbia College (SC), and the University of South Carolina, where she wrote and taught with decision cases. With Wolfer, Runnion was co-recipient of a Social Work Leadership Development Award from the Project on Death in America to support development of this case collection.

Rich Schlauch, M.S.W., L.C.S.W., is Clinical Services Director, Carolina Center for Counseling and Clinical Services, Gastonia, North Carolina.

Georgianne Thornburgh, M.S.W., L.M.S.W., is a retired hospice social worker, Savannah, Georgia.

Jeanette Ucci, M.S.W., is a social worker for Westminster Canterbury Richmond, a continuing care retirement community in Richmond, Virginia.

Terry A. Wolfer, Ph.D., M.S.W., is an associate professor at the College of Social Work, University of South Carolina, Columbia. He teaches social work practice, research and evaluation, and a case-based capstone course. He has coedited previous collections of decision cases on generalist and advanced social work practice, and on spirituality and religion in social work practice. His research interests include social work education, and religion and spirituality in social work practice. With Runnion, Wolfer was co-recipient of a Social Work Leadership Development Award from the Project on Death in America to support development of this case collection.